M
25.50

PACIFIC BAS

Editor: Kaori O'Connor

OTHER BOOKS IN THIS SERIES

James S. de Benneville *Tales of the Samurai*
Isabella Bird *Korea and her neighbours*
Isabella Bird *Six Months in Hawaii*
Katharine Augusta Carl *With the Empress Dowager of China*
Miguel Covarrubias *Island of Bali*
Miguel Covarrubias *Mexico South*
Paul Gauguin *Intimate Journals*
Jukichi Inouye *Home life in Tokyo*
Pierre Loti *Japan: Madame Chrysanthemum*
Pierre Loti *Tahiti: The Marriage of Loti*
Herman Melville *Omoo*
Herman Melville *Typee*
Robert Louis Stevenson *In the South Seas*

THE CRUISE OF THE

SNARK

A PACIFIC VOYAGE

BY JACK LONDON

KPI

LONDON AND NEW YORK

To
CHARMIAN
THE MATE OF THE "SNARK"
WHO TOOK THE WHEEL, NIGHT OR DAY,
WHEN ENTERING
OR LEAVING PORT OR RUNNING A PASSAGE,
WHO TOOK THE WHEEL IN EVERY EMERGENCY, AND
WHO WEPT
AFTER TWO YEARS OF SAILING, WHEN THE
VOYAGE WAS DISCONTINUED

First published in 1911
This edition published in 1986 by KPI Limited
11 New Fetter Lane, London EC4P 4EE
Reprinted 1986

Distributed by
Routledge & Kegan Paul, Associated Book Publishers (UK) Ltd.
11 New Fetter Lane, London EC4P 4EE

Methuen Inc., Routledge & Kegan Paul
29 West 35th Street
New York, NY 10001, USA

Printed in Great Britain by St Edmundsbury Press Ltd,
Bury St Edmunds, Suffolk

ISBN 0 7103 0139 1

CONTENTS

INTRODUCTION

"*L*IFE THAT *lives is life successful.*" With these words from *The Cruise of the Snark*, Jack London summed up the philosophy behind the whirlwind forty years in which he tasted life to the full. Ruggedly handsome, recklessly courageous, he had a sublime confidence that carried him to success against overwhelming odds, and a profound compassion that led to his commitment to improving the lot of those less fortunate than himself. He was a sailor, a tramp, an oyster-pirate, a gold-prospector, a zealous fighter for social reform and the best-known author of this time. The Pacific was his last great love, and his voyage there in the *Snark* was his last great adventure.

Jack London was born John Griffith Chaney in San Francisco on January 12, 1876, the illegitimate son of Flora Wellman and an Irish astrologer called 'Professor' William H. Chaney. The couple parted before their child was born, and when the boy was eight months old Flora married John London, a kindly man who gave Flora's son his name and treated him as his own. Times were hard in the west in the 1870's; San Francisco was full of unemployed men, and John London could not make a living there working as a carpenter. The family moved across the bay and struggled to eke a living on small farms in Alameida, San Mateo and the Livermore valley. Their existence was always precarious, and any small gains were immediately off-set by Flora's get-rich-quick schemes that always got the family into further difficulties. When Jack was ten the family gave up farming and moved to the city of Oakland, where John London found work as a watchman. As their circumstances worsened, Flora sought refuge in spiritualism, conducting seances under the aegis of a spirit guide Indian chieftain called Plume. Life in the London household was chaotic at best, nightmarish at worst. There was never enough money or food, Flora gave way to nervous 'attacks' and provoked constant rows, and her passion for spiritualism became a mania. The young Jack sought refuge in the Oakland public library, where he escaped into books of travel and adventure. When Jack was eleven, John London lost his job, and the boy had to support the family by selling newspapers and doing odd jobs before and after school. When he was thirteen, his formal education stopped altogether, as there was no money to send him on to secondary school.

For a while Jack carried on working at odd jobs, stealing away whenever possible to sail on the Oakland estuary in a leaky skiff he had managed to acquire in secret. The family's needs soon obliged him to take up a job in a cannery where he worked at up to twenty hours at a stretch for ten cents an hour, a brutal existence that came to an end when he became an oyster-pirate. He borrowed money, bought a sloop and joined the small fleet of shadowy sailors who stole from the bay's privately-owned oyster beds by night, and sold their catches cheaply and quickly in the early-morning markets. Just sixteen, his sailing skills and courage won Jack the nickname 'Prince of the Oyster-Pirates'. He made much more money than he had in the cannery and he had freedom and adventure as well, but he became dissatisfied with the life and, after a short time with the Fish Patrol policing fishing in the bay, he returned to doing odd jobs in Oakland. This soon palled and he took to the road as a hobo, sharing his life with other young vagabonds who taught him how to live rough and steal rides on freight trains. On his return, just after his seventeenth birthday, he signed on a sealing schooner for a seven month voyage that took him to Japan. He arrived back with his taste for adventure temporarily sated, knowing he wanted to be a writer but having no idea how to attain his aim. Unemployment was rife, and he was lucky to get a job in a jute mill where he worked under horrible conditions for ten cents an hour. A local newspaper ran a competition for amateur writers – Jack entered, and won first prize and twenty-five dollars with a short story based on his sealing voyage. Elated, he began to write furiously in his spare time, but all his efforts were rejected. He had been lured from the jute mill to a power station, where he worked two shifts a day shovelling coal until he was on the verge of exhaustion. He had been promised a rise in wages and promotion, but he discovered that his employers had been giving him work normally done by two men, and paying him less than either had received, knowing he was desperate for money. He could outwork and out-fight any man, but he could not hope to win against an unjust system. Unable to negotiate better terms, he returned to an aimless round of doing odd jobs and hanging around the estuary.

The continuing economic depression had led to the formation of radical political groups who were determined to give voice to the desperation that was gripping unemployed working men throughout the country. This was a cause after Jack's heart, and he decided to join 'Kelly's army', a thousand-strong group of out-of-work men from the

Bay area who had set out to join in a protest march on Washington D.C. He was just eighteen, and what began as an adventure would turn into a harrowing experience that would change the course of his life.

Jack travelled east using the skills he had learned on the road, riding the rails through Rocky Mountain blizzards until he caught up with Kelly and his men in Nebraska. In the month that Jack was with them the men of Kelly's army were plagued by harsh weather and were finally reduced to living off the land, begging for clothing and shelter as they went, constantly being harrassed by local residents and moved on by the police. When moral and discipline began to deteriorate Jack broke away from the army and rode the rails to New York, where he was arrested for vagrancy. After serving thirty days in jail, where he witnessed scenes of appalling brutality and degradation, he travelled through the east as a hobo, working when he could, begging when he couldn't work and starving when he couldn't beg. Finally he rode the rails back west across Canada, dodging railroad detectives all the way to Vancouver where he found a boat bound for San Francisco and worked his passage home. He would later write of this seven-month trip;

> ". . . I was down in the cellar of society, down in the subterranean depths of misery about which it is neither nice nor proper to speak. I was in the pit, the abyss, the human cesspool, the shambles and the charnel house of our civilization. This is the part of the edifice of society that society chooses to ignore . . . I shall say only that the things I there saw gave me a terrible scare . . ."[1]

Jack arrived back a changed man. The experiences of the previous months had led him to see his personal struggles as part of a larger pattern, and he had become a passionate advocate of social reform. Radical members of Kelly's army had introduced him to Karl Marx's *Communist Manifesto*, and he had found inspiration in its declaration that "The workers have nothing to lose but their chains. They have a world to gain. Workers of the world, unite." He sensed that the lot of the working man could not be improved until the vicious cycle of exploitation in which they were trapped was broken, and he was determined to dedicate himself to helping to bring this about. He had also resolved to devote himself to becoming a writer. The aimless years were over. He finally knew what he wanted in life, and from now on he would always be a man in a hurry.

Education was what he lacked, and he set out to acquire it with a phenomenal energy and determination. At nineteen he entered Oakland High School, working part time to support himself, attending socialist rallies and studying the works of social philosophers like Spencer and Darwin in the public library. He left the high school after a year, dissatisfied with his rate of progress, and soon afterwards he joined the Socialist Party. Over a summer, studying nineteen hours a day, he taught himself enough English, history, mathematics and physics to qualify for the University of California at Berkeley, which he entered in the autumn of 1896, less than two years after he had set out east with Kelly's army. It was a remarkable achievement, and it confirmed him in the belief that there was no mystique about intellectual effort. As he put it succinctly, "*Dig is a wonderful thing, and it will move more mountains than faith ever dreamed of.*"[2] But the college education for which Jack had worked so hard and by which he had set such store proved to be a sad disappointment.

The Berkeley campus of the 1890's was very different to that bastion of radical politics it would become in the 1960's. Jack had expected university to prepare him for life, but he found that his professors and fellow students had no interest in the social problems and new social philosophies that were the very stuff of real life as he knew it. He had assumed the university would be concerned to improve society; instead he found it dedicated to perpetuating a socio-economic system that he knew to be unjust. What mattered at Berkeley was football games, fraternity parties and what he later described as "the passionless pursuit of passionless intelligence"[3]. Bitterly disappointed, he left after only one term.

Jack then worked in a laundry trying to save enough money to buy himself the time to write, but soon realized the hopelessness of his position. In July, 1897 he joined the rush to the Klondike gold fields, travelling by sea as far as the Alaskan coast then packing up through the Chilkoot Pass with a hundred and fifty pound load on his back, shooting the treacherous rapids of Fifty Mile River in a boat he helped to build himself, and finally arriving in the Yukon just as winter set in. He took to the harsh life with alacrity, hiking through trackless wastes and camping in sub-zero temperatures. When the 'white silence' stopped further prospecting until spring, he read and reread the books he had brought with him, including Darwin's *Origin of Species*, Marx's *Capital* and Spencer's *Philosophy of Style*. Of the time he spent among the Indians and prospectors of Alaska he would later say "It was in the Klondike that I found myself. There nobody talks. Everybody thinks. You get your perspective. I got mine."[4]

For all its difficulties, his new life appealed to him far more than the one he had left behind. As he came to see it, life in the wild had a kind of nobility that life in civilization lacked, and if it was brutal it was nonetheless governed by a kind of rough justice that was far more fair than that meted out in city courtrooms or on factory floors. All across America he had seen the worst aspects of a society split by class divisions, and he had been horrified by man's inhumanity to man. On the Alaskan frontier, all men were united against the common enemy, nature. Here a privileged background counted for nothing – courage, strength, self-reliance and intelligence were the only keys to survival. Yet however much he admired these qualities, his compassion and his background made it impossible for him to embrace the doctrine of individualism for which he was, both mentally and physically, so naturally suited. He realized that, taken to extremes, individualism could all too easily lead to the survival of the strong at the expense of the weak; at the very least, it was likely to result in the selfish mentality of every-man-for-himself. He believed that he had the ability to survive and succeed in society as well as on the frontier, but he knew that others were not so fortunate and, like Spencer, he believed that "No one can be perfectly free till all are free; no one can be perfectly moral till all are moral; no one can be perfectly happy till all are happy."[5] He had been to the abyss and lived with its people – if he was to save himself, he must save them also. His study of Marx had persuaded him that the injustices of civilization were due to the capitalist system, and in these early days of Marxist socialism he believed that the workers would rise and throw off their yoke for the ultimate benefit of all. It seemed to him that the individual qualities by which a man might succeed against the odds were very like those needed if the working class was to raise itself. If he drew attention to social problems and celebrated individual effort, he felt he would be furthering the socialist cause that seemed to offer the only hope of bringing about the social changes he so ardently desired.

Now aged twenty-one, Jack returned from Alaska in July, 1893. He had failed to find gold and was suffering badly from scurvy, and he now had the additional responsibility of supporting his mother, for his stepfather had died during his absence in the north. The depression had not improved, so he fell back into the old routine of taking on whatever odd jobs he could find to make ends meet. But the year he had spent away had only deepened his resolve to be a writer, and he set about it as methodically as he had prepared himself for university entrance. He studied the works of his favourite authors Rudyard Kipling and Robert Louis Stevenson, writing out passages from their books longhand by the hour in order to absorb the nuances of their style and technique. He strove to improve his vocabulary, writing unfamiliar words on slips of paper that he strung over his bed so he could read them last thing at night and first thing in the morning. He devised a system of plot construction in which all the elements in a story could be condified and then rearranged, giving rise to endless variations. He experimented with every possible literary form, from ballads and verse to jokes and short stories.

He was working against tremendous odds, and ten years before his chance of success would have been well-nigh impossible. In the latter half of the nineteenth century, American literature had lost touch with the realities of American life. It had become sectional and conservative, devoted to the interests of middle-class East coast society. It took no account of the rise of industrialism and its attendant social problems, the growth of new cities, the development of the mid- and far west, the social discontent that had arisen from years of economic depression, or the fact that the workers now greatly outnumbered any other sector of society. It was sentimental, stultified and steeped in late-Victorian morality; fit reading for a Boston club room or a ladies parlour, but not for a city street. And the fact that both books and magazines were expensively produced put them beyond the reach of any but the comfortable readership for whom they were intended.

But by the early 1890's, a few far-sighted publishers had realized that the working public constituted a huge potential market, and had brought out a new type of publication to attract them. These were the first popular magazines, cheaply priced and based on a lively mixture of short stories, serials and feature articles. Led by *Cosmopolitan* and *McClures*, the new magazines sold well and paid well, and these were the publications that Jack decided to aim for. But although they were meant for the popular market, Jack found that the contents of the magazines fell far short of the vigour and relevance that he felt popular writing should have. As he wrote to a friend, "Our magazines are so goody-goody. This undue care not to bring a blush to the virgin cheek of the young American girl is disgusting."[6] He was determined to write about real life as he knew it, and he was convinced that what he wanted to write about was what the common man wanted and needed to read. He wrote and studied and gradually his own style began to emerge – forceful, direct, simple and devastatingly realistic. Struggle was the theme of all his stories – the struggle of man against nature, man against society, man against beast and man against man. He wrote about poverty and brutality, anger and anguish, sweat and blood. He laid bare a world where comfort and gentility were unknown; he showed human nature at its worst as well as at its best. He sent his work to local magazines and newspapers, and was rewarded with a stream of rejection letters which he kept impaled on a length of wire. He pawned his watch, mackintosh and bicycle and lived on potatoes and beans.

After six months the wire strung with rejection letters was five feet long and Jack was on the verge of despair. As he remembered, "I was at the end of my tether, beaten out, starved, ready to go back to coal shovelling or ahead to suicide."[7] Then a local magazine bought a story, others followed, and in July, 1899 he sold his story *Odyssey of the North* to the prestigious *Atlantic Monthly* magazine. He quickly put together a collection of short stories based on his Klondike experiences and these appeared as his first book, *The Son of the Wolf*, in the spring of 1900. Jack's book hit the literary world like an invigorating blast of arctic air. It brought the era of sentimental fiction to an end and introduced the realism that became the basis of modern American writing. He wrote with the spirit of the new century – bold, brash and sometimes brutal. He broke all the conventions – portrayed rough characters of a type who had not featured in American literature before, used mining camp slang instead of pretty phrases, did not hesitate to portray violence, ugliness and cruelty. Yet at the same time, he celebrated a kind of elemental heroism and courage that only comes to the fore in the face of adversity, and in doing so brought hope and dignity to all those for whom life was a struggle. *The Son of the Wolf* was an immediate popular success and Jack was hailed as a genius, a great artist and a new Kipling.

He carried on working at a phenomenal rate, writing newspaper articles and magazine features as well as more Alaskan short stories. By the end of 1901 he had completed the manuscripts of three books and was exhausted and in need of a change. His opportunity came in the summer of 1901, when a San Francisco newspaper asked him to go to South Africa to report on the aftermath of the Boer War. Jack got as far as London before the assignment was cancelled. What he did instead was to write *The People of the Abyss*, which established him as *the* writer of the working class. It was a searing indictment of conditions in the East End slums of London where he lived disguised as a ragged seaman, encountering disease, despair and death at every turn, sharing all the miseries of the slum dwellers' existence. He was later to say, "Of all my books, I love most *The People of the Abyss*. No other book of mine took so much of my young heart and tears as that study of the economic degradation of the poor."[8] Today, *The People of the Abyss* is recognized as a unique sociological document and a consummate example of the literature of social consciousness, superior in many ways to the writings of Frederick Engels and Robert Tressell. At the time, the book did not sell well outside radical circles, and even did some harm to Jack's burgeoning reputation as an author, but through–

out his life he never allowed considerations of cash or career to prevent him from saying and writing unpopular truths that needed to be told.

Three of Jack's books had been published while he was in London, including *The Children of the Frost*, another collection of Alaskan tales that confirmed his status as the dominant figure in American short story writing. He now decided to concentrate on full-length novels and in one month in the winter of 1902 he wrote *The Call of the Wild*. This story of the cross-bred dog Buck who returns to the wild after being mistreated by man was a huge success, and established Jack as a novelist of international stature. By the following spring he was at work on a second novel, *The Sea Wolf*, a sea adventure that was also a penetrating account of physical and moral brutality between men. On this occasion, some critics found the book cruel and even revolting, stinging Jack into a defense of his work;

> "People find fault with me for my 'disgusting realism'. Life is full of disgusting realism. I know men and women as they are – millions of them yet in the slime state. But I am an evolutionist and therefore a broad optimist, hence my love for the human (in the slime though he be) comes from my knowing him as he is and seeing the divine possibilities ahead of him"[9]

The public agreed with Jack, not with the critics. *The Sea Wolf* was an immediate best seller, and Jack was hailed as America's leading writer.

Although his career was now secure, Jack's financial affairs and private life were in chaos. He never learned to manage his money, and although he was now a highly-paid author his life still followed the precarious pattern set in his penniless youth. He would spend in expectation of what he would receive, then when the money arrived it would be swallowed up by debts and the cycle would begin again. Financial pressures often forced him into unwise measures; he sold *The Call of the Wild* to his publishers outright when he needed cash urgently, while if he had retained his royalty rights he would have earned over $100,000 from the book in just a few years. He had two households to support, his own and that of his mother, and he was unfailingly generous to friends and strangers alike, and to the socialist cause. His financial burdens were increased in the summer of 1903 when he left his wife Bessie Maddern, whom he had married in 1900, and their two young children for Chairman Kittredge, who became his second wife.

He worked at a blistering pace, writing three or more books a year and taking on all the journalistic work he could get as well. He expanded his scope beyond the Klondike and wrote stories based on all his early life experiences. He was the first truly popular author America had ever had, and he was read by millions of farm hands, sailors, factory workers, miners and workers of all kinds who had never taken an interest in literature before. He was one of them, a worker who had lived as they lived, who wrote from experience and who wrote *for* them. His work was full of examples of success against the odds, of hard-fought battles that ended in triumph, and it gave them hope. They valued his realism, and knew they could believe him when he said;

> "I am an idealist who believes in reality, and who therefore, in all I write strive to be real, to keep my own feet and the feet of the readers on the ground, so that no matter how high we dream our dreams will be based on reality."[10]

He had dreamed and succeeded, he had shown them it could be done; he was their hero.

The American Socialist Party did well in the national elections of 1904, and Jack was hopeful that the changes he had worked so hard to bring about might be immanent. No armchair socialist, he threw himself into a round of political activity that culminated in a nation-wide lecture tour in the fall of 1905. His obvious courage and commitment won admiration from many to whom socialism itself was anathema, and even the conservative San Francisco *Bulletin* was moved to observe;

> "The hot sincerity and hatred of wrong that burns in the revolutionary heart of young Jack London is the same spirit that characterized the tea-overboard party in Boston Harbor. It is the spirit that will ultimately reserve for the Republic all that is best, for it is the opposite of the dull spirit of slavish respect for the Established, which slavishness is composed of abasement of mind, and selfishness of character."[11]

But even as he lectured, the party for whom he had done so much was coming to a parting of the ways with its fiery champion.

Jack was a stand-up-and-fight socialist who had expected the party to consolidate the gains of 1904 and move forward with a solid programme of social reform but this did not happen, and he began to have reservations about the direction the American Socialist Party was taking. For their part, the more doctrinaire members of the party began to have reservations about Jack London. They decried his fictional celebrations of individual courage and endeavour as harmful to the concept of class unity. They condemned the non-political journalism he did for newspapers who were not sympathetic to the socialist cause. They even criticized his ownership of the Beauty Ranch, his ranch on the slopes of Sonoma Mountain, twenty-five miles from San Francisco. Jack needed to get away, he needed time to think, and it was now that he conceived of the voyage that is chronicled in *The Cruise of the Snark*.

As a boy he had read and loved Stevenson's South Sea stories and Melville's *Typee*, and he decided to fulfill his boyhood dream of sailing the Pacific. He designed the boat himself, but pressure of work obliged him to leave its construction and outfitting to others who did the work badly, and there were many delays and difficulties before he set sail from San Francisco on April 22, 1907. Once underway, he found that the boat was barely seaworthy, and that the captain had not managed to master the basics of stellar navigation. Jack refused to go back to San Francisco, and the only way to go forward was to take command himself. He studied the navigation charts and texts, set their course and got the *Snark* to Hawaii in twenty-five days. After an extensive refit, the *Snark* left Hawaii on October 7 bound for the Marquesas Islands. This traverse across the prevailing trade winds was theoretically impossible, but the *Snark* sighted the Marquesas in sixty days. After visiting Melville's *Typee* valley, the *Snark* and her crew sailed on to Tahiti, Samoa, Fiji, the New Hebrides and the Solomon Islands, arriving in Sydney, Australia on November 15, 1908.

The *Snark* had been plagued by technical problems throughout the voyage and everyone had suffered from illness in the latter days, but it was the happiest time in Jack's life. Like the Klondike, the Pacific gave him a new perspective, and he fell in love with it with all his heart. In the islands of Polynesia he found a new peace and freedom, and he was struck by the contrast between the easy, care-free lives of the islanders and what he called the 'artificial, wearing lives of the so-called civilized people'.[12] Cut loose from day-to-day pressures and political involvements for the first time and confronted with physical challenges that always brought out the best in him, he was able to gain an independence of mind that allowed him to accept that he was an idealist first and foremost, a socialist only so long as socialism lived up to his ideals. Above all, his Polynesian adventure renewed his faith in individual effort, courage and daring – and it is this theme which runs through *The Cruise of the Snark* like a golden thread, that makes it a book of universal appeal as well as one of the finest accounts of Pacific sailing ever written.

Jack returned from the Pacific in July, 1909. His ranch and his financial and literary affairs had been badly mismanaged in his absence, and he was once again deeply in debt. He set about to rectify matters in the usual way, writing nineteen hours a day until he had re-established himself. His life now centred on the Beauty Ranch where his hospitality was prodigious. He rarely had fewer than a dozen guests at table every night, no tramp who came to the door was ever turned away empty-handed, and he supported a vast number of employees who did very little to earn their keep because he could not bear to refuse anyone a job, as he had so often been refused in his youth. But for all he had accomplished, he was not a happy man. As he put it to a young reporter;

> "You may wonder why I am a pessimist; I often wonder myself. Here I have the most precious thing in the world – the love of a woman; I have beautiful children; I have lots and lots of money; I have fame as a writer; I have many men working for me; I have a beautiful ranch – and still, I am a pessimist. I look at things dispassionately, scientifically, and everything appears almost hopeless; after long years of labor and development, the people are as bad off as ever."[13]

His reservations about the American Socialist Party had been well-founded; they had, he said, become 'mere reformers', interested in nothing more revolutionary than low taxes and economy in government.

By 1913, Jack was making $75,000 a year and spending $100,000. The punishing rate at which he was forced to work had begun to undermine his health, but he refused to stop, saying "*I would rather be ashes than dust! I would rather that my spark should burn out in a brilliant blaze than it should be stifled by dry rot . . . the proper function of man is to live, not to exist. I shall not waste my days in trying to prolong them. I shall use my time.*"[14] He wrote several collections of fine short stories set in the Pacific, spent long holidays in Hawaii, and planned to move there permanently.

By 1916, he had written over fifty books, and was recognized as the most popular author in the world. His final break with the American Socialist Party came in march, 1916 when he tendered the party his formal resignation in a letter written from Hawaii;

> "I am resigning from the Socialist Party because of its lack of fire and fight . . . I believed that the working class, by fighting, by never fusing, by never making terms with the enemy, could emancipate itself. Since the whole trend of socialism in the United States of recent years has been one of peaceableness and com-

promise, I find that my mind refuses further sanction of my remaining a party member. Hence my resignation . . . My final word is that liberty, freedom and independence are royal things that cannot be presented to, nor thrust upon, races or classes. If races and classes cannot rise up and by their own strength of brain and brawn wrest from the world liberty, freedom and independence, they never, in time, can come to these royal possessions – and if such royal things are kindly presented to them by superior individuals, on silver platters, they will not know what to do with them, will fail to make use of them, and will be what they have always been in the past – inferior races and inferior classes."[15]

Eight months later, on November 22, 1916 the man who had always ridden the top of the wave of his life died of uremic poisoning, aged only forty.

In his eighteen years as a writer, he had revolutionized American literature and had worked tirelessly to reform American life by exposing injustice, by instilling a social conscience in the privileged and by giving the under-privileged the courage to better themselves. In its realistic style, commitment to the labour cause and concern with the relative merits of nature and civilization his writing set the pattern for what has been called the 'California school' of literature that was later developed by writers like John Steinbeck, but his work has a significance beyond a purely American context. The political aspect of his writing was always more highly regarded in Europe than in America, and the political insight he showed in his 1908 novel *The Iron Heel* moved Leon Trotsky to observe that London was a better social prophet than Lenin,[16] but the ultimate significance of Jack London's work must be sought in the direction it took in his later years. Of all twentieth-century authors Jack London is the first who can truly be called a Pacific Basin writer. Alaska and California were the setting for his early work, and his writing reflects the thriving frontier spirit of the northwest Pacific rim that is so nearly mirrored in the vigorous cultures of Australia and New Zealand. In going beyond the Pacific coast and into the Pacific itself, he foreshadowed the swing in orientation from Atlantic to Pacific that has been the most important development in American and world politics in recent years, and in marrying the realism of modern writing to the older tradition of Pacific romanticism established by Melville and Stevenson, he laid the foundations for modern Pacific literature.

Finally, Jack London's writing transcends considerations of place, class and politics for it is above all a celebration of life itself, and its

message is a timeless one for men and women everywhere. As he put it
— *"Fight for us or fight against us! Raise your voices one way or another; be alive!"*[17]

KAORI O'CONNOR

FOOTNOTES

1 London, Joan *Jack London And His Times: An Unconventional Biography*, University of Washington Press, Seattle and London, 1968; p 90.
2 ibid; p 172.
3 ibid; p 301.
4 ibid; p 146.
5 from Herbert Spencer's *Social Statistics*; IV. 30. 16.
6 London Ibid; pps 202–3.
7 Barltrop, Robert *Jack London: the Man, the Writer, the Rebel*, Pluto Press, London, 1976; p 66.
8 ibid; p 82.
9 London ibid; p 287.
10 Stone, Irving *Sailor On Horseback: The Biography of Jack London*, Houghton Mifflin Company, The Riverside Press, Cambridge, 1938: p 329.
11 ibid: p 211.
12 Johnson, Martin *Through The South Seas With Jack London*, T. Werner Laurie Ltd, London, 1913; p 226.
13 London ibid; p 336.
14 ibid; p 372.
15 Barltrop ibid; pps 163–4.
16 Martin, Stoddard *California Writers*, The MacMillan Press Ltd, London, 1983; p 23.
17 London ibid; p 301.

THE CRUISE OF THE "SNARK"

CHAPTER I

FOREWORD

IT began in the swimming pool at Glen Ellen. Between swims it was our wont to come out and lie in the sand and let our skins breathe the warm air and soak in the sunshine. Roscoe was a yachtsman. I had followed the sea a bit. It was inevitable that we should talk about boats. We talked about small boats, and the seaworthiness of small boats. We instanced Captain Slocum and his three years' voyage around the world in the *Spray*.

We asserted that we were not afraid to go around the world in a small boat, say forty feet long. We asserted furthermore that we would like to do it. We asserted finally that there was nothing in this world we'd like better than a chance to do it.

"Let us do it," we said . . . in fun.

Then I asked Charmian privily if she'd really care to do it, and she said that it was too good to be true.

The next time we breathed our skins in the sand by the swimming pool I said to Roscoe, " Let us do it."

I was in earnest, and so was he, for he said:

" When shall we start ? "

I had a house to build on the ranch, also an orchard, a vineyard, and several hedges to plant, and a number of other things to do. We thought we would start in four or five years. Then the lure of the adventure began to grip us. Why not start at once ? We'd never be younger, any of us. Let the orchard, vineyard, and hedges be growing up while we were away. When we came back, they would be ready for us, and we could live in the barn while we built the house.

So the trip was decided upon, and the building of the *Snark* began. We named her the *Snark* because we could not think of any other name— this information is given for the benefit of those who otherwise might think there is something occult in the name.

Our friends cannot understand why we make this voyage. They shudder, and moan, and raise their hands. No amount of explanation can make them comprehend that we are moving along the line of least resistance ; that it is easier for us to go down to the sea in a small ship than to remain on dry land, just as it is easier for them to remain on dry land than to go down to the sea in the small ship. This state of mind comes of an undue prominence of the ego. They cannot get away from themselves. They cannot come out of themselves long enough to see that their line of least resistance is not necessarily everybody else's line of least resistance. They make of their own bundle of desires, likes, and dislikes a yardstick wherewith to measure the desires, likes, and dislikes of all creatures. This is unfair. I tell them so. But they cannot get away from their own miserable egos long enough to hear me. They think I am crazy. In return, I am sympathetic. It is a state of mind familiar to me. We are all prone to think there is something wrong with the mental processes of the man who disagrees with us.

The ultimate word is I LIKE. It lies beneath philosophy, and is twined about the heart of life. When philosophy has maundered ponderously for a month, telling the individual what he must do, the individual says, in an instant, "I LIKE," and does something else, and philosophy goes glimmering. It is I LIKE that makes the drunkard drink and the martyr wear a hair shirt; that makes one man a reveller and another man an anchorite; that makes one man pursue fame, another gold, another love, and another God. Philosophy is very often a man's way of explaining his own I LIKE.

But to return to the *Snark*, and why I, for one, want to journey in her around the world. The things I like constitute my set of values. The thing I like most of all is personal achievement—not achievement for the world's applause, but achievement for my own delight. It is the old "I did it! I did it! With my own hands I did it!" But personal achievement, with me, must be concrete. I'd rather win a water-fight in the swimming pool, or remain astride a horse that is trying to get out from under me, than write the great American novel. Each man to his liking. Some other fellow would prefer writing the great American novel to winning the water-fight or mastering the horse.

Possibly the proudest achievement of my life, my moment of highest living, occurred when I was seventeen. I was in a three-masted schooner off the coast of Japan. We were in a typhoon. All hands had been on deck most of the night. I was called from my bunk at seven in the morning to take the wheel. Not a stitch of canvas was set. We were running before it under bare poles, yet the schooner fairly tore along. The seas were all of an eighth of a mile apart, and the wind snatched the whitecaps from their summits, filling the air so thick with driving spray that it was impossible to see more than two waves at a time. The schooner was almost unmanageable, rolling her rail under to starboard and to port, veering and yawing anywhere between south-east and south-west, and threatening, when the huge seas lifted under her quarter, to broach to. Had she broached to, she would ultimately have been reported lost with all hands and no tidings.

I took the wheel. The sailing-master watched me for a space. He was afraid of my youth, feared that I lacked the strength and the nerve. But when he saw me successfully wrestle the schooner through several bouts, he went below to breakfast. Fore and aft, all hands were below at breakfast. Had she broached to, not one of them would ever have reached the deck. For forty minutes I stood there alone at the wheel, in my grasp the wildly careering schooner and the lives of twenty-two men. Once we were pooped. I saw it coming, and, half-drowned, with tons of water crushing me, I checked the schooner's rush to broach to. At the end of the hour, sweating and played out, I was relieved. But I had done it! With my own hands I had done my trick at the wheel and guided a hundred tons of wood and iron through a few million tons of wind and waves.

My delight was in that I had done it—not in the fact that twenty-two men knew I had done it. Within the year over half of them were dead and gone, yet my pride in the thing performed was not diminished by half. I am willing to confess, however, that I do like a small audience. But it must be a very small audience, composed of those who love me and whom I love. When I then accomplish personal achievement, I have a feeling that I am justifying their love for me. But this is quite apart from the delight of the achievement itself. This delight is peculiarly my own and does not depend upon witnesses. When I have done some such thing, I am exalted. I glow all over. I am aware of a pride in myself that is mine, and mine alone. It is organic. Every fibre of me is thrilling with it. It is very natural. It is a mere matter of satisfaction at adjustment to environment. It is success.

Life that lives is life successful, and success is the breath of its nostrils. The achievement of a difficult feat is successful adjustment to a sternly exacting environment. The more difficult the feat, the greater the satisfaction at its accomplishment.   Thus it is with the man who leaps forward from the springboard, out over the swimming pool, and with a backward half-revolution of the body, enters the water head first.   Once he leaves the springboard his environment becomes immediately savage, and savage the penalty it will exact should he fail and strike the water flat.   Of course, the man does not have to run the risk of the penalty.   He could remain on the bank in a sweet and placid environment of summer air, sunshine, and stability.   Only he is not made that way.   In that swift mid-air moment he lives as he could never live on the bank.

As for myself, I'd rather be that man than the fellows who sit on the bank and watch him. That is why I am building the *Snark*.   I am so made.   I like, that is all.   The trip around the world means big moments of living.   Bear with me a moment and look at it.   Here am I, a little animal called a man—a bit of vitalized matter, one hundred and sixty-five pounds of meat and blood, nerve, sinew, bones, and brain,—all of it soft and tender, susceptible to hurt, fallible, and frail.   I strike a light back-handed blow on the nose of an obstreperous horse, and a bone in my hand is broken.   I put my head under the water for five minutes, and I am drowned.   I fall twenty feet through the air, and I am smashed.   I am a creature of temperature.   A few degrees one way, and my fingers and ears and toes blacken and drop off.   A few degrees the other way, and my skin blisters and shrivels away from the raw, quivering flesh.   A few additional degrees either way, and the life and the light in me go out. A drop of poison injected into my body from a snake, and I cease to move—for ever I cease to move. A splinter of lead from a rifle enters my head, and I am wrapped around in the eternal blackness.

Fallible and frail, a bit of pulsating, jelly-like life—it is all I am. About me are the great natural forces—colossal menaces, Titans of destruction, unsentimental monsters that have less concern for me than I have for the grain of sand I crush under my foot. They have no concern at all for me. They do not know me. They are unconscious, unmerciful, and unmoral. They are the cyclones and tornadoes, lightning flashes and cloud-bursts, tide-rips and tidal waves, undertows and waterspouts, great whirls and sucks and eddies, earthquakes and volcanoes, surfs that thunder on rock-ribbed coasts and seas that leap aboard the largest crafts that float, crushing humans to pulp or licking them off into the sea and to death—and these insensate monsters do not know that tiny sensitive creature, all nerves and weaknesses, whom men call Jack London, and who himself thinks he is all right and quite a superior being.

In the maze and chaos of the conflict of these vast and draughty Titans, it is for me to thread my precarious way. The bit of life that is I will exult over them. The bit of life that is I, in so far as it succeeds in baffling them or in bitting them to its service, will imagine that it is godlike. It is good to ride the tempest and feel godlike. I dare to assert that for a finite speck of pulsating jelly to feel godlike is a far more glorious feeling than for a god to feel godlike.

Here is the sea, the wind, and the wave. Here are the seas, the winds, and the waves of all the world. Here is ferocious environment. And here is difficult adjustment, the achievement of which is delight to the small quivering vanity that is I. I like. I am so made. It is my own particular form of vanity, that is all.

There is also another side to the voyage of the *Snark*. Being alive, I want to see, and all the world is a bigger thing to see than one small town or valley. We have done little outlining of the voyage. Only one thing is definite, and that is that our first port of call will be Honolulu. Beyond a few general ideas, we have no thought of our next port after Hawaii. We shall make up our minds as we get nearer. In a general way we know that we shall wander through the South Seas, take in Samoa, New Zealand, Tasmania, Australia, New Guinea, Borneo, and Sumatra, and go on up through the Philippines to Japan. Then will come Korea, China, India, the Red Sea, and the Mediterranean. After that the voyage becomes too vague to describe, though we know a number of things we shall surely do, and we expect to spend from one to several months in every country in Europe.

The *Snark* is to be sailed. There will be a gasolene engine on board, but it will be used only in case of emergency, such as in bad water among reefs and shoals, where a sudden calm in a swift current leaves a sailing-boat helpless. The rig of the *Snark* is to be what is called the "ketch."

The ketch rig is a compromise between the yawl and the schooner. Of late years the yawl rig has proved the best for cruising. The ketch retains the cruising virtues of the yawl, and in addition manages to embrace a few of the sailing virtues of the schooner. The foregoing must be taken with a pinch of salt. It is all theory in my head. I've never sailed a ketch, nor even seen one. The theory commends itself to me. Wait till I get out on the ocean, then I'll be able to tell more about the cruising and sailing qualities of the ketch.

As originally planned, the *Snark* was to be forty feet long on the water-line. But we discovered there was no space for a bath-room, and for that reason we have increased her length to forty-five feet. Her greatest beam is fifteen feet. She has no house and no hold. There is six feet of head-room, and the deck is unbroken save for two companionways and a hatch for'ard. The fact that there is no house to break the strength of the deck will make us feel safer in case great seas thunder their tons of water down on board. A large and roomy cockpit, sunk beneath the deck, with high rail and self-bailing, will make our rough-weather days and nights more comfortable.

There will be no crew. Or, rather, Charmian, Roscoe, and I are the crew. We are going to do the thing with our own hands. With our own hands we're going to circumnavigate the globe. Sail her or sink her, with our own hands we'll do it. Of course there will be a cook and a cabin-boy. Why should we stew over a stove, wash dishes, and set the table? We could stay on land if we wanted to do those things. Besides, we've got to stand watch and work the ship. And also, I've got to work at my trade of writing in order to feed us and to get new sails and tackle and keep the *Snark* in efficient working order. And then there's the ranch ; I've got to keep the vineyard, orchard, and hedges growing.

When we increased the length of the *Snark* in order to get space for a bath-room, we found that all the space was not required by the bath-room. Because of this, we increased the size of the engine. Seventy horse-power our engine is, and since we expect it to drive us along at a nine-knot clip, we do not know the name of a river with a current swift enough to defy us.

We expect to do a lot of inland work. The smallness of the *Snark* makes this possible. When we enter the land, out go the masts and on goes the engine. There are the canals of China, and the Yang-tse River. We shall spend months on them if we can get permission from the government. That will be the one obstacle to our inland voyaging—governmental permission. But if we can get that permission, there is scarcely a limit to the inland voyaging we can do.

When we come to the Nile, why we can go up the Nile. We can go up the Danube to Vienna, up the Thames to London, and we can go up the Seine to Paris and moor opposite the Latin Quarter with a bow-line out to Notre Dame and a stern-line fast to the Morgue. We can leave the Mediterranean and go up the Rhône to Lyons, there enter the Saône, cross from the Saône to the Marne through the Canal de Bourgogne, and from the Marne enter the Seine and go out the Seine at Havre. When we cross the Atlantic to the United States, we can go up the Hudson, pass through the Erie Canal, cross the Great Lakes, leave Lake Michigan at Chicago, gain the Mississippi by way of the Illinois River and the connecting canal, and go down the Mississippi to the Gulf of Mexico. And then there are the great rivers of South America. We'll know something about geography when we get back to California.

People that build houses are often sore perplexed; but if they enjoy the strain of it, I'll advise them to build a boat like the *Snark*. Just consider, for a moment, the strain of detail. Take the engine. What is the best kind of engine —the two cycle? three cycle? four cycle? My lips are mutilated with all kinds of strange jargon, my mind is mutilated with still stranger ideas and is foot-sore and weary from travelling in new and rocky realms of thought.—Ignition methods; shall it be make-and-break or jump-spark? Shall dry cells or storage batteries be used? A storage battery commends itself, but it requires a dynamo. How powerful a dynamo? And when we have installed a dynamo and a storage battery, it is simply ridiculous not to light the boat with electricity. Then comes the discussion of how many lights and how many candle-power. It is a splendid idea. But electric lights will demand a more powerful storage battery, which, in turn, demands a more powerful dynamo.

And now that we've gone in for it, why not have a searchlight? It would be tremendously useful. But the searchlight needs so much electricity that

when it runs it will put all the other lights out of
commission.   Again we travel the weary road in
the quest after more power for storage battery
and dynamo.   And then, when it is finally solved,
some one asks, "What if the engine breaks
down?"   And we collapse.   There are the side-
lights, the binnacle light, and the anchor light.
Our very lives depend upon them.   So we have
to fit the boat throughout with oil lamps as well.

But we are not done with that engine yet.   The
engine is powerful.   We are two small men and a
small woman.   It will break our hearts and our
backs to hoist anchor by hand.   Let the engine
do it.   And then comes the problem of how to
convey power for'ard from the engine to the winch.
And by the time all this is settled, we redistribute
the allotments of space to the engine-room, galley,
bath-room, state-rooms, and cabin, and begin all
over again.   And when we have shifted the
engine, I send off a telegram of gibberish to its
makers at New York, something like this : *Toggle-
joint abandoned change thrust-bearing accordingly
distance from forward side of flywheel to face of
sternpost sixteen feet six inches.*

Just potter around in quest of the best steering
gear, or try to decide whether you will set up
your rigging with old-fashioned lanyards or with
turnbuckles, if you want strain of detail.   Shall
the binnacle be located in front of the wheel in the
centre of the beam, or shall it be located to one
side in front of the wheel?—there's room right
there for a library of sea-dog controversy.   Then
there's the problem of gasolene, fifteen hundred
gallons of it—what are the safest ways to tank it

and pipe it ? and which is the best fire-extinguisher for a gasolene fire ? Then there is the pretty problem of the life-boat and the stowage of the same. And when that is finished, come the cook and cabin-boy to confront one with nightmare possibilities. It is a small boat, and we'll be packed close together. The servant-girl problem of landsmen pales to insignificance. We did select one cabin-boy, and by that much were our troubles eased. And then the cabin-boy fell in love and resigned.

And in the meanwhile how is a fellow to find time to study navigation—when he is divided between these problems and the earning of the money wherewith to settle the problems ? Neither Roscoe nor I know anything about navigation, and the summer is gone, and we are about to start, and the problems are thicker than ever, and the treasury is stuffed with emptiness. Well, anyway, it takes years to learn seamanship, and both of us are seamen. If we don't find the time, we'll lay in the books and instruments and teach ourselves navigation on the ocean between San Francisco and Hawaii.

There is one unfortunate and perplexing phase of the voyage of the *Snark*. Roscoe, who is to be my co-navigator, is a follower of one, Cyrus R. Teed. Now Cyrus R. Teed has a different cosmology from the one generally accepted, and Roscoe shares his views. Wherefore Roscoe believes that the surface of the earth is concave and that we live on the inside of a hollow sphere. Thus, though we shall sail on the one boat, the *Snark*, Roscoe will journey around the world on the inside, while I shall journey around on the outside. But of this, more anon. We threaten to be of the one mind before the voyage is completed. I am confident that I shall convert him into making the journey on the outside, while he is equally confident that before we arrive back in San Francisco I shall be on the inside of the earth. How he is going to get me through the crust I don't know, but Roscoe is ay a masterful man.

P.S.—That engine! While we've got it, and the dynamo, and the storage battery, why not have an ice-machine? Ice in the tropics! It is more necessary than bread. Here goes for the ice-machine! Now I am plunged into chemistry, and my lips hurt, and my mind hurts, and how am I ever to find the time to study navigation?

CHAPTER II

THE INCONCEIVABLE AND MONSTROUS

"SPARE no money," I said to Roscoe. "Let everything on the *Snark* be of the best. And never mind decoration. Plain pine boards is good enough finishing for me. But put the money into the construction. Let the *Snark* be as staunch and strong as any boat afloat. Never mind what it costs to make her staunch and strong; you see that she is made staunch and strong, and I'll go on writing and earning the money to pay for it."

And I did . . . as well as I could ; for the *Snark* ate up money faster than I could earn it. In fact, every little while I had to borrow money with which to supplement my earnings. Now I borrowed one thousand dollars, now I borrowed two thousand dollars, and now I borrowed five thousand dollars. And all the time I went on working every day and sinking the earnings in the venture. I worked Sundays as well, and I took no holidays. But it was worth it. Every time I thought of the *Snark* I knew she was worth it.

For know, gentle reader, the staunchness of the *Snark*. She is forty-five feet long on the water-

27

line.   Her garboard strake is three inches thick ;
her planking two and one-half inches thick ; her
deck-planking two inches thick ; and in all her
planking there are no butts. I know, for I
ordered that planking especially from Puget
Sound.   Then the *Snark* has four water-tight
compartments, which is to say that her length is
broken by three water-tight bulkheads.   Thus,
no matter how large a leak the *Snark* may spring,
only one compartment can fill with water.   The
other three compartments will keep her afloat,
anyway, and, besides, will enable us to mend the
leak.   There is another virtue in these bulkheads.
The last compartment of all, in the very stern,
contains six tanks that carry over one thousand
gallons of gasolene.   Now gasolene is a very
dangerous article to carry in bulk on a small craft
far out on the wide ocean.   But when the six
tanks that do not leak are themselves contained
in a compartment hermetically sealed off from
the rest of the boat, the danger will be seen to be
very small indeed.

The *Snark* is a sail-boat.   She was built
primarily to sail.   But incidentally, as an auxiliary, a seventy-horse-power engine was installed.
This is a good, strong engine.   I ought to know.
I paid for it to come out all the way from New
York City.   Then, on deck, above the engine, is
a windlass.   It is a magnificent affair.   It weighs
several hundred pounds and takes up no end of
deck-room.   You see, it is ridiculous to hoist
up anchor by hand-power when there is a seventy-
horse-power engine on board.   So we installed the
windlass, transmitting power to it from the engine

by means of a gear and castings specially made in a San Francisco foundry.

The *Snark* was made for comfort, and no expense was spared in this regard. There is the bath-room, for instance, small and compact, it is true, but containing all the conveniences of any bath-room upon land. The bath-room is a beautiful dream of schemes and devices, pumps, and levers, and sea-valves. Why, in the course of its building, I used to lie awake nights thinking about that bath-room. And next to the bath-room come the life-boat and the launch. They are carried on deck, and they take up what little space might have been left us for exercise. But then, they beat life insurance ; and the prudent man, even if he has built as staunch and strong a craft as the *Snark*, will see to it that he has a good life-boat as well. And ours is a good one. It is a dandy. It was stipulated to cost one hundred and fifty dollars, and when I came to pay the bill, it turned out to be three hundred and ninety-five dollars. That shows how good a life-boat it is.

I could go on at great length relating the various virtues and excellences of the *Snark*, but I refrain. I have bragged enough as it is, and I have bragged to a purpose, as will be seen before my tale is ended. And please remember its title, " The Inconceivable and Monstrous." It was planned that the *Snark* should sail on October 1, 1906. That she did not so sail was inconceivable and monstrous. There was no valid reason for not sailing except that she was not ready to sail, and there was no conceivable reason why she was not ready. She was promised on November first, on November fifteenth, on December first ; and yet she was never ready. On December first Charmian and I left the sweet, clean Sonoma country and came down to live in the stifling city —but not for long, oh, no, only for two weeks, for we would sail on December fifteenth. And I guess we ought to know, for Roscoe said so, and it was on his advice that we came to the city to stay two weeks. Alas, the two weeks went by, four weeks went by, six weeks went by, eight weeks went by, and we were farther away from sailing than ever. Explain it ? Who ?—me ? I can't. It is the one thing in all my life that I have backed down on. There is no explaining it ; if there were, I'd do it. I, who am an artisan of speech, confess my inability to explain why the *Snark* was not ready. As I have said, and as I must repeat, it was inconceivable and monstrous.

The eight weeks became sixteen weeks, and then, one day, Roscoe cheered us up by saying :

" If we don't sail before April first, you can use my head for a football."

Two weeks later he said, " I'm getting my head in training for that match."

" Never mind," Charmian and I said to each other ; " think of the wonderful boat it is going to be when it is completed."

Whereat we would rehearse for our mutual encouragement the manifold virtues and excellences of the *Snark*. Also, I would borrow more money, and I would get down closer to my desk and write harder, and I refused heroically to take a Sunday off and go out into the hills with my friends. I was building a boat, and by the eternal it was going to be a boat, and a boat spelled out all in capitals—B-O-A-T; and no matter what it cost I didn't care, so long as it was a B O A T.

And, oh, there is one other excellence of the *Snark*, upon which I must brag, namely, her bow. No sea could ever come over it. It laughs at the sea, that bow does; it challenges the sea; it snorts defiance at the sea. And withal it is a beautiful bow; the lines of it are dreamlike; I doubt if ever a boat was blessed with a more beautiful and at the same time a more capable bow. It was made to punch storms. To touch that bow is to rest one's hand on the cosmic nose of things. To look at it is to realize that expense cut no figure where it was concerned. And every time our sailing was delayed, or a new expense was tacked on, we thought of that wonderful bow and were content.

The *Snark* is a small boat. When I figured seven thousand dollars as her generous cost, I was both generous and correct. I have built barns and houses, and I know the peculiar trait such things have of running past their estimated cost. This knowledge was mine, was already mine, when I estimated the probable cost of the building of the *Snark* at seven thousand dollars. Well, she cost thirty thousand. Now don't ask me, please. It is the truth. I signed the cheques and I raised the money. Of course there is no explaining it. Inconceivable and monstrous is what it is, as you will agree, I know, ere my tale is done.

Then there was the matter of delay. I dealt

with forty-seven different kinds of union men and with one hundred and fifteen different firms. And not one union man and not one firm of all the union men and all the firms ever delivered any-thing at the time agreed upon, nor ever was on time for anything except pay-day and bill-collection.   Men pledged me their immortal souls that they would deliver a certain thing on a certain date ; as a rule, after such pledging, they rarely exceeded being three months late in de-livery.   And so it went, and Charmian and I consoled each other by saying what a splendid boat the *Snark* was, so staunch and strong ; also, we would get into the small boat and row around the *Snark,* and gloat over her unbelievably wonderful bow.

" Think," I would say to Charmian, " of a gale off the China coast, and of the *Snark* hove to, that splendid bow of hers driving into the storm. Not a drop will come over that bow.   She'll be as dry as a feather, and we'll be all below playing whist while the gale howls."

And Charmian would press my hand enthusi-astically and exclaim : " It's worth every bit of it—the delay, and expense, and worry, and all the rest.   Oh, what a truly wonderful boat ! "

Whenever I looked at the bow of the *Snark* or thought of her water-tight compartments, I was encouraged. Nobody else, however, was en-couraged.   My friends began to make bets against the various sailing dates of the *Snark*.   Mr. Wiget, who was left behind in charge of our Sonoma ranch, was the first to cash his bet.   He collected on New Year's Day, 1907.   After that the bets came fast and furious. My friends surrounded me like a gang of harpies, making bets against every sailing date I set. I was rash, and I was stubborn. I bet, and I bet, and I continued to bet ; and I paid them all. Why, the women-kind of my friends grew so brave that those among them who never bet before began to bet with me. And I paid them, too.

" Never mind," said Charmian to me ; " just think of that bow and of being hove to on the China Seas."

" You see," I said to my friends, when I paid the latest bunch of wagers, " neither trouble nor cash is being spared in making the *Snark* the most seaworthy craft that ever sailed out through the Golden Gate—that is what causes all the delay."

In the meantime editors and publishers with whom I had contracts pestered me with demands for explanations. But how could I explain to them, when I was unable to explain to myself, or when there was nobody, not even Roscoe, to explain to me ? The newspapers began to laugh at me, and to publish rhymes anent the *Snark's* departure with refrains like, " Not yet, but soon." And Charmian cheered me up by reminding me of the bow, and I went to a banker and borrowed five thousand more. There was one recompense for the delay, however. A friend of mine, who happens to be a critic, wrote a roast of me, of all I had done, and of all I ever was going to do ; and he planned to have it published after I was out on the ocean. I was still on shore when it came out, and he has been busy explaining ever since.

And the time continued to go by.   One thing was becoming apparent, namely, that it was impossible to finish the *Snark* in San Francisco. She had been so long in the building that she was beginning to break down and wear out.   In fact, she had reached the stage where she was breaking down faster than she could be repaired.   She had become a joke.   Nobody took her seriously ; least of all the men who worked on her.   I said we would sail just as she was and finish building her in Honolulu.   Promptly she sprang a leak that had to be attended to before we could sail. I started her for the boat-ways.   Before she got to them she was caught between two huge barges and received a vigorous crushing.   We got her on the ways, and, part way along, the ways spread and dropped her through, stern-first, into the mud.

It was a pretty tangle, a job for wreckers, not boat-builders.   There are two high tides every twenty-four hours, and at every high tide, night and day, for a week, there were two steam tugs pulling and hauling on the *Snark*.   There she was, stuck, fallen between the ways and standing on her stern.   Next, and while still in that predicament, we started to use the gears and castings made in the local foundry whereby power was conveyed from the engine to the windlass.   It was the first time we ever tried to use that windlass.   The castings had flaws ; they shattered asunder, the gears ground together, and the windlass was out of commission.   Following upon that, the seventy-horse-power engine went out of commission.   This engine came from New York ;

so did its bed-plate ; there was a flaw in the bed-plate ; there were a lot of flaws in the bed-plate ; and the seventy-horse-power engine broke away from its shattered foundations, reared up in the air, smashed all connections and fastenings, and fell over on its side. And the *Snark* continued to stick between the spread ways, and the two tugs continued to haul vainly upon her.

" Never mind," said Charmian, " think of what a staunch, strong boat she is."

" Yes," said I, " and of that beautiful bow."

So we took heart and went at it again. The ruined engine was lashed down on its rotten foundation ; the smashed castings and cogs of the power transmission were taken down and stored away—all for the purpose of taking them to Honolulu where repairs and new castings could be made. Somewhere in the dim past the *Snark* had received on the outside one coat of white paint. The intention of the colour was still evident, however, when one got it in the right light. The *Snark* had never received any paint on the inside. On the contrary, she was coated inches thick with the grease and tobacco-juice of the multitudinous mechanics who had toiled upon her. Never mind, we said ; the grease and filth could be planed off, and later, when we fetched Honolulu, the *Snark* could be painted at the same time as she was being rebuilt.

By main strength and sweat we dragged the *Snark* off from the wrecked ways and laid her alongside the Oakland City Wharf. The drays brought all the outfit from home, the books and blankets and personal luggage. Along with this, everything else came on board in a torrent of confusion—wood and coal, water and water-tanks, vegetables, provisions, oil, the life-boat and the launch, all our friends, all the friends of our friends and those who claimed to be their friends, to say nothing of some of the friends of the friends of the friends of our crew. Also there were reporters, and photographers, and strangers, and cranks, and finally, and over all, clouds of coal-dust from the wharf.

We were to sail Sunday at eleven, and Saturday afternoon had arrived. The crowd on the wharf and the coal-dust were thicker than ever. In one pocket I carried a cheque-book, a fountain-pen, a dater, and a blotter; in another pocket I carried between one and two thousand dollars in paper money and gold. I was ready for the creditors, cash for the small ones and cheques for the large ones, and was waiting only for Roscoe to arrive with the balances of the accounts of the hundred and fifteen firms who had delayed me so many months. And then—

And then the inconceivable and monstrous happened once more. Before Roscoe could arrive there arrived another man. He was a United States marshal. He tacked a notice on the *Snark's* brave mast so that all on the wharf could read that the *Snark* had been libelled for debt. The marshal left a little old man in charge of the *Snark*, and himself went away. I had no longer any control of the *Snark*, nor of her wonderful bow. The little old man was now her lord and master, and I learned that I was paying him three dollars a day for being lord and master. Also, I learned the name of the man who had libelled the *Snark*. It was Sellers ; the debt was two hundred and thirty-two dollars ; and the deed was no more than was to be expected from the possessor of such a name. Sellers ! Ye gods ! Sellers !

But who under the sun was Sellers ? I looked in my cheque-book and saw that two weeks before I had made him out a cheque for five hundred dollars. Other cheque-books showed me that during the many months of the building of the *Snark* I had paid him several thousand dollars. Then why in the name of common decency hadn't he tried to collect his miserable little balance instead of libelling the *Snark* ? I thrust my hands into my pockets, and in one pocket encountered the cheque-book and the dater and the pen, and in the other pocket the gold money and the paper money. There was the wherewithal to settle his pitiful account a few score of times and over—why hadn't he given me a chance ? There was no explanation ; it was merely the inconceivable and monstrous.

To make the matter worse, the *Snark* had been libelled late Saturday afternoon ; and though I sent lawyers and agents all over Oakland and San Francisco, neither United States judge, nor United States marshal, nor Mr. Sellers, nor Mr. Sellers' attorney, nor anybody could be found. They were all out of town for the week end. And so the *Snark* did not sail Sunday morning at eleven. The little old man was still in charge, and he said no. And Charmian and I walked out on an opposite wharf and took consolation in the *Snark's* wonderful bow and thought of all the gales and typhoons it would proudly punch.

" A bourgeois trick," I said to Charmian, speaking of Mr. Sellers and his libel ; " a petty trader's panic. But never mind ; our troubles will cease when once we are away from this and out on the wide ocean."

And in the end we sailed away, on Tuesday morning, April 23, 1907. We started rather lame, I confess. We had to hoist anchor by hand, because the power transmission was a wreck. Also, what remained of our seventy-horse-power engine was lashed down for ballast on the bottom of the *Snark*. But what of such things ? They could be fixed in Honolulu, and in the meantime think of the magnificent rest of the boat ! It is true, the engine in the launch wouldn't run, and the life-boat leaked like a sieve ; but then they weren't the *Snark* ; they were mere appurtenances. The things that counted were the water-tight bulk-heads, the solid planking without butts, the bath-room devices—they were the *Snark*. And then there was, greatest of all, that noble, wind-punching bow.

We sailed out through the Golden Gate and set our course south toward that part of the Pacific where we could hope to pick up with the north-east trades. And right away things began to happen. I had calculated that youth was the stuff for a voyage like that of the *Snark*, and I had taken three youths—the engineer, the cook, and the cabin-boy. My calculation was only two-thirds off ; I had forgotten to calculate on seasick youth, and I had two of them, the cook and the cabin-boy. They immediately took to their bunks, and that was the end of their usefulness for a week to come. It will be understood, from the foregoing, that we did not have the hot meals we might have had, nor were things kept clean and orderly down below. But it did not matter very much anyway, for we quickly discovered that our box of oranges had at some time been frozen ; that our box of apples was mushy and spoiling ; that the crate of cabbages, spoiled before it was ever delivered to us, had to go overboard instanter; that kerosene had been spilled on the carrots, and that the turnips were woody and the beets rotten, while the kindling was dead wood that wouldn't burn, and the coal, delivered in rotten potato-sacks, had spilled all over the deck and was washing through the scuppers.

But what did it matter ? Such things were mere accessories. There was the boat—she was all right, wasn't she ? I strolled along the deck and in one minute counted fourteen butts in the beautiful planking ordered specially from Puget Sound in order that there should be no butts in it. Also, that deck leaked, and it leaked badly. It drowned Roscoe out of his bunk and ruined the tools in the engine-room, to say nothing of the provisions it ruined in the galley. Also, the sides of the *Snark* leaked, and the bottom leaked, and we had to pump her every day to keep her afloat. The floor of the galley is a couple of feet above the inside bottom of the *Snark* ; and yet I have stood on the floor of the galley, trying to snatch a cold bite, and been wet to the knees by the water churning around inside four hours after the last pumping.

Then those magnificent water-tight compartments that cost so much time and money—well, they weren't water-tight after all. The water moved free as the air from one compartment to another; furthermore, a strong smell of gasolene from the after compartment leads me to suspect that some one or more of the half-dozen tanks there stored have sprung a leak. The tanks leak, and they are not hermetically sealed in their compartment. Then there was the bath-room with its pumps and levers and sea-valves—it went out of commission inside the first twenty hours. Powerful iron levers broke off short in one's hand when one tried to pump with them. The bath-room was the swiftest wreck of any portion of the *Snark*.

And the iron-work on the *Snark*, no matter what its source, proved to be mush. For instance, the bed-plate of the engine came from New York, and it was mush; so were the casting and gears for the windlass that came from San Francisco. And finally, there was the wrought iron used in the rigging, that carried away in all directions when the first strains were put upon it. Wrought iron, mind you, and it snapped like macaroni.

A gooseneck on the gaff of the mainsail broke short off. We replaced it with the gooseneck from the gaff of the storm trysail, and the second gooseneck broke short off inside fifteen minutes of use, and, mind you, it had been taken from the gaff of the storm trysail, upon which we would have depended in time of storm. At the present moment the *Snark* trails her mainsail like a broken wing, the gooseneck being replaced by a rough lashing. We'll see if we can get honest iron in Honolulu.

Man had betrayed us and sent us to sea in a sieve, but the Lord must have loved us, for we had calm weather in which to learn that we must pump every day in order to keep afloat, and that more trust could be placed in a wooden toothpick than in the most massive piece of iron to be found aboard. As the staunchness and the strength of the *Snark* went glimmering, Charmian and I pinned our faith more and more to the *Snark's* wonderful bow. There was nothing else left to pin to. It was all inconceivable and monstrous, we knew, but that bow, at least, was rational. And then, one evening, we started to heave to.

How shall I describe it? First of all, for the benefit of the tyro, let me explain that heaving to is that sea manœuvre which, by means of short and balanced canvas, compels a vessel to ride bow-on to wind and sea. When the wind is too strong, or the sea is too high, a vessel of the size of the *Snark* can heave to with ease, whereupon there is no more work to do on deck. Nobody needs to steer. The lookout is superfluous. All hands can go below and sleep or play whist.

Well, it was blowing half of a small summer gale, when I told Roscoe we'd heave to. Night was coming on. I had been steering nearly all day, and all hands on deck (Roscoe and Bert and Charmian) were tired, while all hands below were seasick. It happened that we had already put two reefs in the big mainsail. The flying-jib and the jib were taken in, and a reef put in the fore-staysail. The mizzen was also taken in. About this time the flying jib-boom buried itself in a sea and broke short off. I started to put the wheel down in order to heave to. The *Snark* at the moment was rolling in the trough. She continued rolling in the trough. I put the spokes down harder and harder. She never budged from the trough. (The trough, gentle reader, is the most dangerous position of all in which to lay a vessel.) I put the wheel hard down, and still the *Snark* rolled in the trough. Eight points was the nearest I could get her to the wind. I had Roscoe and Bert come in on the main-sheet. The *Snark* rolled on in the trough, now putting her rail under on one side and now under on the other side.

Again the inconceivable and monstrous was showing its grizzly head. It was grotesque, impossible. I refused to believe it. Under double-reefed mainsail and single-reefed staysail the *Snark* refused to heave to. We flattened the mainsail down. It did not alter the *Snark's* course a tenth of a degree. We slacked the mainsail off with no more result. We set a storm trysail on the mizzen, and took in the mainsail. No change. The *Snark* rolled on in the trough. That beautiful bow of hers refused to come up and face the wind.

Next we took in the reefed staysail. Thus, the only bit of canvas left on her was the storm trysail on the mizzen. If anything would bring her bow up to the wind, that would. Maybe you won't believe me when I say it failed, but I do say it failed. And I say it failed because I saw it fail, and not because I believe it failed. I don't believe it did fail. It is unbelievable, and I am not telling you what I believe ; I am telling you what I saw.

Now, gentle reader, what would you do if you were on a small boat, rolling in the trough of the sea, a trysail on that small boat's stern that was unable to swing the bow up into the wind ? Get out the sea-anchor. It's just what we did. We had a patent one, made to order and warranted not to dive. Imagine a hoop of steel that serves to keep open the mouth of a large, conical, canvas bag, and you have a sea-anchor. Well, we made a line fast to the sea-anchor and to the bow of the *Snark*, and then dropped the sea-anchor overboard. It promptly dived. We had a tripping line on it, so we tripped the sea-anchor and hauled it in. We attached a big timber as a float, and dropped the sea-anchor over again. This time it floated. The line to the bow grew taut. The trysail on the mizzen tended to swing the bow into the wind, but, in spite of this tendency, the *Snark* calmly took that sea-anchor in her teeth, and went on ahead, dragging it after her, still in the trough of the sea. And there you are. We even took in the trysail, hoisted the full mizzen in its place, and hauled the full mizzen down flat, and the *Snark* wallowed in the trough and dragged the sea-anchor behind her. Don't believe me. I don't believe it myself. I am merely telling you what I saw.

Now I leave it to you. Who ever heard of a sailing-boat that wouldn't heave to ?—that

wouldn't heave to with a sea-anchor to help it ?
Out of my brief experience with boats I know I
never did.   And I stood on deck and looked on
the naked face of the inconceivable and monstrous
—the *Snark* that wouldn't heave to.   A stormy
night with broken moonlight had come on.
There was a splash of wet in the air, and up to
windward there was a promise of rain-squalls ;
and then there was the trough of the sea, cold
and cruel in the moonlight, in which the *Snark*
complacently rolled.   And then we took in the
sea-anchor and the mizzen, hoisted the reefed
staysail, ran the *Snark* off before it, and went
below—not to the hot meal that should have
awaited us, but to skate across the slush and slime
on the cabin floor, where cook and cabin-boy lay
like dead men in their bunks, and to lie down in
our own bunks, with our clothes on ready for a
call, and to listen to the bilge-water spouting
knee-high on the galley floor.

In the Bohemian Club of San Francisco there
are some crack sailors.   I know, because I heard
them pass judgment on the *Snark* during the
process of her building.   They found only one
vital thing the matter with her, and on this they
were all agreed, namely, that she could not run.
She was all right in every particular, they said,
except that I'd never be able to run her before it
in a stiff wind and sea.   "Her lines," they explained enigmatically, " it is the fault of her lines.
She simply cannot be made to run, that is all."
Well, I wish I'd only had those crack sailors of the
Bohemian Club on board the *Snark* the other
night for them to see for themselves their one,

vital, unanimous judgment absolutely reversed. Run? It is the one thing the *Snark* does to perfection. Run? She ran with a sea-anchor fast for'ard and a full mizzen flattened down aft. Run? At the present moment, as I write this, we are bowling along before it, at a six-knot clip, in the north-east trades. Quite a tidy bit of sea is running. There is nobody at the wheel, the wheel is not even lashed and is set over a half-spoke weather helm. To be precise, the wind is north-east; the *Snark's* mizzen is furled, her mainsail is over to starboard, her head-sheets are hauled flat; and the *Snark's* course is south-south-west. And yet there are men who have sailed the seas for forty years and who hold that no boat can run before it without being steered. They'll call me a liar when they read this; it's what they called Captain Slocum when he said the same of his *Spray*.

As regards the future of the *Snark* I'm all at sea. I don't know. If I had the money or the credit, I'd build another *Snark* that *would* heave to. But I am at the end of my resources. I've got to put up with the present *Snark* or quit—and I can't quit. So I guess I'll have to try to get along with heaving the *Snark* to stern-first. I am waiting for the next gale to see how it will work. I think it can be done. It all depends on how her stern takes the seas. And who knows but that some wild morning on the China Sea, some gray-beard skipper will stare, rub his incredulous eyes and stare again, at the spectacle of a weird, small craft, very much like the *Snark*, hove to stern-first and riding out the gale?

P.S. On my return to California after the voyage, I learned that the *Snark* was forty-three feet on the water-line instead of forty-five. This was due to the fact that the builder was not on speaking terms with the tape-line or two-foot rule.

CHAPTER III

ADVENTURE

NO, adventure is not dead, and in spite of the steam engine and of Thomas Cook & Son. When the announcement of the contemplated voyage of the *Snark* was made, young men of " roving disposition " proved to be legion, and young women as well—to say nothing of the elderly men and women who volunteered for the voyage. Why, among my personal friends there were at least half a dozen who regretted their recent or imminent marriages ; and there was one marriage I know of that almost failed to come off because of the *Snark*.

Every mail to me was burdened with the letters of applicants who were suffocating in the " man-stifled towns," and it soon dawned upon me that a twentieth century Ulysses required a corps of stenographers to clear his correspondence before setting sail. No, adventure is certainly not dead —not while one receives letters that begin : " There is no doubt that when you read this soul-plea from a female stranger in New York City," etc. ; and wherein one learns, a little farther on, that this female stranger weighs only ninety pounds, wants to be cabin-boy, and "yearns to see the countries of the world."

The possession of a "passionate fondness for geography," was the way one applicant expressed the wander-lust that was in him; while another wrote, "I am cursed with an eternal yearning to be always on the move, consequently this letter to you." But best of all was the fellow who said he wanted to come because his feet itched.

There were a few who wrote anonymously, suggesting names of friends and giving said friends' qualifications; but to me there was a hint of something sinister in such proceedings, and I went no further in the matter.

With two or three exceptions, all the hundreds that volunteered for my crew were very much in earnest. Many of them sent their photographs. Ninety per cent. offered to work in any capacity, and ninety-nine per cent. offered to work without salary. "Contemplating your voyage on the *Snark*," said one, "and notwithstanding its attendant dangers, to accompany you (in any capacity whatever) would be the climax of my ambitions." Which reminds me of the young fellow who was "seventeen years old and ambicious," and who, at the end of his letter, earnestly requested "but please do not let this git into the papers or magazines." Quite different was the one who said, "I would be willing to work like hell and not demand pay." Almost all of them wanted me to telegraph, at their expense, my acceptance of their services; and quite a number offered to put up a bond to guarantee their appearance on sailing date.

Some were rather vague in their own minds concerning the work to be done on the *Snark*; as, for instance, the one who wrote: "I am taking the liberty of writing you this note to find out if there would be any possibility of my going with you as one of the crew of your boat to make sketches and illustrations." Several, unaware of the needful work on a small craft like the *Snark*, offered to serve, as one of them phrased it, "as assistant in filing materials collected for books and novels." That's what one gets for being prolific.

"Let me give my qualifications for the job," wrote one. "I am an orphan living with my uncle, who is a hot revolutionary socialist and who says a man without the red blood of adventure is an animated dish-rag." Said another: "I can swim some, though I don't know any of the new strokes. But what is more important than strokes, the water is a friend of mine." "If I was put alone in a sail-boat, I could get her anywhere I wanted to go," was the qualification of a third—and a better qualification than the one that follows, "I have also watched the fish-boats unload." But possibly the prize should go to this one, who very subtly conveys his deep knowledge of the world and life by saying: "My age, in years, is twenty-two."

Then there were the simple, straight-out, homely, and unadorned letters of young boys, lacking in the felicities of expression, it is true, but desiring greatly to make the voyage. These were the hardest of all to decline, and each time I declined one it seemed as if I had struck Youth a slap in the face. They were so earnest, these

boys, they wanted so much to go. " I am sixteen
but large for my age," said one ; and another,
" Seventeen but large and healthy."   " I am as
strong at least as the average boy of my size,"
said an evident weakling.   " Not afraid of any
kind of work," was what many said, while one in
particular, to lure me no doubt by inexpensiveness,
wrote : " I can pay my way to the Pacific coast,
so that part would probably be acceptable to you."
" Going around the world is *the one thing* I want
to do," said one, and it seemed to be the one thing
that a few hundred wanted to do.   " I have no
one who cares whether I go or not," was the
pathetic note sounded by another.   One had sent
his photograph, and speaking of it, said, " I'm a
homely-looking sort of a chap, but looks don't
always count."   And I am confident that the lad
who wrote the following would have turned out
all right : " My age is 19 years, but I am rather
small and consequently won't take up much
room, but I'm tough as the devil."   And there
was one thirteen-year-old applicant that Charmian
and I fell in love with, and it nearly broke our
hearts to refuse him.

But it must not be imagined that most of my
volunteers were boys ; on the contrary, boys
constituted a very small proportion.   There were
men and women from every walk in life.   Physicians, surgeons, and dentists offered in large
numbers to come along, and, like all the professional men, offered to come without pay, to
serve in any capacity, and to pay, even, for the
privilege of so serving.

There was no end of compositors and reporters

who wanted to come, to say nothing of experienced valets, chefs, and stewards. Civil engineers were keen on the voyage ; "lady" companions galore cropped up for Charmian ; while I was deluged with the applications of would-be private secretaries. Many high school and university students yearned for the voyage, and every trade in the working class developed a few applicants, the machinists, electricians, and engineers being especially strong on the trip. I was surprised at the number, who, in musty law offices, heard the call of adventure ; and I was more than surprised by the number of elderly and retired sea captains who were still thralls to the sea. Several young fellows, with millions coming to them later on, were wild for the adventure, as were also several county superintendents of schools.

Fathers and sons wanted to come, and many men with their wives, to say nothing of the young woman stenographer who wrote : " Write immediately if you need me. I shall bring my typewriter on the first train." But the best of all is the following—observe the delicate way in which he worked in his wife : " I thought I would drop you a line of inquiry as to the possibility of making the trip with you, am 24 years of age, married and broke, and a trip of that kind would be just what we are looking for."

Come to think of it, for the average man it must be fairly difficult to write an honest letter of self-recommendation. One of my correspondents was so stumped that he began his letter with the words, " This is a hard task " ; and, after vainly trying to describe his good points, he wound up with,

"It is a hard job writing about one's self." Nevertheless, there was one who gave himself a most glowing and lengthy character, and in conclusion stated that he had greatly enjoyed writing it.

"But suppose this : your cabin-boy could run your engine, could repair it when out of order. Suppose he could take his turn at the wheel, could do any carpenter or machinist work. Suppose he is strong, healthy, and willing to work. Would you not rather have him than a kid that gets seasick and can't do anything but wash dishes ? " It was letters of this sort that I hated to decline. The writer of it, self-taught in English, had been only two years in the United States, and, as he said, "I am not wishing to go with you to earn my living, but I wish to learn and see." At the time of writing to me he was a designer for one of the big motor manufacturing companies ; he had been to sea quite a bit, and had been used all his life to the handling of small boats.

"I have a good position, but it matters not so with me as I prefer travelling," wrote another. "As to salary, look at me, and if I am worth a dollar or two, all right, and if I am not, nothing said. As to my honesty and character, I shall be pleased to show you my employers. Never drink, no tobacco, but to be honest, I myself, after a little more experience, want to do a little writing."

"I can assure you that I am eminently respectable, but find other respectable people tiresome." The man who wrote the foregoing certainly had me guessing, and I am still wondering whether or not he'd have found me tiresome, or what the deuce he did mean.

"I have seen better days than what I am passing through to-day," wrote an old salt, "but I have seen them a great deal worse also."

But the willingness to sacrifice on the part of the man who wrote the following was so touching that I could not accept : "I have a father, a mother, brothers and sisters, dear friends and a lucrative position, and yet I will sacrifice all to become one of your crew."

Another volunteer I could never have accepted was the finicky young fellow who, to show me how necessary it was that I should give him a chance, pointed out that "to go in the ordinary boat, be it schooner or steamer, would be impracticable, for I would have to mix among and live with the ordinary type of seamen, which as a rule is not a clean sort of life."

Then there was the young fellow of twenty-six, who had "run through the gamut of human emotions," and had "done everything from cooking to attending Stanford University," and who, at the present writing, was "A vaquero on a fifty-five-thousand-acre range." Quite in contrast was the modesty of the one who said, "I am not aware of possessing any particular qualities that would be likely to recommend me to your consideration. But should you be impressed, you might consider it worth a few minutes' time to answer. Otherwise, there's always work at the trade. Not expecting, but hoping, I remain, etc."

But I have held my head in both my hands ever

since, trying to figure out the intellectual kinship between myself and the one who wrote : " Long before I knew of you, I had mixed political economy and history and deducted therefrom many of your conclusions in concrete."

Here, in its way, is one of the best, as it is the briefest, that I received : " If any of the present company signed on for cruise happens to get cold feet and you need one more who understands boating, engines, etc., would like to hear from you, etc." Here is another brief one : " Point blank, would like to have the job of cabin-boy on your trip around the world, or any other job on board. Am nineteen years old, weigh one hundred and forty pounds, and am an American."

And here is a good one from a man a " little over five feet long " : " When I read about your manly plan of sailing around the world in a small boat with Mrs. London, I was so much rejoiced that I felt I was planning it myself, and I thought to write you about filling either position of cook or cabin-boy myself, but for some reason I did not do it, and I came to Denver from Oakland to join my friend's business last month, but everything is worse and unfavourable. But fortunately you have postponed your departure on account of the great earthquake, so I finally decided to propose you to let me fill either of the positions. I am not very strong, being a man of a little over five feet long, although I am of sound health and capability."

" I think I can add to your outfit an additional method of utilizing the power of the wind," wrote a well-wisher, " which, while not interfering with ordinary sails in light breezes, will enable you to use the whole force of the wind in its mightiest blows, so that even when its force is so great that you may have to take in every inch of canvas used in the ordinary way, you may carry the fullest spread with my method. With my attachment your craft could not be UPSET."

The foregoing letter was written in San Francisco under the date of April 16, 1906. And two days later, on April 18, came the Great Earthquake. And that's why I've got it in for that earthquake, for it made a refugee out of the man who wrote the letter, and prevented us from ever getting together.

Many of my brother socialists objected to my making the cruise, of which the following is typical: " The Socialist Cause and the millions of oppressed victims of Capitalism has a right and claim upon your life and services. If, however, you persist, then, when you swallow the last mouthful of salt chuck you can hold before sinking, remember that we at least protested."

One wanderer over the world who " could, if opportunity afforded, recount many unusual scenes and events," spent several pages ardently trying to get to the point of his letter, and at last achieved the following : " Still I am neglecting the point I set out to write you about. So will say at once that it has been stated in print that you and one or two others are going to take a cruize around the world in a little fifty- or sixty-foot boat. I therefore cannot get myself to think that a man of your attainments and experience would attempt such a proceeding, which is nothing less than courting death in that way. And even if you were to escape for some time, your whole Person, and those with you would be bruised from the ceaseless motion of a craft of the above size, even if she were padded, a thing not usual at sea." Thank you, kind friend, thank you for that qualification, "a thing not usual at sea." Nor is this friend ignorant of the sea. As he says of himself, "I am not a land-lubber, and I have sailed every sea and ocean." And he winds up his letter with : "Although not wishing to offend, it would be madness to take any woman outside the bay even, in such a craft."

And yet, at the moment of writing this, Charmian is in her state-room at the typewriter, Martin is cooking dinner, Tochigi is setting the table, Roscoe and Bert are caulking the deck, and the *Snark* is steering herself some five knots an hour in a rattling good sea—and the *Snark* is not padded, either.

"Seeing a piece in the paper about your intended trip, would like to know if you would like a good crew, as there is six of us boys all good sailor men, with good discharges from the Navy and Merchant Service, all true Americans all between the ages of 20 and 22, and at present are employed as riggers at the Union Iron Works, and would like very mutch to sail with you."— It was letters like this that made me regret the boat was not larger.

And here writes the one woman in all the world —outside of Charmian—for the cruise : "If you have not succeeded in getting a cook I would like very much to take the trip in that capacity. I am a woman of fifty, healthy and capable, and can do the work for the small company that compose the crew of the *Snark*. I am a very good cook and a very good sailor, and something of a traveller, and the length of the voyage, if of ten years' duration, would suit me better than one. References, etc."

Some day, when I have made a lot of money, I'm going to build a big ship, with room in it for a thousand volunteers. They will have to do all the work of navigating that boat around the world, or they'll stay at home. I believe that they'll work the boat around the world, for I know that Adventure is not dead. I know Adventure is not dead because I have had a long and intimate correspondence with Adventure.

CHAPTER IV

FINDING ONE'S WAY ABOUT

"BUT," our friends objected, "how dare you go to sea without a navigator on board ? You're not a navigator, are you ? "

I had to confess that I was not a navigator, that I had never looked through a sextant in my life, and that I doubted if I could tell a sextant from a nautical almanac. And when they asked if Roscoe was a navigator, I shook my head. Roscoe resented this. He had glanced at the "Epitome," bought for our voyage, knew how to use logarithm tables, had seen a sextant at some time, and, what of this and of his seafaring ancestry, he concluded that he did know navigation. But Roscoe was wrong, I still insist. When a young boy he came from Maine to California by way of the Isthmus of Panama, and that was the only time in his life that he was out of sight of land. He had never gone to a school of navigation, nor passed an examination in the same ; nor had he sailed the deep sea and learned the art from some other navigator. He was a San Francisco Bay yachtsman, where land is always only several miles away and the art of navigation is never employed.

So the *Snark* started on her long voyage without a navigator.   We beat through the Golden Gate on April 23, and headed for the Hawaiian Islands, twenty-one hundred sea-miles away as the gull flies.   And the outcome was our justification. We arrived.   And we arrived, furthermore, without any trouble, as you shall see ; that is, without any trouble to amount to anything.   To begin with, Roscoe tackled the navigating.   He had the theory all right, but it was the first time he had ever applied it, as was evidenced by the erratic behaviour of the *Snark*.   Not but what the *Snark* was perfectly steady on the sea ; the pranks she cut were on the chart.   On a day with a light breeze she would make a jump on the chart that advertised " a wet sail and a flowing sheet," and on a day when she just raced over the ocean, she scarcely changed her position on the chart.   Now when one's boat has logged six knots for twenty-four consecutive hours, it is incontestable that she has covered one hundred and forty-four miles of ocean.   The ocean was all right, and so was the patent log ; as for speed, one saw it with his own eyes.   Therefore, the thing that was not all right was the figuring that refused to boost the *Snark* along over the chart. Not that this happened every day, but that it did happen.   And it was perfectly proper and no more than was to be expected from a first attempt at applying a theory.

The acquisition of the knowledge of navigation has a strange effect on the minds of men.   The average navigator speaks of navigation with deep respect.   To the layman navigation is a deed and awful mystery, which feeling has been generated in him by the deep and awful respect for navigation that the layman has seen displayed by navigators. I have known frank, ingenuous, and modest young men, open as the day, to learn navigation and at once betray secretiveness, reserve, and self-importance, as if they had achieved some tremendous intellectual attainment. The average navigator impresses the layman as a priest of some holy rite. With bated breath, the amateur yachtsman navigator invites one in to look at his chronometer. And so it was that our friends suffered such apprehension at our sailing without a navigator.

During the building of the *Snark*, Roscoe and I had an agreement, something like this : "I'll furnish the books and instruments," I said, " and do you study up navigation now. I'll be too busy to do any studying. Then, when we get to sea, you can teach me what you have learned." Roscoe was delighted. Furthermore, Roscoe was as frank and ingenuous and modest as the young men I have described. But when we got out to sea and he began to practise the holy rite, while I looked on admiringly, a change, subtle and distinctive, marked his bearing. When he shot the sun at noon, the glow of achievement wrapped him in lambent flame. When he went below, figured out his observation, and then returned on deck and announced our latitude and longitude, there was an authoritative ring in his voice that was new to all of us. But that was not the worst of it. He became filled with incommunicable information. And the more he discovered the reasons for the erratic jumps of the *Snark* over the chart, and the less the *Snark* jumped, the more incommunicable and holy and awful became his information. My mild suggestions that it was about time that I began to learn, met with no hearty response, with no offers on his part to help me. He displayed not the slightest intention of living up to our agreement.

Now this was not Roscoe's fault; he could not help it. He had merely gone the way of all the men who learned navigation before him. By an understandable and forgivable confusion of values, plus a loss of orientation, he felt weighted by responsibility, and experienced the possession of power that was like unto that of a god. All his life Roscoe had lived on land, and therefore in sight of land. Being constantly in sight of land, with landmarks to guide him, he had managed, with occasional difficulties, to steer his body around and about the earth. Now he found himself on the sea, wide-stretching, bounded only by the eternal circle of the sky. This circle looked always the same. There were no landmarks. The sun rose to the east and set to the west and the stars wheeled through the night. But who may look at the sun or the stars and say, " My place on the face of the earth at the present moment is four and three-quarter miles to the west of Jones's Cash Store of Smithersville " ? or " I know where I am now, for the Little Dipper informs me that Boston is three miles away on the second turning to the right " ? And yet that was precisely what Roscoe did. That he was astounded by the achievement, is putting it mildly. He stood in reverential awe of himself; he had performed a miraculous feat. The act of finding himself on the face of the waters became a rite, and he felt himself a superior being to the rest of us who knew not this rite and were dependent on him for being shepherded across the heaving and limitless waste, the briny highroad that connects the continents and whereon there are no mile-stones. So, with the sextant he made obeisance to the sun-god, he consulted ancient tomes and tables of magic characters, muttered prayers in a strange tongue that sounded like *Indexerrorparallaxrefraction*, made cabalistic signs on paper, added and carried one, and then, on a piece of holy script called the Grail—I mean, the Chart—he placed his finger on a certain space conspicuous for its blankness and said, "Here we are." When we looked at the blank space and asked, "And where is that?" he answered in the cipher-code of the higher priesthood, "31—15—47 north, 133—5—30 west." And we said "Oh," and felt mighty small.

So I aver, it was not Roscoe's fault. He was like unto a god, and he carried us in the hollow of his hand across the blank spaces on the chart. I experienced a great respect for Roscoe; this respect grew so profound that had he commanded, "Kneel down and worship me," I know that I should have flopped down on the deck and yammered. But, one day, there came a still small thought to me that said: "This is not a god; this is Roscoe, a mere man like myself. What he has done, I can do. Who taught him?

Himself. Go you and do likewise—be your own teacher." And right there Roscoe crashed, and he was high priest of the *Snark* no longer. I invaded the sanctuary and demanded the ancient tomes and magic tables, also the prayer-wheel— the sextant, I mean.

And now, in simple language, I shall describe how I taught myself navigation. One whole afternoon I sat in the cockpit, steering with one hand and studying logarithms with the other. Two afternoons, two hours each, I studied the general theory of navigation and the particular process of taking a meridian altitude. Then I took the sextant, worked out the index error, and shot the sun. The figuring from the data of this observation was child's play. In the " Epitome " and the " Nautical Almanac " were scores of cunning tables, all worked out by mathematicians and astronomers. It was like using interest tables and lightning-calculator tables such as you all know. The mystery was mystery no longer. I put my finger on the chart and announced that that was where we were. I was right too, or at least I was as right as Roscoe, who selected a spot a quarter of a mile away from mine. Even he was willing to split the distance with me. I had exploded the mystery ; and yet, such was the miracle of it, I was conscious of new power in me, and I felt the thrill and tickle of pride. And when Martin asked me, in the same humble and respectful way I had previously asked Roscoe, as to where we were, it was with exaltation and spiritual chest-throwing that I answered in the cipher-code of the higher priesthood and heard Martin's self-abasing and worship-ful "Oh." As for Charmian, I felt that in a new way I had proved my right to her ; and I was aware of another feeling, namely, that she was a most fortunate woman to have a man like me.

I couldn't help it. I tell it as a vindication of Roscoe and all the other navigators. The poison of power was working in me. I was not as other men—most other men ; I knew what they did not know,—the mystery of the heavens, that pointed out the way across the deep. And the taste of power I had received drove me on. I steered at the wheel long hours with one hand, and studied mystery with the other. By the end of the week, teaching myself, I was able to do divers things. For instance, I shot the North Star, at night, of course ; got its altitude, corrected for index error, dip, etc., and found our latitude. And this latitude agreed with the latitude of the previous noon corrected by dead reckoning up to that moment. Proud ? Well, I was even prouder with my next miracle. I was going to turn in at nine o'clock. I worked out the problem, self-instructed, and learned what star of the first magnitude would be passing the meridian around half-past eight. This star proved to be Alpha Crucis. I had never heard of the star before. I looked it up on the star map. It was one of the stars of the Southern Cross. What ! thought I ; have we been sailing with the Southern Cross in the sky of nights and never known it ? Dolts that we are ! Gudgeons and moles ! I couldn't believe it. I went over the problem again, and verified it. Charmian had the wheel from eight till ten that evening.   I told her to keep her eyes open and look due south for the Southern Cross. And when the stars came out, there shone the Southern Cross low on the horizon.   Proud? No medicine man nor high priest was ever prouder. Furthermore, with the prayer-wheel I shot Alpha Crucis and from its altitude worked out our latitude.   And still furthermore, I shot the North Star, too, and it agreed with what had been told me by the Southern Cross.   Proud?   Why, the language of the stars was mine, and I listened and heard them telling me my way over the deep.

Proud?   I was a worker of miracles.   I forgot how easily I had taught myself from the printed page.   I forgot that all the work (and a tremendous work, too) had been done by the master-minds before me, the astronomers and mathematicians, who had discovered and elaborated the whole science of navigation and made the tables in the "Epitome."   I remembered only the everlasting miracle of it—that I had listened to the voices of the stars and been told my place upon the highway of the sea.   Charmian did not know, Martin did not know, Tochigi, the cabin-boy, did not know.   But I told them.   I was God's messenger.   I stood between them and infinity. I translated the high celestial speech into terms of their ordinary understanding.   We were heaven-directed, and it was I who could read the sign-post of the sky!—I! I!

And now, in a cooler moment, I hasten to blab the whole simplicity of it, to blab on Roscoe and the other navigators and the rest of the priesthood. all for fear that I may become even as they, secretive, immodest, and inflated with self-esteem. And I want to say this now: any young fellow with ordinary gray matter, ordinary education, and with the slightest trace of the student-mind, can get the books, and charts, and instruments and teach himself navigation. Now I must not be misunderstood. Seamanship is an entirely different matter. It is not learned in a day, nor in many days; it requires years. Also, navigating by dead reckoning requires long study and practice. But navigating by observations of the sun, moon, and stars, thanks to the astronomers and mathematicians, is child's play. Any average young fellow can teach himself in a week. And yet again I must not be misunderstood. I do not mean to say that at the end of a week a young fellow could take charge of a fifteen-thousand-ton steamer, driving twenty knots an hour through the brine, racing from land to land, fair weather and foul, clear sky or cloudy, steering by degrees on the compass card and making landfalls with most amazing precision. But what I do mean is just this: the average young fellow I have described can get into a staunch sail-boat and put out across the ocean, without knowing anything about navigation, and at the end of the week he will know enough to know where he is on the chart. He will be able to take a meridian observation with fair accuracy, and from that observation, with ten minutes of figuring, work out his latitude and longitude. And, carrying neither freight nor passengers, being under no press to reach his destination, he can jog comfortably along, and if at any time he doubts his own navigation and fears an imminent landfall, he can heave to all night and proceed in the morning.

Joshua Slocum sailed around the world a few years ago in a thirty-seven-foot boat all by himself. I shall never forget, in his narrative of the voyage, where he heartily indorsed the idea of young men, in similar small boats, making similar voyage. I promptly indorsed his idea, and so heartily that I took my wife along. While it certainly makes a Cook's tour look like thirty cents, on top of that, and on top of the fun and pleasure, it is a splendid education for a young man—oh, not a mere education in the things of the world outside, of lands, and peoples, and climates, but an education in the world inside, an education in one's self, a chance to learn one's own self, to get on speaking terms with one's soul. Then there is the training and the disciplining of it. First, naturally, the young fellow will learn his limitations; and next, inevitably, he will proceed to press back those limitations. And he cannot escape returning from such a voyage a bigger and better man. And as for sport, it is a king's sport, taking one's self around the world, doing it with one's own hands, depending on no one but one's self, and at the end, back at the starting-point, contemplating with inner vision the planet rushing through space, and saying, " I did it; with my own hands I did it. I went clear around that whirling sphere, and I can travel alone, without any nurse of a sea-captain to guide my steps across the seas. I may not fly to other stars, but of this star I myself am master."

As I write these lines I lift my eyes and look

seaward. I am on the beach of Waikiki on the
island of Oahu. Far, in the azure sky, the trade-
wind clouds drift low over the blue-green turquoise
of the deep sea. Nearer, the sea is emerald and
light olive-green. Then comes the reef, where the
water is all slaty purple flecked with red. Still
nearer are brighter greens and tans, lying in
alternate stripes and showing where sandbeds lie
between the living coral banks. Through and
over and out of these wonderful colours tumbles
and thunders a magnificent surf. As I say, I lift
my eyes to all this, and through the white crest
of a breaker suddenly appears a dark figure,
erect, a man-fish or a sea-god, on the very forward
face of the crest where the top falls over and down,
driving in toward shore, buried to his loins in
smoking spray, caught up by the sea and flung
landward, bodily, a quarter of a mile. It is a
Kanaka on a surf-board. And I know that when
I have finished these lines I shall be out in that
riot of colour and pounding surf, trying to bit
those breakers even as he, and failing as he never
failed, but living life as the best of us may live it.
And the picture of that coloured sea and that
flying sea-god Kanaka becomes another reason
for the young man to go west, and farther west,
beyond the Baths of Sunset, and still west till he
arrives home again.

But to return. Please do not think that I
already know it all. I know only the rudiments
of navigation. There is a vast deal yet for me
to learn. On the *Snark* there is a score of fascinating books on navigation waiting for me. There
is the danger-angle of Lecky, there is the line of

Sumner, which, when you know least of all where you are, shows most conclusively where you are, and where you are not. There are dozens and dozens of methods of finding one's location on the deep, and one can work years before he masters it all in all its fineness.

Even in the little we did learn there were slips that accounted for the apparently antic behaviour of the *Snark*. On Thursday, May 16, for instance, the trade wind failed us. During the twenty-four hours that ended Friday at noon, by dead reckoning we had not sailed twenty miles. Yet here are our positions, at noon, for the two days, worked out from our observations :

Thursday	20°	57′	9″	N
	152°	40′	30″	W
Friday	21°	15′	33″	N
	154°	12′		W

The difference between the two positions was something like eighty miles. Yet we knew we had not travelled twenty miles. Now our figuring was all right. We went over it several times. What was wrong was the observations we had taken. To take a correct observation requires practice and skill, and especially so on a small craft like the *Snark*. The violently moving boat and the closeness of the observer's eye to the surface of the water are to blame. A big wave that lifts up a mile off is liable to steal the horizon away.

But in our particular case there was another perturbing factor. The sun, in its annual march

north through the heavens, was increasing its
declination.   On the 19th parallel of north latitude
in the middle of May the sun is nearly overhead.
The angle of arc was between eighty-eight and
eighty-nine degrees.   Had it been ninety degrees
it would have been straight overhead.   It was
on another day that we learned a few things about
taking the altitude of the almost perpendicular
sun.   Roscoe started in drawing the sun down
to the eastern horizon, and he stayed by that
point of the compass despite the fact that the
sun would pass the meridian to the south.   I, on
the other hand, started in to draw the sun down
to south-east and strayed away to the south-west.
You see, we were teaching ourselves.   As a result,
at twenty-five minutes past twelve by the ship's
time, I called twelve o'clock by the sun.   Now
this signified that we had changed our location
on the face of the world by twenty-five minutes,
which was equal to something like six degrees of
longitude, or three hundred and fifty miles.   This
showed the *Snark* had travelled fifteen knots per
hour for twenty-four consecutive hours—and we
had never noticed it !   It was absurd and grotesque.   But Roscoe, still looking east, averred
that it was not yet twelve o'clock.   He was bent
on giving us a twenty-knot clip.   Then we began
to train our sextants rather wildly all around the
horizon, and wherever we looked, there was the
sun, puzzlingly close to the sky-line, sometimes
above it and sometimes below it.   In one direction
the sun was proclaiming morning, in another
direction it was proclaiming afternoon.   The sun
was all right—we knew that ; therefore we were

all wrong.   And the rest of the afternoon we spent
in the cockpit reading up the matter in the books
and finding out what was wrong.   We missed the
observation that day, but we didn't the next.
We had learned.

And we learned well, better than for a while we
thought we had.   At the beginning of the second
dog-watch one evening, Charmian and I sat down
on the forecastle-head for a rubber of cribbage.
Chancing to glance ahead, I saw cloud-capped
mountains rising from the sea.   We were rejoiced
at the sight of land, but I was in despair over our
navigation.   I thought we had learned something, yet our position at noon, plus what we had
run since, did not put us within a hundred miles
of land.   But there was the land, fading away
before our eyes in the fires of sunset.   The land
was all right.   There was no disputing it.   Therefore our navigation was all wrong.   But it wasn't.
That land we saw was the summit of Haleakala,
the House of the Sun, the greatest extinct volcano
in the world.   It towered ten thousand feet above
the sea, and it was all of a hundred miles away.
We sailed all night at a seven-knot clip, and in
the morning the House of the Sun was still before
us, and it took a few more hours of sailing to
bring it abreast of us.   "That island is Maui,"
we said, verifying by the chart.   "That next
island sticking out is Molokai, where the lepers
are.   And the island next to that is Oahu.   There
is Makapuu Head now.   We'll be in Honolulu
to-morrow.   Our navigation is all right."

CHAPTER V

THE FIRST LANDFALL

"IT will not be so monotonous at sea," I promised my fellow-voyagers on the *Snark*. "The sea is filled with life. It is so populous that every day something new is happening. Almost as soon as we pass through the Golden Gate and head south we'll pick up with the flying fish. We'll be having them fried for breakfast. We'll be catching bonita and dolphin, and spearing porpoises from the bowsprit. And then there are the sharks—sharks without end."

We passed through the Golden Gate and headed south. We dropped the mountains of California beneath the horizon, and daily the sun grew warmer. But there were no flying fish, no bonita and dolphin. The ocean was bereft of life. Never had I sailed on so forsaken a sea. Always, before, in the same latitudes, had I encountered flying fish.

"Never mind," I said. "Wait till we get off the coast of Southern California. Then we'll pick up the flying fish."

We came abreast of Southern California, abreast of the Peninsula of Lower California, abreast of the coast of Mexico ; and there were no flying fish. Nor was there anything else. No life moved. As the days went by the absence of life became almost uncanny.

"Never mind," I said. "When we do pick up with the flying fish we'll pick up with everything else. The flying fish is the staff of life for all the other breeds. Everything will come in a bunch when we find the flying fish."

When I should have headed the *Snark* southwest for Hawaii, I still held her south. I was going to find those flying fish. Finally the time came when, if I wanted to go to Honolulu, I should have headed the *Snark* due west. Instead of which I kept her south. Not until latitude 19° did we encounter the first flying fish. He was very much alone. I saw him. Five other pairs of eager eyes scanned the sea all day, but never saw another. So sparse were the flying fish that nearly a week more elapsed before the last one on board saw his first flying fish. As for the dolphin, bonita, porpoise, and all the other hordes of life—there weren't any.

Not even a shark broke surface with his ominous dorsal fin. Bert took a dip daily under the bowsprit, hanging on to the stays and dragging his body through the water. And daily he canvassed the project of letting go and having a decent swim. I did my best to dissuade him. But with him I had lost all standing as an authority on sea life.

"If there are sharks," he demanded, "why don't they show up ? "

I assured him that if he really did let go and

have a swim the sharks would promptly appear. This was a bluff on my part. I didn't believe it. It lasted as a deterrent for two days. The third day the wind fell calm, and it was pretty hot. The *Snark* was moving a knot an hour. Bert dropped down under the bowsprit and let go. And now behold the perversity of things. We had sailed across two thousand miles and more of ocean and had met with no sharks. Within five minutes after Bert finished his swim, the fin of a shark was cutting the surface in circles around the *Snark*.

There was something wrong about that shark. It bothered me. It had no right to be there in that deserted ocean. The more I thought about it, the more incomprehensible it became. But two hours later we sighted land and the mystery was cleared up. He had come to us from the land, and not from the uninhabited deep. He had presaged the landfall. He was the messenger of the land.

Twenty-seven days out from San Francisco we arrived at the island of Oahu, Territory of Hawaii. In the early morning we drifted around Diamond Head into full view of Honolulu ; and then the ocean burst suddenly into life. Flying fish cleaved the air in glittering squadrons. In five minutes we saw more of them than during the whole voyage. Other fish, large ones, of various sorts, leaped into the air. There was life everywhere, on sea and shore. We could see the masts and funnels of the shipping in the harbour, the hotels and bathers along the beach at Waikiki, the smoke rising from the dwelling-houses high up

on the volcanic slopes of the Punch Bowl and
Tantalus. The custom-house tug was racing
toward us and a big school of porpoises got under
our bow and began cutting the most ridiculous
capers. The port doctor's launch came charging
out at us, and a big sea turtle broke the surface
with his back and took a look at us. Never was
there such a burgeoning of life. Strange faces
were on our decks, strange voices were speaking,
and copies of that very morning's newspaper, with
cable reports from all the world, were thrust before
our eyes. Incidentally, we read that the *Snark*
and all hands had been lost at sea, and that she
had been a very unseaworthy craft anyway.
And while we read this information a wireless
message was being received by the congressional
party on the summit of Haleakala announcing
the safe arrival of the *Snark*.

It was the *Snark's* first landfall—and such a
landfall! For twenty-seven days we had been
on the deserted deep, and it was pretty hard to
realize that there was so much life in the world.
We were made dizzy by it. We could not take
it all in at once. We were like awakened Rip
Van Winkles, and it seemed to us that we were
dreaming. On one side the azure sea lapped
across the horizon into the azure sky ; on the
other side the sea lifted itself into great breakers
of emerald that fell in a snowy smother upon a
white coral beach. Beyond the beach, green
plantations of sugar-cane undulated gently upward to steeper slopes, which, in turn, became
jagged volcanic crests, drenched with tropic
showers and capped by stupendous masses of

trade-wind clouds. At any rate, it was a most beautiful dream. The *Snark* turned and headed directly in toward the emerald surf, till it lifted and thundered on either hand; and on either hand, scarce a biscuit-toss away, the reef showed its long teeth, pale green and menacing.

Abruptly the land itself, in a riot of olive-greens of a thousand hues, reached out its arms and folded the *Snark* in. There was no perilous passage through the reef, no emerald surf and azure sea—nothing but a warm soft land, a motionless lagoon, and tiny beaches on which swam dark-skinned tropic children. The sea had disappeared. The *Snark's* anchor rumbled the chain through the hawse-pipe, and we lay without movement on a " lineless, level floor." It was all so beautiful and strange that we could not accept it as real. On the chart this place was called Pearl Harbour, but we called it Dream Harbour.

A launch came off to us; in it were members of the Hawaiian Yacht Club, come to greet us and make us welcome, with true Hawaiian hospitality, to all they had. They were ordinary men, flesh and blood and all the rest; but they did not tend to break our dreaming. Our last memories of men were of United States marshals and of panicky little merchants with rusty dollars for souls, who, in a reeking atmosphere of soot and coal-dust, laid grimy hands upon the *Snark* and held her back from her world adventure. But these men who came to meet us were clean men. A healthy tan was on their cheeks, and their eyes were not dazzled and be-spectacled from gazing overmuch at glittering dollar-heaps. No, they merely verified the dream. They clinched it with their unsmirched souls.

So we went ashore with them across a level flashing sea to the wonderful green land. We landed on a tiny wharf, and the dream became more insistent; for know that for twenty-seven days we had been rocking across the ocean on the tiny *Snark*. Not once in all those twenty-seven days had we known a moment's rest, a moment's cessation from movement. This ceaseless movement had become ingrained. Body and brain we had rocked and rolled so long that when we climbed out on the tiny wharf we kept on rocking and rolling. This, naturally, we attributed to the wharf. It was projected psychology. I spraddled along the wharf and nearly fell into the water. I glanced at Charmian, and the way she walked made me sad. The wharf had all the seeming of a ship's deck. It lifted, tilted, heaved, and sank; and since there were no handrails on it, it kept Charmian and me busy avoiding falling in. I never saw such a preposterous little wharf. Whenever I watched it closely, it refused to roll; but as soon as I took my attention off from it, away it went, just like the *Snark*. Once, I caught it in the act, just as it upended, and I looked down the length of it for two hundred feet, and for all the world it was like the deck of a ship ducking into a huge head-sea.

At last, however, supported by our hosts, we negotiated the wharf and gained the land. But the land was no better. The very first thing it did was to tilt up on one side, and far as the eye could see I watched it tilt, clear to its jagged, volcanic backbone, and I saw the clouds above tilt, too. This was no stable, firm-founded land, else it would not cut such capers. It was like all the rest of our landfall, unreal. It was a dream. At any moment, like shifting vapour, it might dissolve away. The thought entered my head that perhaps it was my fault, that my head was swimming or that something I had eaten had disagreed with me. But I glanced at Charmian and her sad walk, and even as I glanced I saw her stagger and bump into the yachtsman by whose side she walked. I spoke to her, and she complained about the antic behaviour of the land.

We walked across a spacious, wonderful lawn and down an avenue of royal palms, and across more wonderful lawn in the gracious shade of stately trees. The air was filled with the songs of birds and was heavy with rich warm fragrances —wafture from great lilies, and blazing blossoms of hibiscus, and other strange gorgeous tropic flowers. The dream was becoming almost impossibly beautiful to us who for so long had seen naught but the restless, salty sea. Charmian reached out her hand and clung to me—for support against the ineffable beauty of it, thought I. But no. As I supported her I braced my legs, while the flowers and lawns reeled and swung around me. It was like an earthquake, only it quickly passed without doing any harm. It was fairly difficult to catch the land playing these tricks. As long as I kept my mind on it, nothing happened. But as soon as my attention was distracted, away it went, the whole panorama, swinging and heaving and tilting at all sorts of angles. Once, however, I turned my head suddenly and caught that stately line of royal palms swinging in a great arc across the sky. But it stopped, just as soon as I caught it, and became a placid dream again.

Next we came to a house of coolness, with great sweeping veranda, where lotus-eaters might dwell. Windows and doors were wide open to the breeze, and the songs and fragrances blew lazily in and out. The walls were hung with tapa-cloths. Couches with grass-woven covers invited everywhere, and there was a grand piano, that played, I was sure, nothing more exciting than lullabies. Servants—Japanese maids in native costume— drifted around and about, noiselessly, like butterflies. Everything was preternaturally cool. Here was no blazing down of a tropic sun upon an unshrinking sea. It was too good to be true. But it was not real. It was a dream-dwelling. I knew, for I turned suddenly and caught the grand piano cavorting in a spacious corner of the room. I did not say anything, for just then we were being received by a gracious woman, a beautiful Madonna, clad in flowing white and shod with sandals, who greeted us as though she had known us always.

We sat at table on the lotus-eating veranda, served by the butterfly maids, and ate strange foods and partook of a nectar called poi. But the dream threatened to dissolve. It shimmered and trembled like an iridescent bubble about to break. I was just glancing out at the green grass and stately trees and blossoms of hibiscus, when suddenly I felt the table move. The table, and the Madonna across from me, and the veranda of the lotus-eaters, the scarlet hibiscus, the greensward and the trees—all lifted and tilted before my eyes, and heaved and sank down into the trough of a monstrous sea. I gripped my chair convulsively and held on. I had a feeling that I was holding on to the dream as well as the chair. I should not have been surprised had the sea rushed in and drowned all that fairyland and had I found myself at the wheel of the *Snark* just looking up casually from the study of logarithms. But the dream persisted. I looked covertly at the Madonna and her husband. They evidenced no perturbation. The dishes had not moved upon the table. The hibiscus and trees and grass were still there. Nothing had changed. I partook of more nectar, and the dream was more real than ever.

" Will you have some iced tea ? " asked the Madonna ; and then her side of the table sank down gently and I said yes to her at an angle of forty-five degrees.

" Speaking of sharks," said her husband, " up at Niihau there was a man——" And at that moment the table lifted and heaved, and I gazed upward at him at an angle of forty-five degrees.

So the luncheon went on, and I was glad that I did not have to bear the affliction of watching Charmian walk. Suddenly, however, a mysterious word of fear broke from the lips of the lotus-eaters. " Ah, ah," thought I, " now the dream goes glimmering." I clutched the chair desperately, resolved to drag back to the reality of the

Snark some tangible vestige of this lotus land.
I felt the whole dream lurching and pulling to be
gone. Just then the mysterious word of fear
was repeated. It sounded like *Reporters*. I
looked and saw three of them coming across the
lawn. Oh, blessed reporters! Then the dream
was indisputably real after all. I glanced out
across the shining water and saw the *Snark* at
anchor, and I remembered that I had sailed in
her from San Francisco to Hawaii, and that this
was Pearl Harbour, and that even then I was
acknowledging introductions and saying, in reply
to the first question, "Yes, we had delightful
weather all the way down."

CHAPTER VI

A ROYAL SPORT

THAT is what it is, a royal sport for the natural kings of earth. The grass grows right down to the water at Waikiki Beach, and within fifty feet of the everlasting sea. The trees also grow down to the salty edge of things, and one sits in their shade and looks seaward at a majestic surf thundering in on the beach to one's very feet. Half a mile out, where is the reef, the white-headed combers thrust suddenly skyward out of the placid turquoise-blue and come rolling in to shore. One after another they come, a mile long, with smoking crests, the white battalions of the infinite army of the sea. And one sits and listens to the perpetual roar, and watches the unending procession, and feels tiny and fragile before this tremendous force expressing itself in fury and foam and sound. Indeed, one feels microscopically small, and the thought that one may wrestle with this sea raises in one's imagination a thrill of apprehension, almost of fear. Why, they are a mile long, these bull-mouthed monsters, and they weigh a thousand tons, and they charge in to shore faster than a man can run. What chance ? No chance at all, is the verdict of the shrinking ego ; and one sits, and looks, and listens, and thinks the grass and the shade are a pretty good place in which to be.

And suddenly, out there where a big smoker lifts skyward, rising like a sea-god from out of the welter of spume and churning white, on the giddy, toppling, overhanging and downfalling, precarious crest appears the dark head of a man. Swiftly he rises through the rushing white. His black shoulders, his chest, his loins, his limbs— all is abruptly projected on one's vision. Where but the moment before was only the wide desolation and invincible roar, is now a man, erect, full-statured, not struggling frantically in that wild movement, not buried and crushed and buffeted by those mighty monsters, but standing above them all, calm and superb, poised on the giddy summit, his feet buried in the churning foam, the salt smoke rising to his knees, and all the rest of him in the free air and flashing sunlight, and he is flying through the air, flying forward, flying fast as the surge on which he stands. He is a Mercury—a brown Mercury. His heels are winged, and in them is the swiftness of the sea. In truth, from out of the sea he has leaped upon the back of the sea, and he is riding the sea that roars and bellows and cannot shake him from its back. But no frantic outreaching and balancing is his. He is impassive, motionless as a statue carved suddenly by some miracle out of the sea's depth from which he rose. And straight on toward shore he flies on his winged heels and the white crest of the breaker. There is a wild burst of foam, a long tumultuous rushing sound as the breaker falls futile and spent on the beach at your feet ; and there, at your feet steps calmly ashore a Kanaka, burnt golden and brown by the tropic sun. Several minutes ago he was a speck a quarter of a mile away. He has "bitted the bull-mouthed breaker" and ridden it in, and the pride in the feat shows in the carriage of his magnificent body as he glances for a moment carelessly at you who sit in the shade of the shore. He is a Kanaka—and more, he is a man, a member of the kingly species that has mastered matter and the brutes and lorded it over creation.

And one sits and thinks of Tristram's last wrestle with the sea on that fatal morning ; and one thinks further, to the fact that that Kanaka has done what Tristram never did, and that he knows a joy of the sea that Tristram never knew. And still further one thinks. It is all very well, sitting here in cool shade of the beach, but you are a man, one of the kingly species, and what that Kanaka can do, you can do yourself. Go to. Strip off your clothes that are a nuisance in this mellow clime. Get in and wrestle with the sea ; wing your heels with the skill and power that reside in you ; bit the sea's breakers, master them, and ride upon their backs as a king should.

And that is how it came about that I tackled surf-riding. And now that I have tackled it, more than ever do I hold it to be a royal sport. But first let me explain the physics of it. A wave is a communicated agitation. The water that composes the body of a wave does not move. If it did, when a stone is thrown into a pond and the ripples spread away in an ever widening circle, there would appear at the centre an ever increasing hole. No, the water that composes the body of a wave is stationary. Thus, you may watch a particular portion of the ocean's surface and you will see the same water rise and fall a thousand times to the agitation communicated by a thousand successive waves. Now imagine this communicated agitation moving shoreward. As the bottom shoals, the lower portion of the wave strikes land first and is stopped. But water is fluid, and the upper portion has not struck anything, wherefore it keeps on communicating its agitation, keeps on going. And when the top of the wave keeps on going, while the bottom of it lags behind, something is bound to happen. The bottom of the wave drops out from under and the top of the wave falls over, forward, and down, curling and cresting and roaring as it does so. It is the bottom of a wave striking against the top of the land that is the cause of all surfs.

But the transformation from a smooth undulation to a breaker is not abrupt except where the bottom shoals abruptly. Say the bottom shoals gradually for from quarter of a mile to a mile, then an equal distance will be occupied by the transformation. Such a bottom is that off the beach of Waikiki, and it produces a splendid surf-riding surf. One leaps upon the back of a breaker just as it begins to break, and stays on it as it continues to break all the way in to shore.

And now to the particular physics of surf-riding. Get out on a flat board, six feet long, two feet wide, and roughly oval in shape. Lie down upon it like a small boy on a coaster and

paddle with your hands out to deep water, where
the waves begin to crest.   Lie out there quietly
on the board.   Sea after sea breaks before,
behind, and under and over you, and rushes in
to shore, leaving you behind.   When a wave
crests, it gets steeper.   Imagine yourself, on your
board, on the face of that steep slope.   If it stood
still, you would slide down just as a boy slides
down a hill on his coaster.   "But," you object,
"the wave doesn't stand still."   Very true, but
the water composing the wave stands still, and
there you have the secret.   If ever you start
sliding down the face of that wave, you'll keep on
sliding and you'll never reach the bottom.   Please
don't laugh.   The face of that wave may be only
six feet, yet you can slide down it a quarter of a
mile, or half a mile, and not reach the bottom.
For, see, since a wave is only a communicated
agitation or impetus, and since the water that
composes a wave is changing every instant, new
water is rising into the wave as fast as the wave
travels.   You slide down this new water, and
yet remain in your old position on the wave,
sliding down the still newer water that is rising
and forming the wave.   You slide precisely as
fast as the wave travels.   If it travels fifteen
miles an hour, you slide fifteen miles an hour.
Between you and shore stretches a quarter of
mile of water.   As the wave travels, this water
obligingly heaps itself into the wave, gravity
does the rest, and down you go, sliding the whole
length of it.   If you still cherish the notion, while
sliding, that the water is moving with you, thrust
your arms into it and attempt to paddle ; you

will find that you have to be remarkably quick
to get a stroke, for that water is dropping astern
just as fast as you are rushing ahead.

And now for another phase of the physics of
surf-riding. All rules have their exceptions. It
is true that the water in a wave does not travel
forward. But there is what may be called the
send of the sea. The water in the overtoppling
crest does move forward, as you will speedily
realize if you are slapped in the face by it, or if
you are caught under it and are pounded by one
mighty blow down under the surface panting and
gasping for half a minute. The water in the top
of a wave rests upon the water in the bottom of
the wave. But when the bottom of the wave
strikes the land, it stops, while the top goes on.
It no longer has the bottom of the wave to hold
it up. Where was solid water beneath it, is now
air, and for the first time it feels the grip of gravity,
and down it falls, at the same time being torn
asunder from the lagging bottom of the wave
and flung forward. And it is because of this that
riding a surf-board is something more than a
mere placid sliding down a hill. In truth, one
is caught up and hurled shoreward as by some
Titan's hand.

I deserted the cool shade, put on a swimming
suit, and got hold of a surf-board. It was too
small a board. But I didn't know, and nobody
told me. I joined some little Kanaka boys in
shallow water, where the breakers were well spent
and small—a regular kindergarten school. I
watched the little Kanaka boys. When a likely-
looking breaker came along, they flopped upon

their stomachs on their boards, kicked like mad
with their feet, and rode the breaker in to the
beach. I tried to emulate them. I watched
them, tried to do everything that they did, and
failed utterly. The breaker swept past, and I
was not on it. I tried again and again. I kicked
twice as madly as they did, and failed. Half a
dozen would be around. We would all leap on
our boards in front of a good breaker. Away
our feet would churn like the stern-wheels of
river steamboats, and away the little rascals
would scoot while I remained in disgrace behind.

I tried for a solid hour, and not one wave could
I persuade to boost me shoreward. And then
arrived a friend, Alexander Hume Ford, a globe
trotter by profession, bent ever on the pursuit of
sensation. And he had found it at Waikiki.
Heading for Australia, he had stopped off for a
week to find out if there were any thrills in surf-
riding, and he had become wedded to it. He
had been at it every day for a month and could
not yet see any symptoms of the fascination
lessening on him. He spoke with authority.

"Get off that board," he said. "Chuck it
away at once. Look at the way you're trying to
ride it. If ever the nose of that board hits
bottom, you'll be disembowelled. Here, take my
board. It's a man's size."

I am always humble when confronted by
knowledge. Ford knew. He showed me how
properly to mount his board. Then he waited
for a good breaker, gave me a shove at the right
moment, and started me in. Ah, delicious moment when I felt that breaker grip and fling me.

On I dashed, a hundred and fifty feet, and subsided with the breaker on the sand. From that moment I was lost. I waded back to Ford with his board. It was a large one, several inches thick, and weighed all of seventy-five pounds. He gave me advice, much of it. He had had no one to teach him, and all that he had laboriously learned in several weeks he communicated to me in half an hour. I really learned by proxy. And inside of half an hour I was able to start myself and ride in. I did it time after time, and Ford applauded and advised. For instance, he told me to get just so far forward on the board and no farther. But I must have got some farther, for as I came charging in to land, that miserable board poked its nose down to bottom, stopped abruptly, and turned a somersault, at the same time violently severing our relations. I was tossed through the air like a chip and buried ignominiously under the downfalling breaker. And I realized that if it hadn't been for Ford, I'd have been disembowelled. That particular risk is part of the sport, Ford says. Maybe he'll have it happen to him before he leaves Waikiki, and then, I feel confident, his yearning for sensation will be satisfied for a time.

When all is said and done, it is my steadfast belief that homicide is worse than suicide, especially if, in the former case, it is a woman. Ford saved me from being a homicide. "Imagine your legs are a rudder," he said. "Hold them close together, and steer with them." A few minutes later I came charging in on a comber. As I neared the beach, there, in the water, up to her waist, dead in front of me, appeared a woman. How was I to stop that comber on whose back I was ? It looked like a dead woman. The board weighed seventy-five pounds, I weighed a hundred and sixty-five. The added weight had a velocity of fifteen miles per hour. The board and I constituted a projectile. I leave it to the physicists to figure out the force of the impact upon that poor, tender woman. And then I remembered my guardian angel, Ford. "Steer with your legs!" rang through my brain. I steered with my legs, I steered sharply, abruptly, with all my legs and with all my might. The board sheered around broadside on the crest. Many things happened simultaneously. The wave gave me a passing buffet, a light tap as the taps of waves go, but a tap sufficient to knock me off the board and smash me down through the rushing water to bottom, with which I came in violent collision and upon which I was rolled over and over. I got my head out for a breath of air and then gained my feet. There stood the woman before me. I felt like a hero. I had saved her life. And she laughed at me. It was not hysteria. She had never dreamed of her danger. Anyway, I solaced myself, it was not I but Ford that saved her, and I didn't have to feel like a hero. And besides, that leg-steering was great. In a few minutes more of practice I was able to thread my way in and out past several bathers and to remain on top my breaker instead of going under it.

"To-morrow," Ford said, "I am going to take you out into the blue water."

I looked seaward where he pointed, and saw

the great smoking combers that made the breakers I had been riding look like ripples. I don't know what I might have said had I not recollected just then that I was one of a kingly species. So all that I did say was, "All right, I'll tackle them to-morrow."

The water that rolls in on Waikiki Beach is just the same as the water that laves the shores of all the Hawaiian Islands ; and in ways, especially from the swimmer's standpoint, it is wonderful water. It is cool enough to be comfortable, while it is warm enough to permit a swimmer to stay in all day without experiencing a chill. Under the sun or the stars, at high noon or at midnight, in midwinter or in midsummer, it does not matter when, it is always the same temperature—not too warm, not too cold, just right. It is wonderful water, salt as old ocean itself, pure and crystal-clear. When the nature of the water is considered, it is not so remarkable after all that the Kanakas are one of the most expert of swimming races.

So it was, next morning, when Ford came along, that I plunged into the wonderful water for a swim of indeterminate length. Astride of our surf-boards, or, rather, flat down upon them on our stomachs, we paddled out through the kindergarten where the little Kanaka boys were at play. Soon we were out in deep water where the big smokers came roaring in. The mere struggle with them, facing them and paddling seaward over them and through them, was sport enough in itself. One had to have his wits about him, for it was a battle in which mighty blows were struck, on one side, and in which cunning

was used on the other side—a struggle between
insensate force and intelligence. I soon learned
a bit. When a breaker curled over my head, for
a swift instant I could see the light of day through
its emerald body ; then down would go my head,
and I would clutch the board with all my strength.
Then would come the blow, and to the onlooker
on shore I would be blotted out. In reality the
board and I have passed through the crest and
emerged in the respite of the other side. I should
not recommend those smashing blows to an invalid
or delicate person. There is weight behind them,
and the impact of the driven water is like a sand-
blast. Sometimes one passes through half a
dozen combers in quick succession, and it is just
about that time that he is liable to discover new
merits in the stable land and new reasons for
being on shore.

Out there in the midst of such a succession of
big smoky ones, a third man was added to our
party, one Freeth. Shaking the water from my
eyes as I emerged from one wave and peered ahead
to see what the next one looked like, I saw him
tearing in on the back of it, standing upright on
his board, carelessly poised, a young god bronzed
with sunburn. We went through the wave on
the back of which he rode. Ford called to him.
He turned an airspring from his wave, rescued
his board from its maw, paddled over to us and
joined Ford in showing me things. One thing in
particular I learned from Freeth, namely, how
to encounter the occasional breaker of exceptional
size that rolled in. Such breakers were really
ferocious, and it was unsafe to meet them on top

of the board. But Freeth showed me, so that whenever I saw one of that calibre rolling down on me, I slid off the rear end of the board and dropped down beneath the surface, my arms over my head and holding the board. Thus, if the wave ripped the board out of my hands and tried to strike me with it (a common trick of such waves), there would be a cushion of water a foot or more in depth, between my head and the blow. When the wave passed, I climbed upon the board and paddled on. Many men have been terribly injured, I learn, by being struck by their boards.

The whole method of surf-riding and surf-fighting, I learned, is one of non-resistance. Dodge the blow that is struck at you. Dive through the wave that is trying to slap you in the face. Sink down, feet first, deep under the surface, and let the big smoker that is trying to smash you go by far overhead. Never be rigid. Relax. Yield yourself to the waters that are ripping and tearing at you. When the undertow catches you and drags you seaward along the bottom, don't struggle against it. If you do, you are liable to be drowned, for it is stronger than you. Yield yourself to that undertow. Swim with it, not against it, and you will find the pressure removed. And, swimming with it, fooling it so that it does not hold you, swim upward at the same time. It will be no trouble at all to reach the surface.

The man who wants to learn surf-riding must be a strong swimmer, and he must be used to going under the water. After that, fair strength and common-sense are all that is required. The

force of the big comber is rather unexpected.
There are mix-ups in which board and rider are
torn apart and separated by several hundred feet.
The surf-rider must take care of himself. No
matter how many riders swim out with him, he
cannot depend upon any of them for aid. The
fancied security I had in the presence of Ford
and Freeth made me forget that it was my first
swim out in deep water among the big ones. I
recollected, however, and rather suddenly, for
a big wave came in, and away went the two men
on its back all the way to shore. I could have been
drowned a dozen different ways before they got
back to me.

One slides down the face of a breaker on his
surf-board, but he has to get started to sliding.
Board and rider must be moving shoreward at a
good rate before the wave overtakes them. When
you see the wave coming that you want to ride in,
you turn tail to it and paddle shoreward with all
your strength, using what is called the windmill
stroke. This is a sort of spurt performed immediately in front of the wave. If the board is
going fast enough, the wave accelerates it, and
the board begins its quarter-of-a-mile slide.

I shall never forget the first big wave I caught
out there in the deep water. I saw it coming,
turned my back on it and paddled for dear life.
Faster and faster my board went, till it seemed
my arms would drop off. What was happening
behind me I could not tell. One cannot look
behind and paddle the windmill stroke. I heard
the crest of the wave hissing and churning, and
then my board was lifted and flung forward. I

scarcely knew what happened the first half-minute. Though I kept my eyes open, I could not see anything, for I was buried in the rushing white of the crest. But I did not mind. I was chiefly conscious of ecstatic bliss at having caught the wave. At the end of the half-minute, however, I began to see things, and to breathe. I saw that three feet of the nose of my board was clear out of water and riding on the air. I shifted my weight forward, and made the nose come down. Then I lay, quite at rest in the midst of the wild movement, and watched the shore and the bathers on the beach grow distinct. I didn't cover quite a quarter of a mile on that wave, because, to prevent the board from diving, I shifted my weight back, but shifted it too far and fell down the rear slope of the wave.

It was my second day at surf-riding, and I was quite proud of myself. I stayed out there four hours, and when it was over, I was resolved that on the morrow I'd come in standing up. But that resolution paved a distant place. On the morrow I was in bed. I was not sick, but I was very unhappy, and I was in bed. When describing the wonderful water of Hawaii I forgot to describe the wonderful sun of Hawaii. It is a tropic sun, and, furthermore, in the first part of June, it is an overhead sun. It is also an insidious, deceitful sun. For the first time in my life I was sunburned unawares. My arms, shoulders, and back had been burned many times in the past and were tough; but not so my legs. And for four hours I had exposed the tender backs of my legs, at right-angles, to that perpendicular Hawaiian sun. It was not until after I got ashore that I discovered the sun had touched me. Sunburn at first is merely warm ; after that it grows intense and the blisters come out. Also, the joints, where the skin wrinkles, refuse to bend. That is why I spent the next day in bed. I couldn't walk. And that is why, to-day, I am writing this in bed. It is easier to than not to. But to-morrow, ah, to-morrow, I shall be out in that wonderful water, and I shall come in standing up, even as Ford and Freeth. And if I fail to-morrow, I shall do it the next day, or the next. Upon one thing I am resolved : the *Snark* shall not sail from Honolulu until I, too, wing my heels with the swiftness of the sea, and become a sun-burned, skin-peeling Mercury.

CHAPTER VII

THE LEPERS OF MOLOKAI

WHEN the *Snark* sailed along the windward coast of Molokai, on her way to Honolulu, I looked at the chart, then pointed to a low-lying peninsula backed by a tremendous cliff varying from two to four thousand feet in height, and said : " The pit of hell, the most cursed place on earth." I should have been shocked, if, at that moment, I could have caught a vision of myself a month later, ashore in the most cursed place on earth and having a disgracefully good time along with eight hundred of the lepers who were likewise having a good time. Their good time was not disgraceful ; but mine was, for in the midst of so much misery it was not meet for me to have a good time. That is the way I felt about it, and my only excuse is that I couldn't help having a good time.

For instance, in the afternoon of the Fourth of July all the lepers gathered at the race-track for the sports. I had wandered away from the Superintendent and the physicians in order to get a snapshot of the finish of one of the races. It was an interesting race, and partisanship ran high. Three horses were entered, one ridden by a Chinese,

one by an Hawaiian, and one by a Portuguese
boy. All three riders were lepers ; so were the
judges and the crowd. The race was twice
around the track. The Chinese and the Hawaiian
got away together and rode neck and neck, the
Portuguese boy toiling along two hundred feet
behind. Around they went in the same positions.
Halfway around on the second and final lap the
Chinese pulled away and got one length ahead of
the Hawaiian. At the same time the Portuguese
boy was beginning to crawl up.. But it looked
hopeless. The crowd went wild. All the lepers
were passionate lovers of horseflesh. The Portuguese boy crawled nearer and nearer. I went
wild, too. They were on the home stretch. The
Portuguese boy passed the Hawaiian. There was
a thunder of hoofs, a rush of the three horses
bunched together, the jockeys plying their whips,
and every last onlooker bursting his throat, or
hers, with shouts and yells. Nearer, nearer, inch
by inch, the Portuguese boy crept up, and passed,
yes, passed, winning by a head from the Chinese.
I came to myself in a group of lepers. They were
yelling, tossing their hats, and dancing around
like fiends. So was I. When I came to I was
waving my hat and murmuring ecstatically :
" By golly, the boy wins ! The boy wins ! "
I tried to check myself. I assured myself that
I was witnessing one of the horrors of Molokai,
and that it was shameful for me, under such
circumstances, to be so light-hearted and light-
headed. But it was no use. The next event was
a donkey-race, and it was just starting ; so was
the fun. The last donkey in was to win the race,

and what complicated the affair was that no rider rode his own donkey. They rode one another's donkeys, the result of which was that each man strove to make the donkey he rode beat his own donkey ridden by some one else. Naturally, only men possessing very slow or extremely obstreperous donkeys had entered them for the race. One donkey had been trained to tuck in its legs and lie down whenever its rider touched its sides with his heels. Some donkeys strove to turn around and come back ; others developed a penchant for the side of the track, where they stuck their heads over the railing and stopped ; while all of them dawdled. Halfway around the track one donkey got into an argument with its rider. When all the rest of the donkeys had crossed the wire, that particular donkey was still arguing. He won the race, though his rider lost it and came in on foot. And all the while nearly a thousand lepers were laughing uproariously at the fun. Anybody in my place would have joined with them in having a good time.

All the foregoing is by way of preamble to the statement that the horrors of Molokai, as they have been painted in the past, do not exist. The Settlement has been written up repeatedly by sensationalists, and usually by sensationalists who have never laid eyes on it. Of course, leprosy is leprosy, and it is a terrible thing ; but so much that is lurid has been written about Molokai that neither the lepers, nor those who devote their lives to them, have received a fair deal. Here is a case in point. A newspaper writer, who, of course, had never been near the Settlement, vividly described Superintendent McVeigh, crouching in a grass hut and being besieged nightly by starving lepers on their knees, wailing for food. This hair-raising account was copied by the press all over the United States and was the cause of many indignant and protesting editorials. Well, I lived and slept for five days in Mr. McVeigh's " grass hut " (which was a comfortable wooden cottage, by the way ; and there isn't a grass house in the whole Settlement), and I heard the lepers wailing for food—only the wailing was peculiarly harmonious and rhythmic, and it was accompanied by the music of stringed instruments, violins, guitars, *ukuleles*, and banjos. Also, the wailing was of various sorts. The leper brass band wailed, and two singing societies wailed, and lastly a quintet of excellent voices wailed. So much for a lie that should never have been printed. The wailing was the serenade which the glee clubs always give Mr. McVeigh when he returns from a trip to Honolulu.

Leprosy is not so contagious as is imagined. I went for a week's visit to the Settlement, and I took my wife along—all of which would not have happened had we had any apprehension of contracting the disease. Nor did we wear long, gauntleted gloves and keep apart from the lepers. On the contrary, we mingled freely with them, and before we left, knew scores of them by sight and name. The precautions of simple cleanliness seem to be all that is necessary. On returning to their own houses, after having been among and handling lepers, the non-lepers, such as the physicians and the superintendent, merely wash their faces and hands with mildly antiseptic soap and change their coats.

That a leper is unclean, however, should be insisted upon; and the segregation of lepers, from what little is known of the disease, should be rigidly maintained. On the other hand, the awful horror with which the leper has been regarded in the past, and the frightful treatment he has received, have been unnecessary and cruel. In order to dispel some of the popular misapprehensions of leprosy, I want to tell something of the relations between the lepers and non-lepers as I observed them at Molokai. On the morning after our arrival Charmian and I attended a shoot of the Kalaupapa Rifle Club, and caught our first glimpse of the democracy of affliction and alleviation that obtains. The club was just beginning a prize shoot for a cup put up by Mr. McVeigh, who is also a member of the club, as also are Dr. Goodhue and Dr. Hollmann, the resident physicians (who, by the way, live in the Settlement with their wives). All about us, in the shooting booth, were the lepers. Lepers and non-lepers were using the same guns, and all were rubbing shoulders in the confined space. The majority of the lepers were Hawaiians. Sitting beside me on a bench was a Norwegian. Directly in front of me, in the stand, was an American, a veteran of the Civil War, who had fought on the Confederate side. He was sixty-five years of age, but that did not prevent him from running up a good score. Strapping Hawaiian policemen, lepers, khaki-clad, were also shooting, as were

Portuguese, Chinese, and *kokuas*—the latter are native helpers in the Settlement who are non-lepers. And on the afternoon that Charmian and I climbed the two-thousand-foot *pali* and looked our last upon the Settlement, the superintendent, the doctors, and the mixture of nationalities and of diseased and non-diseased were all engaged in an exciting baseball game.

Not so was the leper and his greatly misunderstood and feared disease treated during the middle ages in Europe. At that time the leper was considered legally and politically dead. He was placed in a funeral procession and led to the church, where the burial service was read over him by the officiating clergyman. Then a spadeful of earth was dropped upon his chest and he was dead—living dead. While this rigorous treatment was largely unnecessary, nevertheless, one thing was learned by it. Leprosy was unknown in Europe until it was introduced by the returning Crusaders, whereupon it spread slowly until it had seized upon large numbers of the people. Obviously, it was a disease that could be contracted by contact. It was a contagion, and it was equally obvious that it could be eradicated by segregation. Terrible and monstrous as was the treatment of the leper in those days, the great lesson of segregation was learned. By its means leprosy was stamped out.

And by the same means leprosy is even now decreasing in the Hawaiian Islands. But the segregation of the lepers on Molokai is not the horrible nightmare that has been so often exploited by *yellow* writers. In the first place, the

leper is not torn ruthlessly from his family.
When a suspect is discovered, he is invited by
the Board of Health to come to the Kalihi re-
ceiving station at Honolulu. His fare and all
expenses are paid for him. He is first passed
upon by microscopical examination by the
bacteriologist of the Board of Health. If the
bacillus leprœ is found, the patient is examined
by the Board of Examining Physicians, five in
number. If found by them to be a leper, he is
so declared, which finding is later officially
confirmed by the Board of Health, and the leper is
ordered straight to Molokai. Furthermore, during
the thorough trial that is given his case, the
patient has the right to be represented by a
physician whom he can select and employ for
himself. Nor, after having been declared a
leper, is the patient immediately rushed off to
Molokai. He is given ample time, weeks, and
even months, sometimes, during which he stays
at Kalihi and winds up or arranges all his business
affairs. At Molokai, in turn, he may be visited
by his relatives, business agents, etc., though
they are not permitted to eat and sleep in his
house. Visitors' houses, kept " clean," are maintained for this purpose.

I saw an illustration of the thorough trial given
the suspect, when I visited Kalihi with Mr.
Pinkham, president of the Board of Health. The
suspect was an Hawaiian, seventy years of age,
who for thirty-four years had worked in Honolulu
as a pressman in a printing office. The bacteriologist had decided that he was a leper, the Examining Board had been unable to make up its

mind, and that day all had come out to Kalihi to make another examination.

When at Molokai, the declared leper has the privilege of re-examination, and patients are continually coming back to Honolulu for that purpose. The steamer that took me to Molokai had on board two returning lepers, both young women, one of whom had come to Honolulu to settle up some property she owned, and the other had come to Honolulu to see her sick mother. Both had remained at Kalihi for a month.

The Settlement of Molokai enjoys a far more delightful climate than even Honolulu, being situated on the windward side of the island in the path of the fresh north-east trades. The scenery is magnificent ; on one side is the blue sea, on the other the wonderful wall of the *pali*, receding here and there into beautiful mountain valleys. Everywhere are grassy pastures over which roam the hundreds of horses which are owned by the lepers. Some of them have their own carts, rigs, and traps. In the little harbour of Kalaupapa lie fishing boats and a steam launch, all of which are privately owned and operated by lepers. Their bounds upon the sea are, of course, determined ; otherwise no restriction is put upon their sea-faring. Their fish they sell to the Board of Health, and the money they receive is their own. While I was there, one night's catch was four thousand pounds.

And as these men fish, others farm. All trades are followed. One leper, a pure Hawaiian, is the boss painter. He employs eight men, and takes contracts for painting buildings from the Board of Health. He is a member of the Kalaupapa Rifle Club, where I met him, and I must confess that he was far better dressed than I. Another man, similarly situated, is the boss carpenter. Then, in addition to the Board of Health store, there are little privately owned stores, where those with shopkeeper's souls may exercise their peculiar instincts. The Assistant Superintendent, Mr. Waiamau, a finely educated and able man, is a pure Hawaiian and a leper. Mr. Bartlett, who is the present storekeeper, is an American who was in business in Honolulu before he was struck down by the disease. All that these men earn is that much in their own pockets. If they do not work, they are taken care of anyway by the territory, given food, shelter, clothes, and medical attendance. The Board of Health carries on agriculture, stock-raising, and dairying, for local use, and employment at fair wages is furnished to all that wish to work. They are not compelled to work, however, for they are the wards of the territory. For the young, and the very old, and the helpless there are homes and hospitals.

Major Lee, an American and long a marine engineer for the Inter Island Steamship Company, I met actively at work in the new steam laundry, where he was busy installing the machinery. I met him often, afterwards, and one day he said to me:

" Give us a good breeze about how we live here. For heaven's sake write us up straight. Put your foot down on this chamber-of-horrors rot and all the rest of it. We don't like being misrepresented. We've got some feelings. Just tell the world how we really are in here."

Man after man that I met in the Settlement, and woman after woman, in one way or another expressed the same sentiment. It was patent that they resented bitterly the sensational and untruthful way in which they have been exploited in the past.

In spite of the fact that they are afflicted by disease, the lepers form a happy colony, divided into two villages and numerous country and seaside homes, of nearly a thousand souls. They have six churches, a Young Men's Christian Association building, several assembly halls, a band stand, a race-track, baseball grounds, shooting ranges, an athletic club, numerous glee clubs, and two brass bands.

"They are so contented down there," Mr. Pinkham told me, "that you can't drive them away with a shot-gun."

This I later verified for myself. In January of this year, eleven of the lepers, on whom the disease, after having committed certain ravages, showed no further signs of activity, were brought back to Honolulu for re-examination. They were loath to come ; and, on being asked whether or not they wanted to go free if found clean of leprosy, one and all answered, "Back to Molokai."

In the old days, before the discovery of the leprosy bacillus, a small number of men and women, suffering from various and wholly different diseases, were adjudged lepers and sent to Molokai. Years afterward they suffered great consternation when the bacteriologists declared that they were not afflicted with leprosy and never had been. They fought against being sent away from

Molokai, and in one way or another, as helpers and nurses, they got jobs from the Board of Health and remained. The present jailer is one of these men. Declared to be a non-leper, he accepted, on salary, the charge of the jail, in order to escape being sent away.

At the present moment, in Honolulu, there is a bootblack. He is an American negro. Mr. McVeigh told me about him. Long ago, before the bacteriological tests, he was sent to Molokai as a leper. As a ward of the state he developed a superlative degree of independence and fomented much petty mischief. And then, one day, after having been for years a perennial source of minor annoyances, the bacteriological test was applied, and he was declared a non-leper.

" Ah, ha ! " chortled Mr. McVeigh. " Now I've got you ! Out you go on the next steamer and good riddance ! "

But the negro didn't want to go. Immediately he married an old woman, in the last stages of leprosy, and began petitioning the Board of Health for permission to remain and nurse his sick wife. There was no one, he said pathetically, who could take care of his poor wife as well as he could. But they saw through his game, and he was deported on the steamer and given the freedom of the world. But he preferred Molokai. Landing on the leeward side of Molokai, he sneaked down the *pali* one night and took up his abode in the Settlement. He was apprehended, tried and convicted of trespass, sentenced to pay a small fine, and again deported on the steamer with the warning that if he trespassed again, he would be fined one hundred dollars and be sent to prison in Honolulu.   And now, when Mr. McVeigh comes up to Honolulu, the bootblack shines his shoes for him and says :

" Say, Boss, I lost a good home down there. Yes, sir, I lost a good home." Then his voice sinks to a confidential whisper as he says, " Say, Boss, can't I go back ?   Can't you fix it for me so as I can go back ? "

He had lived nine years on Molokai, and he had had a better time there than he has ever had, before and after, on the outside.

As regards the fear of leprosy itself, nowhere in the Settlement among lepers, or non-lepers, did I see any sign of it.   The chief horror of leprosy obtains in the minds of those who have never seen a leper and who do not know anything about the disease.   At the hotel at Waikiki a lady expressed shuddering amazement at my having the hardi-hood to pay a visit to the Settlement.   On talking with her I learned that she had been born in Honolulu, had lived there all her life, and had never laid eyes on a leper.   That was more than I could say of myself in the United States, where the segregation of lepers is loosely enforced and where I have repeatedly seen lepers on the streets of large cities.

Leprosy is terrible, there is no getting away from that ; but from what little I know of the disease and its degree of contagiousness, I would by far prefer to spend the rest of my days in Molokai than in any tuberculosis sanatorium.   In every city and county hospital for poor people in the United States, or in similar institutions in other countries, sights as terrible as those in Molokai can be witnessed, and the sum total of these sights is vastly more terrible. For that matter, if it were given me to choose between being compelled to live in Molokai for the rest of my life, or in the East End of London, the East Side of New York, or the Stockyards of Chicago, I would select Molokai without debate. I would prefer one year of life in Molokai to five years of life in the above-mentioned cesspools of human degradation and misery.

In Molokai the people are happy. I shall never forget the celebration of the Fourth of July I witnessed there. At six o'clock in the morning the " horribles " were out, dressed fantastically, astride horses, mules, and donkeys (their own property), and cutting capers all over the Settlement. Two brass bands were out as well. Then there were the *pa-u* riders, thirty or forty of them, Hawaiian women all, superb horsewomen dressed gorgeously in the old, native riding costume, and dashing about in twos and threes and groups. In the afternoon Charmian and I stood in the judge's stand and awarded the prizes for horsemanship and costume to the *pa-u* riders. All about were the hundreds of lepers, with wreaths of flowers on heads and necks and shoulders, looking on and making merry. And always, over the brows of hills and across the grassy level stretches, appearing and disappearing, were the groups of men and women, gaily dressed, on galloping horses, horses and riders flower-bedecked and flower-garlanded, singing, and laughing, and riding like the wind. And as I stood in the

judge's stand and looked at all this, there came
to my recollection the lazar house of Havana,
where I had once beheld some two hundred lepers,
prisoners inside four restricted walls until they
died.   No, there are a few thousand places I
wot of in this world over which I would select
Molokai as a place of permanent residence.   In
the evening we went to one of the leper assembly
halls, where, before a crowded audience, the
singing societies contested for prizes, and where
the night wound up with a dance.   I have seen
the Hawaiians living in the slums of Honolulu,
and, having seen them, I can readily understand
why the lepers, brought up from the Settlement
for re-examination, shouted one and all, "Back to
Molokai!"

One thing is certain.   The leper in the Settlement is far better off than the leper who lies in
hiding outside.   Such a leper is a lonely outcast,
living in constant fear of discovery and slowly
and surely rotting away.   The action of leprosy
is not steady.   It lays hold of its victim, commits
a ravage, and then lies dormant for an indeterminate period.   It may not commit another
ravage for five years, or ten years, or forty years,
and the patient may enjoy uninterrupted good
health.   Rarely, however, do these first ravages
cease of themselves.   The skilled surgeon is
required, and the skilled surgeon cannot be called
in for the leper who is in hiding.   For instance,
the first ravage may take the form of a perforating
ulcer in the sole of the foot.   When the bone is
reached, necrosis sets in.   If the leper is in hiding,
he cannot be operated upon, the necrosis will

continue to eat its way up the bone of the leg, and in a brief and horrible time that leper will die of gangrene or some other terrible complication. On the other hand, if that same leper is in Molokai, the surgeon will operate upon the foot, remove the ulcer, cleanse the bone, and put a complete stop to that particular ravage of the disease. A month after the operation the leper will be out riding horseback, running foot races, swimming in the breakers, or climbing the giddy sides of the valleys for mountain apples. And as has been stated before, the disease, lying dormant, may not again attack him for five, ten, or forty years.

The old horrors of leprosy go back to the conditions that obtained before the days of antiseptic surgery, and before the time when physicians like Dr. Goodhue and Dr. Hollmann went to live at the Settlement. Dr. Goodhue is the pioneer surgeon there, and too much praise cannot be given him for the noble work he has done. I spent one morning in the operating room with him and of the three operations he performed, two were on men, newcomers, who had arrived on the same steamer with me. In each case, the disease had attacked in one spot only. One had a perforating ulcer in the ankle, well advanced, and the other man was suffering from a similar affliction, well advanced, under his arm. Both cases were well advanced because the man had been on the outside and had not been treated. In each case, Dr. Goodhue put an immediate and complete stop to the ravage, and in four weeks those two men will be as well and able-bodied as they ever were in their lives. The only difference between them and you or me is that the disease is lying dormant in their bodies and may at any future time commit another ravage.

Leprosy is as old as history. References to it are found in the earliest written records. And yet to-day practically nothing more is known about it than was known then. This much was known then, namely, that it was contagious and that those afflicted by it should be segregated. The difference between then and now is that to-day the leper is more rigidly segregated and more humanely treated. But leprosy itself still remains the same awful and profound mystery. A reading of the reports of the physicians and specialists of all countries reveals the baffling nature of the disease. These leprosy specialists are unanimous on no one phase of the disease. They do not know. In the past they rashly and dogmatically generalized. They generalize no longer. The one possible generalization that can be drawn from all the investigation that has been made is that leprosy is *feebly contagious*. But in what manner it is feebly contagious is not known. They have isolated the bacillus of leprosy. They can determine by bacteriological examination whether or not a person is a leper ; but they are as far away as ever from knowing how that bacillus finds its entrance into the body of a non-leper. They do not know the length of time of incubation. They have tried to inoculate all sorts of animals with leprosy, and have failed.

They are baffled in the discovery of a serum wherewith to fight the disease. And in all their work, as yet, they have found no clue, no cure. Sometimes there have been blazes of hope, theories of causation and much heralded cures, but every time the darkness of failure quenched the flame. A doctor insists that the cause of leprosy is a long-continued fish diet, and he proves his theory voluminously till a physician from the highlands of India demands why the natives of that district should therefore be afflicted by leprosy when they have never eaten fish, nor all the generations of their fathers before them. A man treats a leper with a certain kind of oil or drug, announces a cure, and five, ten, or forty years afterwards the disease breaks out again. It is this trick of leprosy lying dormant in the body for indeterminate periods that is responsible for many alleged cures. But this much is certain : *as yet there has been no authentic case of a cure.*

Leprosy is *feebly contagious*, but how is it contagious ? An Austrian physician has inoculated himself and his assistants with leprosy and failed to catch it. But this is not conclusive, for there is the famous case of the Hawaiian murderer, who had his sentence of death commuted to life imprisonment on his agreeing to be inoculated with the *bacillus leprœ.* Some time after inoculation, leprosy made its appearance, and the man died a leper on Molokai. Nor was this conclusive, for it was discovered that at the time he was inoculated several members of his family were already suffering from the disease on Molokai. He may have contracted the disease from them, and it may have been well along in its mysterious period of incubation at the time he was officially

inoculated. Then there is the case of that hero
of the Church, Father Damien, who went to
Molokai a clean man and died a leper. There
have been many theories as to how he contracted
leprosy, but nobody knows. He never knew
himself. But every chance that he ran has
certainly been run by a woman at present living
in the Settlement; who has lived there many
years; who has had five leper husbands, and had
children by them; and who is to-day, as she
always has been, free of the disease.

As yet no light has been shed upon the mystery
of leprosy. When more is learned about the
disease, a cure for it may be expected. Once an
efficacious serum is discovered, and leprosy, because it is so feebly contagious, will pass away
swiftly from the earth. The battle waged with
it will be short and sharp. In the meantime, how
to discover that serum, or some other unguessed
weapon? In the present it is a serious matter.
It is estimated that there are half a million lepers,
not segregated, in India alone. Carnegie libraries,
Rockefeller universities, and many similar bene-
factions are all very well; but one cannot help
thinking how far a few thousands of dollars would
go, say in the leper Settlement of Molokai. The
residents there are accidents of fate, scapegoats
to some mysterious natural law of which man
knows nothing, isolated for the welfare of their
fellows who else might catch the dread disease,
even as they have caught it, nobody knows how.
Not for their sakes merely, but for the sake of
future generations, a few thousands of dollars
would go far in a legitimate and scientific

search after a cure for leprosy, for a serum, or for some undreamed discovery that will enable the medical world to exterminate the *bacillus lepræ*. There's the place for your money, you philanthropists.

CHAPTER VIII

THE HOUSE OF THE SUN

THERE are hosts of people who journey like restless spirits round and about this earth in search of seascapes and landscapes and the wonders and beauties of nature. They overrun Europe in armies ; they can be met in droves and herds in Florida and the West Indies, at the Pyramids, and on the slopes and summits of the Canadian and American Rockies ; but in the House of the Sun they are as rare as live and wriggling dinosaurs. Haleakala is the Hawaiian name for "the House of the Sun." It is a noble dwelling, situated on the Island of Maui ; but so few tourists have ever peeped into it, much less entered it, that their number may be practically reckoned as zero. Yet I venture to state that for natural beauty and wonder the nature-lover may see dissimilar things as great as Haleakala, but no greater, while he will never see elsewhere anything more beautiful or wonderful. Honolulu is six days' steaming from San Francisco ; Maui is a night's run on the steamer from Honolulu ; and six hours more if he is in a hurry, can bring the traveller to Kolikoli, which is ten thousand and thirty-two feet above the sea and which stands

116

hard by the entrance portal to the House of the Sun. Yet the tourist comes not, and Haleakala sleeps on in lonely and unseen grandeur.

Not being tourists, we of the *Snark* went to Haleakala. On the slopes of that monster mountain there is a cattle ranch of some fifty thousand acres, where we spent the night at an altitude of two thousand feet. The next morning it was boots and saddles, and with cow-boys and pack-horses we climbed to Ukulele, a mountain ranch-house, the altitude of which, fifty-five hundred feet, gives a severely temperate climate, compelling blankets at night and a roaring fireplace in the living-room. Ukulele, by the way, is the Hawaiian for " jumping flea " as it is also the Hawaiian for a certain musical instrument that may be likened to a young guitar. It is my opinion that the mountain ranch-house was named after the young guitar. We were not in a hurry, and we spent the day at Ukulele, learnedly discussing altitudes and barometers and shaking our particular barometer whenever any one's argument stood in need of demonstration. Our barometer was the most graciously acquiescent instrument I have ever seen. Also, we gathered mountain raspberries, large as hen's eggs and larger, gazed up the pasture-covered lava slopes to the summit of Haleakala, forty-five hundred feet above us, and looked down upon a mighty battle of the clouds that was being fought beneath us, ourselves in the bright sunshine.

Every day and every day this unending battle goes on. Ukiukiu is the name of the trade-wind that comes raging down out of the north-east and hurls itself upon Haleakala. Now Haleakala is so bulky and tall that it turns the north-east trade-wind aside on either hand, so that in the lee of Haleakala no trade-wind blows at all. On the contrary, the wind blows in the counter direction, in the teeth of the north-east trade. This wind is called Naulu. And day and night and always Ukiukiu and Naulu strive with each other, advancing, retreating, flanking, curving, curling, and turning and twisting, the conflict made visible by the cloud-masses plucked from the heavens and hurled back and forth in squadrons, battalions, armies, and great mountain ranges. Once in a while, Ukiukiu, in mighty gusts, flings immense cloud-masses clear over the summit of Haleakala ; whereupon Naulu craftily captures them, lines them up in new battle-formation, and with them smites back at his ancient and eternal antagonist. Then Ukiukiu sends a great cloud-army around the eastern side of the mountain. It is a flanking movement, well executed. But Naulu, from his lair on the leeward side, gathers the flanking army in, pulling and twisting and dragging it, hammering it into shape, and sends it charging back against Ukiukiu around the western side of the mountain. And all the while, above and below the main battle-field, high up the slopes toward the sea, Ukiukiu and Naulu are continually sending out little wisps of cloud, in ragged skirmish line, that creep and crawl over the ground, among the trees and through the canyons, and that spring upon and capture one another in sudden ambuscades and sorties. And sometimes Ukiukiu or Naulu, abruptly sending out a heavy

charging column, captures the ragged little
skirmishers or drives them skyward, turning over
and over, in vertical whirls, thousands of feet in
the air.

But it is on the western slopes of Haleakala that
the main battle goes on.   Here Naulu masses his
heaviest formations and wins his greatest victories.
Ukiukiu grows weak toward late afternoon, which
is the way of all trade-winds, and is driven backward by Naulu.   Naulu's generalship is excellent.
All day he has been gathering and packing away
immense reserves.   As the afternoon draws on,
he welds them into a solid column, sharp-pointed,
miles in length, a mile in width, and hundreds of
feet thick.   This column he slowly thrusts forward
into the broad battle-front of Ukiukiu, and slowly
and surely Ukiukiu, weakening fast, is split
asunder.   But it is not all bloodless.   At times
Ukiukiu struggles wildly, and with fresh acces-
sions of strength from the limitless north-east,
smashes away half a mile at a time of Naulu's
column and sweeps it off and away toward West
Maui.   Sometimes, when the two charging armies
meet end-on, a tremendous perpendicular whirl
results, the cloud-masses, locked together, mount-
ing thousands of feet into the air and turning over
and over.   A favourite device of Ukiukiu is to
send a low, squat formation, densely packed,
forward along the ground and under Naulu.
When Ukiukiu is under, he proceeds to buck.
Naulu's mighty middle gives to the blow and
bends upward, but usually he turns the attacking
column back upon itself and sets it milling.   And
all the while the ragged little skirmishers, stray and

detached, sneak through the trees and canyons, crawl along and through the grass, and surprise one another with unexpected leaps and rushes ; while above, far above, serene and lonely in the rays of the setting sun, Haleakala looks down upon the conflict.   And so, the night.   But in the morning, after the fashion of trade-winds, Ukiukiu gathers strength and sends the hosts of Naulu rolling back in confusion and rout.   And one day is like another day in the battle of the clouds, where Ukiukiu and Naulu strive eternally on the slopes of Haleakala.

Again in the morning, it was boots and saddles, cow-boys and packhorses, and the climb to the top began.   One packhorse carried twenty gallons of water, slung in five-gallon bags on either side ; for water is precious and rare in the crater itself, in spite of the fact that several miles to the north and east of the crater-rim more rain comes down than in any other place in the world.   The way led upward across countless lava flows, without regard for trails, and never have I seen horses with such perfect footing as that of the thirteen that composed our outfit.   They climbed or dropped down perpendicular places with the sureness and coolness of mountain goats, and never a horse fell or baulked.

There is a familiar and strange illusion experienced by all who climb isolated mountains. The higher one climbs, the more of the earth's surface becomes visible, and the effect of this is that the horizon seems up-hill from the observer. This illusion is especially notable on Haleakala, for the old volcano rises directly from the sea, without buttresses or connecting ranges. In consequence, as fast as we climbed up the grim slope of Haleakala, still faster did Haleakala, ourselves, and all about us, sink down into the centre of what appeared a profound abyss. Everywhere, far above us, towered the horizon. The ocean sloped down from the horizon to us. The higher we climbed, the deeper did we seem to sink down, the farther above us shone the horizon, and the steeper pitched the grade up to that horizontal line where sky and ocean met. It was weird and unreal, and vagrant thoughts of Simm's Hole and of the volcano through which Jules Verne journeyed to the centre of the earth flitted through one's mind.

And then, when at last we reached the summit of that monster mountain, which summit was like the bottom of an inverted cone situated in the centre of an awful cosmic pit, we found that we were at neither top nor bottom. Far above us was the heaven-towering horizon, and far beneath us, where the top of the mountain should have been, was a deeper deep, the great crater, the House of the Sun. Twenty-three miles around stretched the dizzy walls of the crater. We stood on the edge of the nearly vertical western wall, and the floor of the crater lay nearly half a mile beneath. This floor, broken by lava-flows and cinder-cones, was as red and fresh and uneroded as if it were but yesterday that the fires went out. The cinder-cones, the smallest over four hundred feet in height and the largest over nine hundred, seemed no more than puny little sand-hills, so mighty was the magnitude of the setting. Two gaps, thousands of feet deep, broke the rim of the crater, and through these Ukiukiu vainly strove to drive his fleecy herds of trade-wind clouds. As fast as they advanced through the gaps, the heat of the crater dissipated them into thin air, and though they advanced always, they got nowhere.

It was a scene of vast bleakness and desolation, stern, forbidding, fascinating. We gazed down upon a place of fire and earthquake. The tie-ribs of earth lay bare before us. It was a workshop of nature still cluttered with the raw beginnings of world-making. Here and there great dikes of primordial rock had thrust themselves up from the bowels of earth, straight through the molten surface-ferment that had evidently cooled only the other day. It was all unreal and unbelievable. Looking upward, far above us (in reality beneath us) floated the cloud-battle of Ukiukiu and Naulu. And higher up the slope of the seeming abyss, above the cloud-battle, in the air and sky, hung the islands of Lanai and Molokai. Across the crater, to the south-east, still apparently looking upward, we saw ascending, first, the turquoise sea, then the white surf-line of the shore of Hawaii ; above that the belt of trade-clouds, and next, eighty miles away, rearing their stupendous bulks out of the azure sky, tipped with snow, wreathed with cloud, trembling like a mirage, the peaks of Mauna Kea and Mauna Loa hung poised on the wall of heaven.

It is told that long ago, one Maui, the son of Hina, lived on what is now known as West Maui. His mother, Hina, employed her time in the

making of *kapas*. She must have made them at
night, for her days were occupied in trying to dry
the *kapas*. Each morning, and all morning, she
toiled at spreading them out in the sun. But no
sooner were they out, than she began taking them
in, in order to have them all under shelter for the
night. For know that the days were shorter
then than now. Maui watched his mother's
futile toil and felt sorry for her. He decided to do
something—oh, no, not to help her hang out and
take in the *kapas*. He was too clever for that.
His idea was to make the sun go slower. Perhaps
he was the first Hawaiian astronomer. At any
rate, he took a series of observations of the sun
from various parts of the island. His conclusion
was that the sun's path was directly across
Haleakala. Unlike Joshua, he stood in no need of
divine assistance. He gathered a huge quantity
of coconuts, from the fibre of which he braided
a stout cord, and in one end of which he made
a noose, even as the cow-boys of Haleakala do to
this day. Next he climbed into the House of the
Sun and laid in wait. When the sun came
tearing along the path, bent on completing its
journey in the shortest time possible, the valiant
youth threw his lariat around one of the sun's
largest and strongest beams. He made the sun
slow down some ; also, he broke the beam short
off. And he kept on roping and breaking off
beams till the sun said it was willing to listen to
reason. Maui set forth his terms of peace, which
the sun accepted, agreeing to go more slowly
thereafter. Wherefore Hina had ample time in
which to dry her *kapas*, and the days are longer

than they used to be, which last is quite in accord with the teachings of modern astronomy.

We had a lunch of jerked beef and hard *poi* in a stone corral, used of old time for the night-impounding of cattle being driven across the island.   Then we skirted the rim for half a mile and began the descent into the crater.   Twenty-five hundred feet beneath lay the floor, and down a steep slope of loose volcanic cinders we dropped, the sure-footed horses slipping and sliding, but always keeping their feet.   The black surface of the cinders, when broken by the horses' hoofs, turned to a yellow ochre dust, virulent in appearance and acid of taste, that arose in clouds. There was a gallop across a level stretch to the mouth of a convenient blow-hole, and then the descent continued in clouds of volcanic dust, winding in and out among cinder-cones, brick-red, old rose, and purplish black of colour.   Above us, higher and higher, towered the crater-walls, while we journeyed on across innumerable lava-flows, turning and twisting a devious way among the adamantine billows of a petrified sea.   Saw-toothed waves of lava vexed the surface of this weird ocean, while on either hand arose jagged crests and spiracles of fantastic shape.   Our way led on past a bottomless pit and along and over the main stream of the latest lava-flow for seven miles.

At the lower end of the crater was our camping spot, in a small grove of *olapa* and *kolea* trees, tucked away in a corner of the crater at the base of walls that rose perpendicularly fifteen hundred feet.   Here was pasturage for the horses, but no water, and first we turned aside and picked our way across a mile of lava to a known water-hole in a crevice in the crater-wall. The water-hole was empty. But on climbing fifty feet up the crevice, a pool was found containing half a dozen barrels of water. A pail was carried up, and soon a steady stream of the precious liquid was running down the rock and filling the lower pool, while the cow-boys below were busy fighting the horses back, for there was room for one only to drink at a time. Then it was on to camp at the foot of the wall, up which herds of wild goats scrambled and blatted, while the tent arose to the sound of rifle-firing. Jerked beef, hard *poi*, and broiled kid were the menu. Over the crest of the crater, just above our heads, rolled a sea of clouds, driven on by Ukiukiu. Though this sea rolled over the crest unceasingly, it never blotted out nor dimmed the moon, for the heat of the crater dissolved the clouds as fast as they rolled in. Through the moonlight, attracted by the camp-fire, came the crater cattle to peer and challenge. They were rolling fat, though they rarely drank water, the morning dew on the grass taking its place. It was because of this dew that the tent made a welcome bedchamber, and we fell asleep to the chanting of *hulas* by the unwearied Hawaiian cow-boys, in whose veins, no doubt, ran the blood of Maui, their valiant forebear.

The camera cannot do justice to the House of the Sun. The sublimated chemistry of photography may not lie, but it certainly does not tell all the truth. The Koolau Gap may be faithfully reproduced, just as it impinged on the retina of the

camera, yet in the resulting picture the gigantic
scale of things would be missing.   Those walls that
seem several hundred feet in height are almost as
many thousand ; that entering wedge of cloud is a
mile and a half wide in the gap itself, while beyond
the gap it is a veritable ocean ; and that fore-
ground of cinder-cone and volcanic ash, mushy
and colourless in appearance, is in truth gorgeous-
hued in brick-red, terra-cotta, rose, yellow ochre,
and purplish black.   Also, words are a vain thing
and drive to despair.   To say that a crater-wall
is two thousand feet high is to say just precisely
that it is two thousand feet high ; but there is a
vast deal more to that crater-wall than a mere
statistic.   The sun is ninety-three millions of miles
distant, but to mortal conception the adjoining
county is farther away.   This frailty of the human
brain is hard on the sun.   It is likewise hard on
the House of the Sun.   Haleakala has a message
of beauty and wonder for the human soul that
cannot be delivered by proxy.   Kolikoli is six
hours from Kahului ; Kahului is a night's run
from Honolulu ; Honolulu is six days from San
Francisco ; and there you are.

We climbed the crater-walls, put the horses
over impossible places, rolled stones, and shot
wild goats.   I did not get any goats.   I was too
busy rolling stones.   One spot in particular I
remember, where we started a stone the size of a
horse.   It began the descent easy enough, rolling
over, wobbling, and threatening to stop ; but in
a few minutes it was soaring through the air two
hundred feet at a jump.   It grew rapidly smaller
until it struck a slight slope of volcanic sand, over

which it darted like a startled jackrabbit, kicking
up behind it a tiny trail of yellow dust. Stone
and dust diminished in size, until some of the
party said the stone had stopped. That was
because they could not see it any longer. It had
vanished into the distance beyond their ken.
Others saw it rolling farther on—I know I did;
and it is my firm conviction that that stone is
still rolling.

Our last day in the crater, Ukiukiu gave us a
taste of his strength. He smashed Naulu back
all along the line, filled the House of the Sun to
overflowing with clouds, and drowned us out.
Our rain-gauge was a pint cup under a tiny hole
in the tent. That last night of storm and rain
filled the cup, and there was no way of measuring
the water that spilled over into the blankets.
With the rain-gauge out of business there was no
longer any reason for remaining; so we broke
camp in the wet-gray of dawn, and plunged eastward across the lava to the Kaupo Gap. East
Maui is nothing more or less than the vast lava
stream that flowed long ago through the Kaupo
Gap; and down this stream we picked our way
from an altitude of six thousand five hundred feet
to the sea. This was a day's work in itself for
the horses; but never were there such horses.
Safe in the bad places, never rushing, never losing
their heads, as soon as they found a trail wide
and smooth enough to run on, they ran. There
was no stopping them until the trail became bad
again, and then they stopped of themselves.
Continuously, for days, they had performed the
hardest kind of work, and fed most of the time on

grass foraged by themselves at night while we slept, and yet that day they covered twenty-eight leg-breaking miles and galloped into Hana like a bunch of colts. Also, there were several of them, reared in the dry region on the leeward side of Haleakala, that had never worn shoes in all their lives. Day after day, and all day long, unshod, they had travelled over the sharp lava, with the extra weight of a man on their backs, and their hoofs were in better condition than those of the shod horses.

The scenery between Vieiras's (where the Kaupo Gap empties into the sea) and Hana, which we covered in half a day, is well worth a week or a month; but, wildly beautiful as it is, it becomes pale and small in comparison with the wonderland that lies beyond the rubber plantations between Hana and the Honomanu Gulch. Two days were required to cover this marvellous stretch, which lies on the windward side of Haleakala. The people who dwell there call it the "ditch country," an unprepossessing name, but it has no other. Nobody else ever comes there. Nobody else knows anything about it. With the exception of a handful of men, whom business has brought there, nobody has heard of the ditch country of Maui. Now a ditch is a ditch, assumably muddy, and usually traversing uninteresting and monotonous landscapes. But the Nahiku Ditch is not an ordinary ditch. The windward side of Haleakala is serried by a thousand precipitous gorges, down which rush as many torrents, each torrent of which achieves a score of cascades and waterfalls before it reaches the sea. More rain comes

down here than in any other region in the world.
In 1904 the year's downpour was four hundred
and twenty inches. Water means sugar, and
sugar is the backbone of the territory of Hawaii,
wherefore the Nahiku Ditch, which is not a ditch,
but a chain of tunnels. The water travels under-
ground, appearing only at intervals to leap a
gorge, travelling high in the air on a giddy flume
and plunging into and through the opposing
mountain. This magnificent waterway is called a
" ditch," and with equal appropriateness can
Cleopatra's barge be called a box-car.

There are no carriage roads through the ditch
country, and before the ditch was built, or bored,
rather, there was no horse-trail. Hundreds of
inches of rain annually, on fertile soil, under a
tropic sun, means a steaming jungle of vegetation.
A man, on foot, cutting his way through, might
advance a mile a day, but at the end of a week
he would be a wreck, and he would have to crawl
hastily back if he wanted to get out before the
vegetation overran the passage way he had cut.
O'Shaughnessy was the daring engineer who
conquered the jungle and the gorges, ran the ditch,
and made the horse-trail. He built enduringly,
in concrete and masonry, and made one of the
most remarkable water-farms in the world.
Every little runlet and dribble is harvested and
conveyed by subterranean channels to the main
ditch. But so heavily does it rain at times, that
countless spillways let the surplus escape to the sea.

The horse-trail is not very wide. Like the
engineer who built it, it dares anything. Where
the ditch plunges through the mountain, it climbs

over ; and where the ditch leaps a gorge on a
flume, the horse-trail takes advantage of the
ditch and crosses on top of the flume. That
careless trail thinks nothing of travelling up or
down the faces of precipices.   It gouges its narrow
way out of the wall, dodging around waterfalls
or passing under them where they thunder down
in white fury ; while straight overhead the wall
rises hundreds of feet, and straight beneath it
sinks a thousand.   And those marvellous mountain horses are as unconcerned as the trail.   They
fox-trot along it as a matter of course, though the
footing is slippery with rain, and they will gallop
with their hind feet slipping over the edge if you
let them.   I advise only those with steady nerves
and cool heads to tackle the Nahiku Ditch trail.
One of our cow-boys was noted as the strongest
and bravest on the big ranch. He had ridden
mountain horses all his life on the rugged western
slopes of Haleakala.   He was first in the horse-
breaking ; and when the others hung back, as a
matter of course, he would go in to meet a wild
bull in the cattle-pen. He had a reputation.
But he had never ridden over the Nahiku Ditch.
It was there he lost his reputation. When he
faced the first flume, spanning a hair-raising gorge,
narrow, without railings, with a bellowing waterfall above, another below, and directly beneath
a wild cascade, the air filled with driving spray
and rocking to the clamour and rush of sound and
motion—well, that cow-boy dismounted from his
horse, explained briefly that he had a wife and two
children, and crossed over on foot, leading the
horse behind him.

The only relief from the flumes was the precipices ; and the only relief from the precipices was
the flumes, except where the ditch was far under
ground, in which case we crossed one horse and
rider at a time, on primitive log-bridges that
swayed and teetered and threatened to carry
away.   I confess that at first I rode such places
with my feet loose in the stirrups, and that on the
sheer walls I saw to it, by a definite, conscious act
of will, that the foot in the outside stirrup, overhanging the thousand feet of fall, was exceedingly
loose.   I say " at first " ;   for, as in the crater
itself we quickly lost our conception of magnitude,
so, on the Nahiku Ditch, we quickly lost our
apprehension of depth.   The ceaseless iteration
of height and depth produced a state of consciousness in which height and depth were accepted
as the ordinary conditions of existence ;   and
from the horse's back to look sheer down four
hundred or five hundred feet became quite
commonplace and non-productive of thrills.   And
as carelessly as the trail and the horses, we swung
along the dizzy heights and ducked around or
through the waterfalls.

And such a ride !   Falling water was everywhere.   We rode above the clouds, under the
clouds, and through the clouds !   and every now
and then a shaft of sunshine penetrated like a
search-light to the depths yawning beneath us,
or flashed upon some pinnacle of the crater-rim
thousands of feet above.   At every turn of the
trail a waterfall or a dozen waterfalls, leaping
hundreds of feet through the air, burst upon our
vision.   At our first night's camp, in the Keanæ

Gulch, we counted thirty-two waterfalls from a single viewpoint. The vegetation ran riot over that wild land. There were forests of koa and kolea trees, and candlenut trees ; and then there were the trees called ohia-ai, which bore red mountain apples, mellow and juicy and most excellent to eat. Wild bananas grew everywhere, clinging to the sides of the gorges, and, overborne by their great bunches of ripe fruit, falling across the trail and blocking the way. And over the forest surged a sea of green life, the climbers of a thousand varieties, some that floated airily, in lacelike filaments, from the tallest branches ; others that coiled and wound about the trees like huge serpents ; and one, the ei-ei, that was for all the world like a climbing palm, swinging on a thick stem from branch to branch and tree to tree and throttling the supports whereby it climbed. Through the sea of green, lofty tree-ferns thrust their great delicate fronds, and the lehua flaunted its scarlet blossoms. Underneath the climbers, in no less profusion, grew the warm-coloured, strangely-marked plants that in the United States one is accustomed to seeing pre-ciously conserved in hot-houses. In fact, the ditch country of Maui is nothing more nor less than a huge conservatory. Every familiar variety of fern flourishes, and more varieties that are unfamiliar, from the tiniest maidenhair to the gross and voracious staghorn, the latter the terror of the woodsmen, interlacing with itself in tangled masses five or six feet deep and covering acres.

Never was there such a ride. For two days it lasted, when we emerged into rolling country, and, along an actual wagon-road, came home to the ranch at a gallop. I know it was cruel to gallop the horses after such a long, hard journey ; but we blistered our hands in vain effort to hold them in. That's the sort of horses they grow on Haleakala. At the ranch there was great festival of cattle-driving, branding, and horse-breaking. Overhead Ukiukiu and Naulu battled valiantly, and far above, in the sunshine, towered the mighty summit of Haleakala.

CHAPTER IX

A PACIFIC TRAVERSE

Sandwich Islands to Tahiti.—There is great difficulty in making this passage across the trades. The whalers and all others speak with great doubt of fetching Tahiti from the Sandwich Islands. Capt. Bruce says that a vessel should keep to the northward until she gets a start of wind before bearing for her destination. In his passage between them in November, 1837, he had no variables near the line in coming south, and never could make easting on either tack, though he endeavoured by every means to do so.

So say the sailing directions for the South Pacific Ocean; and that is all they say. There is not a word more to help the weary voyager in making this long traverse—nor is there any word at all concerning the passage from Hawaii to the Marquesas, which lie some eight hundred miles to the northeast of Tahiti and which are the more difficult to reach by just that much. The reason for the lack of directions is, I imagine, that no voyager is supposed to make himself weary by attempting so impossible a traverse. But the impossible did not deter the

Snark,—principally because of the fact that we did not read that particular little paragraph in the sailing directions until after we had started. We sailed from Hilo, Hawaii, on October 7, and arrived at Nuka-hiva, in the Marquesas, on December 6. The distance was two thousand miles as the crow flies, while we actually travelled at least four thousand miles to accomplish it, thus proving for once and for ever that the shortest distance between two points is not always a straight line. Had we headed directly for the Marquesas, we might have travelled five or six thousand miles.

Upon one thing we were resolved : we would not cross the Line west of 130° west longitude. For here was the problem. To cross the Line to the west of that point, if the southeast trades were well around to the southeast, would throw us so far to leeward of the Marquesas that a head-beat would be maddeningly impossible. Also, we had to remember the equatorial current, which moves west at a rate of anywhere from twelve to seventy-five miles a day. A pretty pickle, indeed, to be to leeward of our destination with such a current in our teeth. No ; not a minute, nor a second, west of 130° west longitude would we cross the Line. But since the southeast trades were to be expected five or six degrees north of the Line (which, if they were well around to the southeast or south-southeast, would necessitate our sliding off toward south-southwest), we should have to hold to the eastward, north of the Line, and north of the southeast trades, until we gained at least 128° west longitude.

I have forgotten to mention that the seventy-horse-power gasolene engine, as usual, was not working, and that we could depend upon wind alone. Neither was the launch engine working. And while I am about it, I may as well confess that the five-horse-power, which ran the lights, fans, and pumps, was also on the sick-list. A striking title for a book haunts me, waking and sleeping. I should like to write that book some day and to call it "Around the World with Three Gasolene Engines and a Wife." But I am afraid I shall not write it, for fear of hurting the feelings of some of the young gentlemen of San Francisco, Honolulu, and Hilo, who learned their trades at the expense of the *Snark's* engines.

It looked easy on paper. Here was Hilo and there was our objective, 128° west longitude. With the northeast trade blowing we could travel a straight line between the two points, and even slack our sheets off a goodly bit. But one of the chief troubles with the trades is that one never knows just where he will pick them up and just in what direction they will be blowing. We picked up the northeast trade right outside of Hilo harbour, but the miserable breeze was away around into the east. Then there was the north equatorial current setting westward like a mighty river. Furthermore, a small boat, by the wind and bucking into a big headsea, does not work to advantage. She jogs up and down and gets nowhere. Her sails are full and straining, every little while she presses her lee-rail under, she flounders, and bumps, and splashes, and that is all. Whenever she begins to gather way, she runs

ker-chug into a big mountain of water and is
brought to a standstill. So, with the *Snark*, the
resultant of her smallness, of the trade around
into the east, and of the strong equatorial current,
was a long sag south. Oh, she did not go quite
south. But the easting she made was distressing.
On October 11, she made forty miles easting ;
October 12, fifteen miles ; October 13, no easting ; October 14, thirty miles ; October 15, twenty-
three miles ; October 16, eleven miles ; and on
October 17, she actually went to the westward
four miles. Thus, in a week, she made one
hundred and fifteen miles easting, which was
equivalent to sixteen miles a day. But, between
the longitude of Hilo and 128° west longitude is
a difference of twenty-seven degrees, or, roughly,
sixteen hundred miles. At sixteen miles a day,
one hundred days would be required to accomplish this distance. And even then, our objective,
128° west longitude, was five degrees north of the
Line, while Nuka-hiva, in the Marquesas, lay nine
degrees south of the Line and twelve degrees to
the west !

There remained only one thing to do—to work
south out of the trade and into the variables. It
is true that Captain Bruce found no variables on
his traverse, and that he " never could make
easting on either tack." It was the variables or
nothing with us, and we prayed for better luck
than he had had. The variables constitute the
belt of ocean lying between the trades and the
doldrums, and are conjectured to be the draughts
of heated air which rise in the doldrums, flow high
in the air counter to the trades, and gradually

sink down till they fan the surface of the ocean where they are found. And they are found . . . where they are found ; for they are wedged between the trades and the doldrums, which same shift their territory from day to day and month to month.

We found the variables in 11° north latitude, and 11° north latitude we hugged jealously. To the south lay the doldrums. To the north lay the northeast trade that refused to blow from the northeast. The days came and went, and always they found the *Snark* somewhere near the eleventh parallel. The variables were truly variable. A light head-wind would die away and leave us rolling in a calm for forty-eight hours. Then a light head-wind would spring up, blow for three hours, and leave us rolling in another calm for forty-eight hours. Then—hurrah !—the wind would come out of the west, fresh, beautifully fresh, and send the *Snark* along, wing and wing, her wake bubbling, the log-line straight astern. At the end of half an hour, while we were preparing to set the spinnaker, with a few sickly gasps the wind would die away. And so it went. We wagered optimistically on every favourable fan of air that lasted over five minutes ; but it never did any good. The fans faded out just the same.

But there were exceptions. In the variables, if you wait long enough, something is bound to happen, and we were so plentifully stocked with food and water that we could afford to wait. On October 26, we actually made one hundred and three miles of easting, and we talked about it for days afterwards. Once we caught a moderate gale from the south, which blew itself out in eight hours, but it helped us to seventy-one miles of easting in that particular twenty-four hours. And then, just as it was expiring, the wind came straight out from the north (the directly opposite quarter), and fanned us along over another degree of easting.

In years and years no sailing vessel has attempted this traverse, and we found ourselves in the midst of one of the loneliest of the Pacific solitudes. In the sixty days we were crossing it we sighted no sail, lifted no steamer's smoke above the horizon. A disabled vessel could drift in this deserted expanse for a dozen generations, and there would be no rescue. The only chance of rescue would be from a vessel like the *Snark*, and the *Snark* happened to be there principally because of the fact that the traverse had been begun before the particular paragraph in the sailing directions had been read. Standing upright on deck, a straight line drawn from the eye to the horizon would measure three miles and a half. Thus, seven miles was the diameter of the circle of the sea in which we had our centre. Since we remained always in the centre, and since we constantly were moving in some direction, we looked upon many circles. But all circles looked alike. No tufted islets, gray headlands, nor glistening patches of white canvas ever marred the symmetry of that unbroken curve. Clouds came and went, rising up over the rim of the circle, flowing across the space of it, and spilling away and down across the opposite rim.

The world faded as the procession of the weeks marched by. The world faded until at last there ceased to be any world except the little world of the *Snark*, freighted with her seven souls and floating on the expanse of the waters. Our memories of the world, the great world, became like dreams of former lives we had lived somewhere before we came to be born on the *Snark*. After we had been out of fresh vegetables for some time, we mentioned such things in much the same way I have heard my father mention the vanished apples of his boyhood. Man is a creature of habit, and we on the *Snark* had got the habit of the *Snark*. Everything about her and aboard her was as a matter of course, and anything different would have been an irritation and an offence.

There was no way by which the great world could intrude. Our bell rang the hours, but no caller ever rang it. There were no guests to dinner, no telegrams, no insistent telephone jangles invading our privacy. We had no engagements to keep, no trains to catch, and there were no morning newspapers over which to waste time in learning what was happening to our fifteen hundred million other fellow-creatures.

But it was not dull. The affairs of our little world had to be regulated, and, unlike the great world, our world had to be steered in its journey through space. Also, there were cosmic disturbances to be encountered and baffled, such as do not afflict the big earth in its frictionless orbit through the windless void. And we never knew, from moment to moment, what was going to happen next. There were spice and variety enough and to spare. Thus, at four in the morning, I relieve Hermann at the wheel.

" East-northeast," he gives me the course. " She's eight points off, but she ain't steering."

Small wonder. The vessel does not exist that can be steered in so absolute a calm.

" I had a breeze a little while ago—maybe it will come back again," Hermann says hopefully, ere he starts forward to the cabin and his bunk.

The mizzen is in and fast furled. In the night, what of the roll and the absence of wind, it had made life too hideous to be permitted to go on rasping at the mast, smashing at the tackles, and buffeting the empty air into hollow outbursts of sound. But the big mainsail is still on, and the staysail, jib, and flying-jib are snapping and slashing at their sheets with every roll. Every star is out. Just for luck I put the wheel hard over in the opposite direction to which it had been left by Hermann, and I lean back and gaze up at the stars. There is nothing else for me to do. There is nothing to be done with a sailing vessel rolling in a stark calm.

Then I feel a fan on my cheek, faint, so faint, that I can just sense it ere it is gone. But another comes, and another, until a real and just perceptible breeze is blowing. How the *Snark's* sails manage to feel it is beyond me, but feel it they do, as she does as well, for the compass card begins slowly to revolve in the binnacle. In reality, it is not revolving at all. It is held by terrestrial magnetism in one place, and it is the *Snark* that is revolving, pivoted upon that delicate cardboard device that floats in a closed vessel of alcohol.

So the *Snark* comes back on her course. The breath increases to a tiny puff. The *Snark* feels the weight of it and actually heels over a trifle. There is flying scud overhead, and I notice the stars being blotted out. Walls of darkness close in upon me, so that, when the last star is gone, the darkness is so near that it seems I can reach out and touch it on every side. When I lean toward it, I can feel it loom against my face. Puff follows puff, and I am glad the mizzen is furled. Phew ! that was a stiff one ! The *Snark* goes over and down until her lee-rail is buried and the whole Pacific Ocean is pouring in. Four or five of these gusts make me wish that the jib and flying-jib were in. The sea is picking up, the gusts are growing stronger and more frequent, and there is a splatter of wet in the air. There is no use in attempting to gaze to windward. The wall of blackness is within arm's length. Yet I cannot help attempting to see and gauge the blows that are being struck at the *Snark*. There is something ominous and menacing up there to windward, and I have a feeling that if I look long enough and strong enough, I shall divine it. Futile feeling. Between two gusts I leave the wheel and run forward to the cabin companionway, where I light matches and consult the barometer. " 29-90 " it reads. That sensitive instrument refuses to take notice of the disturbance which is humming with a deep, throaty voice in the rigging. I get back to the wheel just in time to meet another gust, the strongest yet.

Well, anyway, the wind is abeam and the *Snark* is on her course, eating up easting. That at least is well.

The jib and flying-jib bother me, and I wish they were in. She would make easier weather of it, and less risky weather likewise. The wind snorts, and stray raindrops pelt like birdshot. I shall certainly have to call all hands, I conclude ; then conclude the next instant to hang on a little longer. Maybe this is the end of it, and I shall have called them for nothing. It is better to let them sleep. I hold the *Snark* down to her task, and from out of the darkness, at right angles, comes a deluge of rain accompanied by shrieking· wind. Then everything eases except the blackness, and I rejoice in that I have not called the men.

No sooner does the wind ease than the sea picks up. The combers are breaking now, and the boat is tossing like a cork. Then out of the blackness the gusts come harder and faster than before. If only I knew what was up there to windward in the blackness ! The *Snark* is making heavy weather of it, and her lee-rail is buried oftener than not. More shrieks and snorts of wind. Now, if ever, is the time to call the men. I *will* call them, I resolve. Then there is a burst of rain, a slackening of the wind, and I do not call. But it is rather lonely, there at the wheel, steering a little world through howling blackness. It is quite a responsibility to be all alone on the surface of a little world in time of stress, doing the thinking for its sleeping inhabitants. I recoil from the responsibility as more gusts begin to strike and as a sea licks along the weather rail and splashes over into the cockpit. The salt water seems strangely warm to my body and is shot through with ghostly nodules of phosphorescent light. I shall surely call all hands to shorten sail. Why should they sleep? I am a fool to have any compunctions in the matter. My intellect is arrayed against my heart. It was my heart that said, "Let them sleep." Yes, but it was my intellect that backed up my heart in that judgment. Let my intellect then reverse the judgment; and, while I am speculating as to what particular entity issued that command to my intellect, the gusts die away. Solicitude for mere bodily comfort has no place in practical seamanship, I conclude sagely; but study the feel of the next series of gusts and do not call the men. After all, it *is* my intellect, behind everything, procrastinating, measuring its knowledge of what the *Snark* can endure against the blows being struck at her, and waiting the call of all hands against the striking of still severer blows.

Daylight, gray and violent, steals through the cloud-pall and shows a foaming sea that flattens under the weight of recurrent and increasing squalls. Then comes the rain, filling the windy valleys of the sea with milky smoke and further flattening the waves, which but wait for the easement of wind and rain to leap more wildly than before. Come the men on deck, their sleep out, and among them Hermann, his face on the broad grin in appreciation of the breeze of wind I have picked up. I turn the wheel over to Warren and start to go below, pausing on the way to rescue the galley stovepipe which has gone adrift. I am barefooted, and my toes have had an excellent education in the art of clinging ; but, as the rail buries itself in a green sea, I suddenly sit down on the streaming deck. Hermann good-naturedly elects to question my selection of such a spot. Then comes the next roll, and he sits down, suddenly, and without premeditation. The *Snark* heels over and down, the rail takes it green, and Hermann and I, clutching the precious stovepipe, are swept down into the lee-scuppers. After that I finish my journey below, and while changing my clothes grin with satisfaction—the *Snark* is making easting.

No, it is not all monotony. When we had worried along our easting to 126° west longitude, we left the variables and headed south through the doldrums, where was much calm weather and where, taking advantage of every fan of air, we were often glad to make a score of miles in as many hours. And yet, on such a day, we might pass through a dozen squalls and be surrounded by dozens more. And every squall was to be regarded as a bludgeon capable of crushing the *Snark*. We were struck sometimes by the centres and sometimes by the sides of these squalls, and we never knew just where or how we were to be hit. The squall that rose up, covering half the heavens, and swept down upon us, as likely as not split into two squalls which passed us harmlessly on either side ; while the tiny, innocent-looking squall that appeared to carry no more than a hogshead of water and a pound of wind, would abruptly assume cyclopean proportions, deluging us with rain and overwhelming us with wind. Then there were treacherous squalls that went boldly astern and sneaked back upon us from a mile to leeward. Again, two squalls would tear along, one on each side of us, and we would get a fillip from each of them. Now a gale certainly grows tiresome after a few hours, but squalls never. The thousandth squall in one's experience is as interesting as the first one, and perhaps a bit more so. It is the tyro who has no apprehension of them. The man of a thousand squalls respects a squall. He knows what they are.

It was in the doldrums that our most exciting event occurred. On November 20, we discovered that through an accident we had lost over one-half of the supply of fresh water that remained to us. Since we were at that time forty-three days out from Hilo, our supply of fresh water was not large. To lose over half of it was a catastrophe. On close allowance, the remnant of water we possessed would last twenty days. But we were in the doldrums; there was no telling where the southeast trades were, nor where we would pick them up.

The handcuffs were promptly put upon the pump, and once a day the water was portioned out. Each of us received a quart for personal use, and eight quarts were given to the cook. Enters now the psychology of the situation. No sooner had the discovery of the water shortage been made than I, for one, was afflicted with a burning thirst. It seemed to me that I had never been so thirsty in my life. My little quart of water I could easily have drunk in one draught, and to refrain from doing so required a severe exertion of will. Nor was I alone in this. All of us talked water, thought water, and dreamed water when we slept. We examined the charts for possible islands to which to run in extremity, but there were no such islands. The Marquesas were the nearest, and they were the other side of the Line, and of the doldrums, too, which made it even worse. We were in 3° north latitude, while the Marquesas were in 9° south latitude—a difference of over a thousand miles. Furthermore, the Marquesas lay some fourteen degrees to the west of our longitude. A pretty pickle for a handful of creatures sweltering on the ocean in the heat of tropic calms.

We rigged lines on either side between the main and mizzen riggings. To these we laced the big deck awning, hoisting it up aft with a sailing pennant so that any rain it might collect would run forward where it could be caught. Here and there squalls passed across the circle of the sea. All day we watched them, now to port or starboard, and again ahead or astern. But never one came near enough to wet us. In the afternoon a big one bore down upon us. It spread out across the ocean as it approached, and we could see it emptying countless thousands of gallons into the salt sea. Extra attention was paid to the awning and then we waited. Warren, Martin, and Hermann made a vivid picture. Grouped together, holding on to the rigging, swaying to the roll, they were gazing intently at the squall. Strain, anxiety, and yearning were in every

posture of their bodies. Beside them was the
dry and empty awning. But they seemed to
grow limp and to droop as the squall broke in half,
one part passing on ahead, the other drawing
astern and going to leeward.

But that night came rain. Martin, whose
psychological thirst had compelled him to drink
his quart of water early, got his mouth down to
the lip of the awning and drank the deepest
draught I ever have seen drunk. The precious
water came down in bucketfuls and tubfuls, and
in two hours we caught and stored away in the
tanks one hundred and twenty gallons. Strange
to say, in all the rest of our voyage to the Marquesas not another drop of rain fell on board. If
that squall had missed us, the handcuffs would
have remained on the pump, and we would have
busied ourselves with utilizing our surplus gasolene
for distillation purposes.

Then there was the fishing. One did not have
to go in search of it, for it was there at the rail.
A three-inch steel hook, on the end of a stout line,
with a piece of white rag for bait, was all that
was necessary to catch bonitas weighing from ten
to twenty-five pounds. Bonitas feed on flying-
fish, wherefore they are unaccustomed to nibbling
at the hook. They strike as gamely as the
gamest fish in the sea, and their first run is
something that no man who has ever caught them
will forget. Also, bonitas are the veriest cannibals. The instant one is hooked he is attacked
by his fellows. Often and often we hauled them
on board with fresh, clean-bitten holes in them
the size of teacups.

One school of bonitas, numbering many thousands, stayed with us day and night for more than three weeks. Aided by the *Snark*, it was great hunting ; for they cut a swath of destruction through the ocean half a mile wide and fifteen hundred miles in length. They ranged along abreast of the *Snark* on either side, pouncing upon the flying-fish her forefoot scared up. Since they were continually pursuing astern the flying-fish that survived for several flights, they were always overtaking the *Snark*, and at any time one could glance astern and on the front of a breaking wave see scores of their silvery forms coasting down just under the surface. When they had eaten their fill, it was their delight to get in the shadow of the boat, or of her sails, and a hundred or so were always to be seen lazily sliding along and keeping cool.

But the poor flying-fish ! Pursued and eaten alive by the bonitas and dolphins, they sought flight in the air, where the swooping seabirds drove them back into the water. Under heaven there was no refuge for them. Flying-fish do not play when they essay the air. It is a life-and-death affair with them. A thousand times a day we could lift our eyes and see the tragedy played out. The swift, broken circling of a guny might attract one's attention. A glance beneath shows the back of a dolphin breaking the surface in a wild rush. Just in front of its nose a shimmering palpitant streak of silver shoots from the water into the air—a delicate, organic mechanism of flight, endowed with sensation, power of direction, and love of life. The guny swoops for it and misses, and the flying-fish, gaining its altitude by rising, kite-like, against the wind, turns in a half-circle and skims off to leeward, gliding on the bosom of the wind.   Beneath it, the wake of the dolphin shows in churning foam.   So he follows, gazing upward with large eyes at the flashing breakfast that navigates an element other than his own.   He cannot rise to so lofty occasion, but he is a thorough-going empiricist, and he knows, sooner or later, if not gobbled up by the guny, that the flying-fish must return to the water. And then—breakfast.   We used to pity the poor winged fish.   It was sad to see such sordid and bloody slaughter.   And then, in the night watches, when a forlorn little flying-fish struck the mainsail and fell gasping and splattering on the deck, we would rush for it just as eagerly, just as greedily, just as voraciously, as the dolphins and bonitas. For know that flying-fish are most toothsome for breakfast.   It is always a wonder to me that such dainty meat does not build dainty tissue in the bodies of the devourers.   Perhaps the dolphins and bonitas are coarser-fibred because of the high speed at which they drive their bodies in order to catch their prey.   But then again, the flying-fish drive their bodies at high speed, too.

Sharks we caught occasionally, on large hooks, with chain-swivels, bent on a length of small rope. And sharks meant pilot-fish, and remoras, and various sorts of parasitic creatures. Regular man-eaters some of the sharks proved, tiger-eyed and with twelve rows of teeth, razor-sharp.   By the way, we of the *Snark* are agreed that we have eaten many fish that will not compare with baked shark smothered in tomato dressing. In the calms we occasionally caught a fish called " haké " by the Japanese cook. And once, on a spoon-hook trolling a hundred yards astern, we caught a snake-like fish, over three feet in length and not more than three inches in diameter, with four fangs in his jaw. He proved the most delicious fish—delicious in meat and flavour—that we have ever eaten on board.

The most welcome addition to our larder was a green sea-turtle, weighing a full hundred pounds and appearing on the table most appetizingly in steaks, soups, and stews, and finally in a wonderful curry which tempted all hands into eating more rice than was good for them. The turtle was sighted to windward, calmly sleeping on the surface in the midst of a huge school of curious dolphins. It was a deep-sea turtle of a surety, for the nearest land was a thousand miles away. We put the *Snark* about and went back for him, Hermann driving the granes into his head and neck. When hauled aboard, numerous remora were clinging to his shell, and out of the hollows at the roots of his flippers crawled several large crabs. It did not take the crew of the *Snark* longer than the next meal to reach the unanimous conclusion that it would willingly put the *Snark* about any time for a turtle.

But it is the dolphin that is the king of deep-sea fishes. Never is his colour twice quite the same. Swimming in the sea, an ethereal creature of palest azure, he displays in that one guise a miracle of colour. But it is nothing compared with the displays of which he is capable. At one time he will appear green—pale green, deep green, phosphorescent green ; at another time blue—deep blue, electric blue, all the spectrum of blue. Catch him on a hook, and he turns to gold, yellow gold, all gold. Haul him on deck, and he excels the spectrum, passing through inconceivable shades of blues, greens, and yellows, and then, suddenly, turning a ghostly white, in the midst of which are bright blue spots, and you suddenly discover that he is speckled like a trout. Then back from white he goes, through all the range of colours, finally turning to a mother-of-pearl.

For those who are devoted to fishing, I can recommend no finer sport than catching dolphin. Of course, it must be done on a thin line with reel and pole. A No. 7, O'Shaughnessy tarpon hook is just the thing, baited with an entire flying-fish. Like the bonita, the dolphin's fare consists of flying-fish, and he strikes like lightning at the bait. The first warning is when the reel screeches and you see the line smoking out at right angles to the boat. Before you have time to entertain anxiety concerning the length of your line, the fish rises into the air in a succession of leaps. Since he is quite certain to be four feet long or over, the sport of landing so gamey a fish can be realized. When hooked, he invariably turns golden. The idea of the series of leaps is to rid himself of the hook, and the man who has made the strike must be of iron or decadent if his heart does not beat with an extra flutter when he beholds such gorgeous fish, glittering in golden mail and shaking itself like a stallion in each mid-air leap. 'Ware slack ! If you don't, on one of those leaps the hook will be flung out and twenty feet away. No slack, and away he will go on another run, culminating in another series of leaps. About this time one begins to worry over the line, and to wish that he had had nine hundred feet on the reel originally instead of six hundred. With careful playing the line can be saved, and after an hour of keen excitement the fish can be brought to gaff. One such dolphin I landed on the *Snark* measured four feet and seven inches.

Hermann caught dolphins more prosaically. A hand-line and a chunk of shark-meat were all he needed. His hand-line was very thick, but on more than one occasion it parted and lost the fish. One day a dolphin got away with a lure of Hermann's manufacture, to which were lashed four O'Shaughnessy hooks. Within an hour the same dolphin was landed with the rod, and on dissecting him the four hooks were recovered. The dolphins, which remained with us over a month, deserted us north of the line, and not one was seen during the remainder of the traverse.

So the days passed. There was so much to be done that time never dragged. Had there been little to do, time could not have dragged with such wonderful seascapes and cloudscapes—dawns that were like burning imperial cities under rainbows that arched nearly to the zenith; sunsets that bathed the purple sea in rivers of rose-coloured light, flowing from a sun whose diverging, heaven-climbing rays were of the purest blue. Overside, in the heat of the day, the sea was an azure satiny fabric, in the depths of which the sunshine focussed in funnels of light. Astern, deep down, when there was a breeze, bubbled a procession of milky-turquoise ghosts—the foam flung down by the hull of the *Snark* each time she floundered against a sea. At night the wake was phosphorescent fire, where the medusa slime resented our passing bulk, while far down could be observed the unceasing flight of comets, with long, undulating, nebulous tails—caused by the passage of the bonitas through the resentful medusa slime. And now and again, from out of the darkness on either hand, just under the surface, larger phosphorescent organisms flashed up like electric lights, marking collisions with the careless bonitas skurrying ahead to the good hunting just beyond our bowsprit.

We made our easting, worked down through the doldrums, and caught a fresh breeze out of south-by-west. Hauled up by the wind, on such a slant, we would fetch past the Marquesas far away to the westward. But the next day, on Tuesday, November 26, in the thick of a heavy squall, the wind shifted suddenly to the southeast. It was the trade at last. There were no more squalls, naught but fine weather, a fair wind, and a whirling log, with sheets slacked off and with spinnaker and mainsail swaying and bellying on either side. The trade backed more and more, until it blew out of the northeast, while we steered a steady course to the southwest. Ten days of this, and on the morning of December 6, at five o'clock, we sighted land "just where it ought to have been," dead ahead. We passed to leeward of Ua-huka, skirted the southern edge of Nuka-hiva, and that night, in driving squalls and inky darkness, fought our way in to an anchorage in the narrow bay of Taiohae. The anchor rumbled down to the blatting of wild goats on the cliffs, and the air we breathed was heavy with the perfume of flowers. The traverse was accomplished. Sixty days from land to land, across a lonely sea above whose horizons never rise the straining sails of ships.

CHAPTER X

TYPEE

TO the eastward Ua-huka was being blotted out by an evening rain-squall that was fast overtaking the *Snark*. But that little craft, her big spinnaker filled by the southeast trade, was making a good race of it. Cape Martin, the southeasternmost point of Nuku-hiva, was abeam, and Comptroller Bay was opening up as we fled past its wide entrance, where Sail Rock, for all the world like the spritsail of a Columbia River salmon-boat, was making brave weather of it in the smashing southeast swell.

" What do you make that out to be ? " I asked Hermann, at the wheel.

" A fishing-boat, sir," he answered after careful scrutiny.

Yet on the chart it was plainly marked, " Sail Rock."

But we were more interested in the recesses of Comptroller Bay, where our eyes eagerly sought out the three bights of land and centred on the midmost one, where the gathering twilight showed the dim walls of a valley extending inland. How often we had pored over the chart and centred always on that midmost bight and on the valley it opened—the Valley of Typee. "Taipi" the chart spelled it, and spelled it correctly, but I prefer "Typee," and I shall always spell it "Typee." When I was a little boy, I read a book spelled in that manner—Herman Melville's "Typee"; and many long hours I dreamed over its pages. Nor was it all dreaming. I resolved there and then, mightily, come what would, that when I had gained strength and years, I, too, would voyage to Typee. For the wonder of the world was penetrating to my tiny consciousness— the wonder that was to lead me to many lands, and that leads and never palls. The years passed, but Typee was not forgotten. Returned to San Francisco from a seven months' cruise in the North Pacific, I decided the time had come. The brig *Galilee* was sailing for the Marquesas, but her crew was complete and I, who was an able seaman before the mast and young enough to be over-weeningly proud of it, was willing to condescend to ship as cabin-boy in order to make the pilgrimage to Typee. Of course, the *Galilee* would have sailed from the Marquesas without me, for I was bent on finding another Fayaway and another Kory-Kory. I doubt that the captain read desertion in my eye. Perhaps even the berth of cabin-boy was already filled. At any rate, I did not get it.

Then came the rush of years, filled brimming with projects, achievements, and failures; but Typee was not forgotten, and here I was now, gazing at its misty outlines till the squall swooped down and the *Snark* dashed on into the driving smother. Ahead, we caught a glimpse and took the compass bearing of Sentinel Rock, wreathed with pounding surf. Then it, too, was effaced by the rain and darkness. We steered straight for it, trusting to hear the sound of breakers in time to sheer clear. We had to steer for it. We had naught but a compass bearing with which to orientate ourselves, and if we missed Sentinel Rock, we missed Taiohae Bay, and we would have to throw the *Snark* up to the wind and lie off and on the whole night—no pleasant prospect for voyagers weary from a sixty days' traverse of the vast Pacific solitude, and land-hungry, and fruit-hungry, and hungry with an appetite of years for the sweet vale of Typee.

Abruptly, with a roar of sound, Sentinel Rock loomed through the rain dead ahead. We altered our course, and, with mainsail and spinnaker bellying to the squall, drove past. Under the lee of the rock the wind dropped us, and we rolled in an absolute calm. Then a puff of air struck us, right in our teeth, out of Taiohae Bay. It was in spinnaker, up mizzen, all sheets by the wind, and we were moving slowly ahead, heaving the lead and straining our eyes for the fixed red light on the ruined fort that would give us our bearings to anchorage. The air was light and baffling, now east, now west, now north, now south ; while from either hand came the roar of unseen breakers. From the looming cliffs arose the blatting of wild goats, and overhead the first stars were peeping mistily through the ragged train of the passing squall. At the end of two hours, having come a mile into the bay, we dropped anchor in eleven fathoms. And so we came to Taiohae.

In the morning we awoke in fairyland. The *Snark* rested in a placid harbour that nestled in a vast amphitheatre, the towering, vine-clad walls of which seemed to rise directly from the water. Far up, to the east, we glimpsed the thin line of a trail, visible in one place, where it scoured across the face of the wall.

" The path by which Toby escaped from Typee ! " we cried.

We were not long in getting ashore and astride horses, though the consummation of our pilgrimage had to be deferred for a day. Two months at sea, bare-footed all the time, without space in which to exercise one's limbs, is not the best preliminary to leather shoes and walking. Besides, the land had to cease its nauseous rolling before we could feel fit for riding goat-like horses over giddy trails. So we took a short ride to break in, and crawled through thick jungle to make the acquaintance of a venerable moss-grown idol, where had foregathered a German trader and a Norwegian captain to estimate the weight of said idol, and to speculate upon depreciation in value caused by sawing him in half. They treated the old fellow sacrilegiously, digging their knives into him to see how hard he was and how deep his mossy mantle, and commanding him to rise up and save them trouble by walking down to the ship himself. In lieu of which, nineteen Kanakas slung him on a frame of timbers and toted him to the ship, where, battened down under hatches, even now he is cleaving the South Pacific Hornward and toward Europe—the ultimate abiding-place for all good heathen idols, save for the few in America and one in particular who grins beside me as I write, and who, barring shipwreck, will grin somewhere in my neighbourhood until I die. And he will win out. He will be grinning when I am dust.

Also, as a preliminary, we attended a feast, where one Taiara Tamarii, the son of an Hawaiian sailor who deserted from a whaleship, commemorated the death of his Marquesan mother by roasting fourteen whole hogs and inviting in the village. So we came along, welcomed by a native herald, a young girl, who stood on a great rock and chanted the information that the banquet was made perfect by our presence—which information she extended impartially to every arrival. Scarcely were we seated, however, when she changed her tune, while the company manifested intense excitement. Her cries became eager and piercing. From a distance came answering cries, in men's voices, which blended into a wild, barbaric chant that sounded incredibly savage, smacking of blood and war. Then, through vistas of tropical foliage appeared a procession of savages, naked save for gaudy loin-cloths. They advanced slowly, uttering deep guttural cries of triumph and exaltation. Slung from young saplings carried on their shoulders were mysterious objects of considerable weight, hidden from view by wrappings of green leaves.

Nothing but pigs, innocently fat and roasted to a turn, were inside those wrappings, but the men were carrying them into camp in imitation of old times when they carried in "long-pig." Now long-pig is not pig. Long-pig is the Polynesian euphemism for human flesh ; and these descendants of man-eaters, a king's son at their head, brought in the pigs to table as of old their grandfathers had brought in their slain enemies. Every now and then the procession halted in order that the bearers should have every advantage in uttering particularly ferocious shouts of victory, of contempt for their enemies, and of gustatory desire. So Melville, two generations ago, witnessed the bodies of slain Happar warriors, wrapped in palm-leaves, carried to banquet at the Ti. At another time, at the Ti, he " observed a curiously carved vessel of wood," and on looking into it his eyes " fell upon the disordered members of a human skeleton, the bones still fresh with moisture, and with particles of flesh clinging to them here and there."

Cannibalism has often been regarded as a fairy story by ultracivilized men, who dislike, perhaps, the notion that their own savage forebears have somewhere in the past been addicted to similar practices. Captain Cook was rather sceptical upon the subject, until, one day, in a harbour of New Zealand, he deliberately tested the matter. A native happened to have brought on board, for sale, a nice, sun-dried head. At Cook's orders strips of the flesh were cut away and handed to the native, who greedily devoured them. To say the least, Captain Cook was a rather thorough-going empiricist. At any rate, by that act he supplied one ascertained fact of which science had been badly in need. Little did he dream of the existence of a certain group of islands, thousands of miles away, where in subsequent days there would arise a curious suit at law, when an old chief of Maui would be charged with defamation of character because he persisted in asserting that his body was the living repository of Captain Cook's great toe. It is said that the plaintiffs failed to prove that the old chief was *not* the tomb of the navigator's great toe, and that the suit was dismissed.

I suppose I shall not have the chance in these degenerate days to see any long-pig eaten, but at least I am already the possessor of a duly certified Marquesan calabash, oblong in shape, curiously carved, over a century old, from which has been drunk the blood of two shipmasters. One of those captains was a mean man. He sold a decrepit whale-boat, as good as new what of the fresh white paint, to a Marquesan chief. But no sooner had the captain sailed away than the whale-boat dropped to pieces. It was his fortune, some time afterwards, to be wrecked, of all places, on that particular island. The Marquesan chief was ignorant of rebates and discounts; but he had a primitive sense of equity and an equally primitive conception of the economy of nature, and he balanced the account by eating the man who had cheated him.

We started in the cool dawn for Typee, astride ferocious little stallions that pawed and screamed and bit and fought one another quite oblivious of the fragile humans on their backs and of the slippery boulders, loose rocks, and yawning gorges. The way led up an ancient road through a jungle of *hau* trees. On every side were the vestiges of a one-time dense population. Where-ever the eye could penetrate the thick growth, glimpses were caught of stone walls and of stone foundations, six to eight feet in height, built solidly throughout, and many yards in width and depth. They formed great stone platforms, upon which, at one time, there had been houses. But the houses and the people were gone, and huge trees sank their roots through the platforms and towered over the under-running jungle These foundations are called *pae-paes*—the *pi-pis* of Melville, who spelled phonetically.

The Marquesans of the present generation lack the energy to hoist and place such huge stones. Also, they lack incentive. There are plenty of *pae-paes* to go around, with a few thousand unoccupied ones left over. Once or twice, as we ascended the valley, we saw magnificent *pae-paes* bearing on their general surface pitiful little straw huts, the proportions being similar to a voting booth perched on the broad foundation of the Pyramid of Cheops. For the Marquesans are perishing, and, to judge from conditions at Taiohae, the one thing that retards their destruction is the infusion of fresh blood. A pure Marquesan is a rarity. They seem to be all half-breeds and strange conglomerations of dozens of different races. Nineteen able labourers are all the trader at Taiohae can muster for the loading of copra on shipboard, and in their veins runs the blood of English, American, Dane, German, French, Corsican, Spanish, Portuguese, Chinese, Hawaiian, Paumotan, Tahitian, and Easter Islander. There are more races than there are persons, but it is a wreckage of races at best.

Life faints and stumbles and gasps itself away. In this warm, equable clime—a truly terrestrial paradise—where are never extremes of temperature and where the air is like balm, kept ever pure by the ozone-laden southeast trade, asthma, phthisis, and tuberculosis flourish as luxuriantly as the vegetation. Everywhere, from the few grass huts, arises the racking cough or exhausted groan of wasted lungs. Other horrible diseases prosper as well, but the most deadly of all are those that attack the lungs. There is a form of consumption called "galloping," which is especially dreaded. In two months' time it reduces the strongest man to a skeleton under a grave-cloth. In valley after valley the last inhabitant has passed and the fertile soil has relapsed to jungle. In Melville's day the valley of Hapaa (spelled by him "Happar") was peopled by a strong and warlike tribe. A generation later, it contained but two hundred persons. To-day it is an untenanted, howling, tropical wilderness.

We climbed higher and higher in the valley, our unshod stallions picking their steps on the disintegrating trail, which led in and out through the abandoned *pae-paes* and insatiable jungle. The sight of red mountain apples, the *ohias*, familiar to us from Hawaii, caused a native to be sent climbing after them. And again he climbed for cocoanuts. I have drunk the cocoanuts of Jamaica and of Hawaii, but I never knew how delicious such draught could be till I drank it here in the Marquesas. Occasionally we rode under wild limes and oranges—great trees which had survived the wilderness longer than the motes of humans who had cultivated them.

We rode through endless thickets of yellow-pollened cassi—if riding it could be called ; for those fragrant thickets were inhabited by wasps. And such wasps ! Great yellow fellows the size of small canary birds, darting through the air with behind them drifting a bunch of legs a couple of inches long.   A stallion abruptly stands on his forelegs and thrusts his hindlegs skyward. He withdraws them from the sky long enough to make one wild jump ahead, and then returns them to their index position.   It is nothing.   His thick hide has merely been punctured by a flaming lance of wasp virility.   Then a second and a third stallion, and all the stallions, begin to cavort on their forelegs over the precipitous landscape. Swat ! A white-hot poniard penetrates my cheek. Swat again ! I am stabbed in the neck. I am bringing up the rear and getting more than my share. There is no retreat, and the plunging horses ahead, on a precarious trail, promise little safety. My horse overruns Charmian's horse, and that sensitive creature, fresh-stung at the psycho-logical moment, planks one of his hoofs into my horse and the other hoof into me. I thank my stars that he is not steel-shod, and half-arise from the saddle at the impact of another flaming dagger. I am certainly getting more than my share, and so is my poor horse, whose pain and panic are only exceeded by mine.

" Get out of the way ! I'm coming ! " I shout, frantically dashing my cap at the winged vipers around me.

On one side of the trail the landscape rises straight up. On the other side it sinks straight down. The only way to get out of my way is to keep on going. How that string of horses kept their feet is a miracle ; but they dashed ahead, over-running one another, galloping, trotting, stumbling, jumping, scrambling, and kicking methodically skyward every time a wasp landed on them. After a while we drew breath and counted our injuries. And this happened not once, nor twice, but time after time. Strange to say, it never grew monotonous. I know that I, for one, came through each brush with the undiminished zest of a man flying from sudden death. No ; the pilgrim from Taiohae to Typee will never suffer from *ennui* on the way.

At last we arose above the vexation of wasps. It was a matter of altitude, however, rather than of fortitude. All about us lay the jagged backbones of ranges, as far as the eye could see, thrusting their pinnacles into the trade-wind clouds. Under us, from the way we had come, the *Snark* lay like a tiny toy on the calm water of Taiohae Bay. Ahead we could see the inshore indentation of Comptroller Bay. We dropped down a thousand feet, and Typee lay beneath us. " Had a glimpse of the gardens of paradise been revealed to me I could scarcely have been more ravished with the sight "—so said Melville on the moment of his first view of the valley. He saw a garden. We saw a wilderness. Where were the hundred groves of the breadfruit tree he saw ? We saw jungle, nothing but jungle, with the exception of two grass huts and several clumps of cocoanuts breaking the primordial green mantle. Where was the *Ti* of Mehevi, the bachelors' hall, the palace where women were taboo, and where he ruled with his lesser chieftains, keeping the half-dozen dusty and torpid ancients to remind them of the valorous past ? From the swift stream no sounds arose of maids and matrons pounding *tapa*. And where was the hut that old Narheyo eternally builded ? In vain I looked for him perched ninety feet from the ground in some tall cocoanut, taking his morning smoke.

We went down a zigzag trail under overarching, matted jungle, where great butterflies drifted by in the silence. No tattooed savage with club and javelin guarded the path ; and when we forded the stream, we were free to roam where we pleased. No longer did the taboo, sacred and merciless, reign in that sweet vale. Nay, the taboo still did reign, a new taboo, for when we approached too near the several wretched native women, the taboo was uttered warningly. And it was well. They were lepers. The man who warned us was afflicted horribly with elephantiasis. All were suffering from lung trouble. The valley of Typee was the abode of death, and the dozen survivors of the tribe were gasping feebly the last painful breaths of the race.

Certainly the battle had not been to the strong, for once the Typeans were very strong, stronger than the Happars, stronger than the Taiohaeans, stronger than all the tribes of Nuku-hiva. The word " typee," or, rather, " taipi," originally signified an eater of human flesh. But since all the Marquesans were human-flesh eaters, to be so designated was the token that the Typeans were the human-flesh eaters par excellence. Not alone to Nuku-hiva did the Typean reputation for bravery and ferocity extend. In all the islands of the Marquesas the Typeans were named with dread. Man could not conquer them. Even the French fleet that took possession of the Marquesas left the Typeans alone. Captain Porter, of the frigate *Essex*, once invaded the valley. His sailors and marines were reinforced by two thousand warriors of Happar and Taiohae. They penetrated quite a distance into the valley, but met with so fierce a resistance that they were glad to retreat and get away in their flotilla of boats and war-canoes.

Of all inhabitants of the South Seas, the Marquesans were adjudged the strongest and the most beautiful. Melville said of them : " I was especially struck by the physical strength and beauty they displayed. . . . In beauty of form they surpassed anything I had ever seen. Not a single instance of natural deformity was observable in all the throng attending the revels. . . . Every individual appeared free from those blemishes which sometimes mar the effect of an otherwise perfect form. But their physical excellence did not merely consist in an exemption from these evils ; nearly every individual of their number might have been taken for a sculptor's model." Mendaña, the discoverer of the Marquesas, described the natives as wondrously beautiful to behold. Figueroa, the chronicler of his voyage, said of them : " In complexion they were nearly white ; of good stature and finely formed." Captain Cook called the Marquesans the most splendid islanders in the South Seas. The men were described as "in almost every instance of lofty stature, scarcely ever less than six feet in height."

And now all this strength and beauty has departed, and the valley of Typee is the abode of some dozen wretched creatures, afflicted by leprosy, elephantiasis, and tuberculosis. Melville estimated the population at two thousand, not taking into consideration the small adjoining valley of Ho-o-u-mi. Life has rotted away in this wonderful garden spot, where the climate is as delightful and healthful as any to be found in the world. Not alone were the Typeans physically magnificent; they were pure. Their air did not contain the bacilli and germs and microbes of disease that fill our own air. And when the white men imported in their ships these various microorganisms of disease, the Typeans crumpled up and went down before them.

When one considers the situation, one is almost driven to the conclusion that the white race flourishes on impurity and corruption. Natural selection, however, gives the explanation. We of the white race are the survivors and the descendants of the thousands of generations of survivors in the war with the micro-organisms. Whenever one of us was born with a constitution peculiarly receptive to these minute enemies, such a one promptly died. Only those of us survived who could withstand them. We who are alive are the immune, the fit—the ones best constituted to live in a world of hostile micro-organisms. The poor Marquesans had undergone no such selection. They were not immune. And they, who had made a custom of eating their enemies, were now eaten by enemies so microscopic as to be invisible, and against whom no war of dart and javelin was possible. On the other hand, had there been a few hundred thousand Marquesans to begin with, there might have been sufficient survivors to lay the foundation for a new race—a regenerated race, if a plunge into a festering bath of organic poison can be called regeneration.

We unsaddled our horses for lunch, and after we had fought the stallions apart—mine with several fresh chunks bitten out of his back—and after we had vainly fought the sand-flies, we ate bananas and tinned meats, washed down by generous draughts of cocoanut milk. There was little to be seen. The jungle had rushed back and engulfed the puny works of man. Here and there *pai-pais* were to be stumbled upon, but there were no inscriptions, no hieroglyphics, no clues to the past they attested—only dumb stones, builded and carved by hands that were forgotten dust. Out of the *pai-pais* grew great trees, jealous of the wrought work of man, splitting and scattering the stones back into the primeval chaos.

We gave up the jungle and sought the stream with the idea of evading the sand-flies. Vain hope! To go in swimming one must take off his clothes. The sand-flies are aware of the fact, and they lurk by the river bank in countless myriads. In the native they are called the *nau-nau*, which is pronounced "now-now." They are certainly well named, for they are the insistent present. There is no past nor future when they fasten upon one's epidermis, and I am willing to wager that Omar Khayyám could never have written the Rubáiyát in the valley of Typee —it would have been psychologically impossible. I made the strategic mistake of undressing on the edge of a steep bank where I could dive in but could not climb out. When I was ready to dress, I had a hundred yards' walk on the bank before I could reach my clothes. At the first step, fully ten thousand *nau-naus* landed upon me. At the second step I was walking in a cloud. By the third step the sun was dimmed in the sky. After that I don't know what happened. When I arrived at my clothes, I was a maniac. And here enters my grand tactical error. There is only one rule of conduct in dealing with *nau-naus*. Never swat them. Whatever you do, don't swat them. They are so vicious that in the instant of annihilation they eject their last atom of poison into your carcass. You must pluck them delicately, between thumb and forefinger, and persuade them gently to remove their proboscides from your quivering flesh. It is like pulling teeth. But the difficulty was that the teeth sprouted faster than I could pull them, so I swatted, and, so doing, filled myself full with their poison. This was a week ago. At the present moment I resemble a sadly neglected smallpox convalescent.

Ho-o-u-mi is a small valley, separated from Typee by a low ridge, and thither we started when we had knocked our indomitable and insatiable riding-animals into submission. As it was, Warren's mount, after a mile run, selected the most dangerous part of the trail for an exhibition that kept us all on the anxious seat for fully five minutes. We rode by the mouth of Typee valley and gazed down upon the beach from which Melville escaped. There was where the whale-boat lay on its oars close in to the surf; and there was where Karakoee, the taboo Kanaka, stood in the water and trafficked for the sailor's life. There, surely, was where Melville gave Fayaway the parting embrace ere he dashed for the boat. And there was the point of land from which Mehevi and Mow-mow and their following swam off to intercept the boat, only to have their wrists gashed by sheath-knives when they laid hold of the gunwale, though it was reserved for Mow-mow to receive the boat-hook full in the throat from Melville's hands.

We rode on to Ho-o-u-mi. So closely was Melville guarded that he never dreamed of the existence of this valley, though he must continually have met its inhabitants, for they belonged to Typee. We rode through the same abandoned *pae-paes*, but as we neared the sea we found a profusion of cocoanuts, breadfruit trees, and taro patches, and fully a dozen grass dwellings. In one of these we arranged to pass the night, and preparations were immediately put on foot for a feast. A young pig was promptly despatched, and while he was being roasted among hot stones, and while chickens were stewing in cocoanut milk, I persuaded one of the cooks to climb an unusually tall cocoanut palm. The cluster of nuts at the top was fully one hundred and twenty-five feet from the ground, but that

native strode up to the tree, seized it in both
hands, jack-knived at the waist so that the soles
of his feet rested flatly against the trunk, and
then he walked right straight up without stopping.
There were no notches in the tree. He had no
ropes to help him. He merely walked up the
tree, one hundred and twenty-five feet in the air,
and cast down the nuts from the summit. Not
every man there had the physical stamina for
such a feat, or the lungs, rather, for most of them
were coughing their lives away. Some of the
women kept up a ceaseless moaning and groaning,
so badly were their lungs wasted. Very few of
either sex were full-blooded Marquesans. They
were mostly half-breeds and three-quarter-breeds
of French, English, Danish, and Chinese extrac-
tion. At the best, these infusions of fresh blood
merely delayed the passing, and the results led
one to wonder whether it was worth while.

The feast was served on a broad *pae-pae*, the
rear portion of which was occupied by the house
in which we were to sleep. The first course was
raw fish and *poi-poi*, the latter sharp and more
acrid of taste than the *poi* of Hawaii, which is
made from taro. The *poi-poi* of the Marquesas
is made from breadfruit. The ripe fruit, after the
core is removed, is placed in a calabash and
pounded with a stone pestle into a stiff, sticky
paste. In this stage of the process, wrapped in
leaves, it can be buried in the ground, where it will
keep for years. Before it can be eaten, however,
further processes are necessary. A leaf-covered
package is placed among hot stones, like the pig,
and thoroughly baked. After that it is mixed

with cold water and thinned out—not thin enough to run, but thin enough to be eaten by sticking one's first and second fingers into it. On close acquaintance it proves a pleasant and most healthful food. And breadfruit, ripe and well boiled or roasted! It is delicious. Breadfruit and taro are kingly vegetables, the pair of them, though the former is patently a misnomer and more resembles a sweet potato than anything else, though it is not mealy like a sweet potato, nor is it so sweet.

The feast ended, we watched the moon rise over Typee. The air was like balm, faintly scented with the breath of flowers. It was a magic night, deathly still, without the slightest breeze to stir the foliage; and one caught one's breath and felt the pang that is almost hurt, so exquisite was the beauty of it. Faint and far could be heard the thin thunder of the surf upon the beach. There were no beds; and we drowsed and slept wherever we thought the floor softest. Near by, a woman panted and moaned in her sleep, and all about us the dying islanders coughed in the night.

CHAPTER XI

THE NATURE MAN

I FIRST met him on Market Street in San Francisco. It was a wet and drizzly afternoon, and he was striding along, clad solely in a pair of abbreviated knee-trousers and an abbreviated shirt, his bare feet going slick-slick through the pavement-slush. At his heels trooped a score of excited gamins. Every head—and there were thousands—turned to glance curiously at him as he went by. And I turned, too. Never had I seen such lovely sunburn. He was all sunburn, of the sort a blond takes on when his skin does not peel. His long yellow hair was burnt, so was his beard, which sprang from a soil unploughed by any razor. He was a tawny man, a golden-tawny man, all glowing and radiant with the sun. Another prophet, thought I, come up to town with a message that will save the world.

A few weeks later I was with some friends in their bungalow in the Piedmont hills overlooking San Francisco Bay. "We've got him, we've got him," they barked. "We caught him up a tree; but he's all right now, he'll feed from the hand.

Come on and see him." So I accompanied them up a dizzy hill, and in a rickety shack in the midst of a eucalyptus grove found my sunburned prophet of the city pavements.

He hastened to meet us, arriving in the whirl and blur of a handspring. He did not shake hands with us; instead, his greeting took the form of stunts. He turned more handsprings. He twisted his body sinuously, like a snake, until, having sufficiently limbered up, he bent from the hips, and, with legs straight and knees touching, beat a tattoo on the ground with the palms of his hands. He whirligigged and pirouetted, dancing and cavorting round like an inebriated ape. All the sun-warmth of his ardent life beamed in his face. I am so happy, was the song without words he sang.

He sang it all evening, ringing the changes on it with an endless variety of stunts. "A fool! a fool! I met a fool in the forest!" thought I. And a worthy fool he proved. Between handsprings and whirligigs he delivered his message that would save the world. It was twofold. First, let suffering humanity strip off its clothing and run wild in the mountains and valleys; and, second, let the very miserable world adopt phonetic spelling. I caught a glimpse of the great social problems being settled by the city populations swarming naked over the landscape, to the popping of shot-guns, the barking of ranch-dogs, and countless assaults with pitchforks wielded b irate farmers.

The years passed, and, one sunny morning, the *Snark* poked her nose into a narrow opening in a reef that smoked with the crashing impact of the trade-wind swell, and beat slowly up Papeete harbour. Coming off to us was a boat, flying a yellow flag. We knew it contained the port doctor. But quite a distance off, in its wake, was a tiny outrigger canoe that puzzled us. It was flying a red flag. I studied it through the glasses, fearing that it marked some hidden danger to navigation, some recent wreck or some buoy or beacon that had been swept away. Then the doctor came on board. After he had examined the state of our health and been assured that we had no live rats hidden away in the *Snark*, I asked him the meaning of the red flag. "Oh, that is Darling," was the answer.

And then Darling, Ernest Darling, flying the red flag that is indicative of the brotherhood of man, hailed us. "Hello, Jack!" he called. "Hello, Charmian!" He paddled swiftly nearer, and I saw that he was the tawny prophet of the Piedmont hills. He came over the side, a sun-god clad in a scarlet loin-cloth, with presents of Arcady and greeting in both his hands—a bottle of golden honey and a leaf-basket filled with great golden mangoes, golden bananas specked with freckles of deeper gold, golden pine-apples and golden limes, and juicy oranges minted from the same precious ore of sun and soil. And in this fashion, under the southern sky, I met once more Darling, the Nature Man.

Tahiti is one of the most beautiful spots in the world, inhabited by thieves and robbers and liars, also by several honest and truthful men and women. Wherefore, because of the blight cast upon Tahiti's wonderful beauty by the spidery human vermin that infest it, I am minded to write, not of Tahiti, but of the Nature Man. He, at least, is refreshing and wholesome. The spirit that emanates from him is so gentle and sweet that it would harm nothing, hurt nobody's feelings save the feelings of a predatory and plutocratic capitalist.

"What does this red flag mean?" I asked.

"Socialism, of course."

"Yes, yes, I know that," I went on; "but what does it mean in your hands?"

"Why, that I've found my message."

"And that you are delivering it to Tahiti?" I demanded incredulously.

"Sure," he answered simply; and later on I found that he was, too.

When we dropped anchor, lowered a small boat into the water, and started ashore, the Nature Man joined us. Now, thought I, I shall be pestered to death by this crank. Waking or sleeping I shall never be quit of him until I sail away from here.

But never in my life was I more mistaken. I took a house and went to live and work in it, and the Nature Man never came near me. He was waiting for the invitation. In the meantime he went aboard the *Snark* and took possession of her library, delighted by the quantity of scientific books, and shocked, as I learned afterwards, by the inordinate amount of fiction. The Nature Man never wastes time on fiction.

After a week or so, my conscience smote me, and I invited him to dinner at a downtown hotel.

He arrived, looking unwontedly stiff and uncomfortable in a cotton jacket. When invited to peel it off, he beamed his gratitude and joy, and did so, revealing his sun-gold skin, from waist to shoulder, covered only by a piece of fish-net of coarse twine and large of mesh. A scarlet loin-cloth completed his costume. I began my acquaintance with him that night, and during my long stay in Tahiti that acquaintance ripened into friendship.

" So you write books," he said, one day when, tired and sweaty, I finished my morning's work.

" I, too, write books," he announced.

Aha, thought I, now at last is he going to pester me with his literary efforts. My soul was in revolt. I had not come all the way to the South Seas to be a literary bureau.

" This is the book I write," he explained, smashing himself a resounding blow on the chest with his clenched fist. " The gorilla in the African jungle pounds his chest till the noise of it can be heard half a mile away."

" A pretty good chest," quoth I, admiringly ; " it would even make a gorilla envious."

And then, and later, I learned the details of the marvellous book Ernest Darling had written. Twelve years ago he lay close to death. He weighed but ninety pounds, and was too weak to speak. The doctors had given him up. His father, a practising physician, had given him up. Consultations with other physicians had been held upon him. There was no hope for him. Overstudy (as a school-teacher and as a university student) and two successive attacks of pneumonia were responsible for his breakdown. Day by day he was losing strength. He could extract no nutrition from the heavy foods they gave him ; nor could pellets and powders help his stomach to do the work of digestion. Not only was he a physical wreck, but he was a mental wreck. His mind was overwrought. He was sick and tired of medicine, and he was sick and tired of persons. Human speech jarred upon him. Human attentions drove him frantic. The thought came to him that since he was going to die, he might as well die in the open, away from all the bother and irritation. And behind this idea lurked a sneaking idea that perhaps he would not die after all if only he could escape from the heavy foods, the medicines, and the well-intentioned persons who made him frantic.

So Ernest Darling, a bag of bones and a death's-head, a perambulating corpse, with just the dimmest flutter of life in it to make it perambulate, turned his back upon men and the habitations of men and dragged himself for five miles through the brush, away from the city of Portland, Oregon. Of course he was crazy. Only a lunatic would drag himself out of his death-bed.

But in the brush, Darling found what he was looking for—rest. Nobody bothered him with beefsteaks and pork. No physicians lacerated his tired nerves by feeling his pulse, nor tormented his tired stomach with pellets and powders. He began to feel soothed. The sun was shining warm, and he basked in it. He had the feeling that the sunshine was an elixir of health. Then it seemed to him that his whole wasted wreck of a body was crying for the sun. He stripped off his clothes and bathed in the sunshine. He felt better. It had done him good—the first relief in weary months of pain.

As he grew better, he sat up and began to take notice. All about him were the birds fluttering and chirping, the squirrels chattering and playing. He envied them their health and spirits, their happy, care-free existence. That he should contrast their condition with his was inevitable; and that he should question why they were splendidly vigorous while he was a feeble, dying wraith of a man, was likewise inevitable. His conclusion was the very obvious one, namely, that they lived naturally, while he lived most unnaturally; therefore, if he intended to live, he must return to nature.

Alone, there in the brush, he worked out his problem and began to apply it. He stripped off his clothing and leaped and gambolled about, running on all fours, climbing trees; in short, doing physical stunts,—and all the time soaking in the sunshine. He imitated the animals. He built a nest of dry leaves and grasses in which to sleep at night, covering it over with bark as a protection against the early fall rains. "Here is a beautiful exercise," he told me, once, flapping his arms mightily against his sides; "I learned it from watching the roosters crow." Another time I remarked the loud, sucking intake with which he drank cocoanut-milk. He explained that he had noticed the cows drinking that way and concluded there must be something in it. He tried it and found it good, and thereafter he drank only in that fashion.

He noted that the squirrels lived on fruits and nuts. He started on a fruit-and-nut diet, helped out by bread, and he grew stronger and put on weight. For three months he continued his primordial existence in the brush, and then the heavy Oregon rains drove him back to the habitations of men. Not in three months could a ninety-pound survivor of two attacks of pneumonia develop sufficient ruggedness to live through an Oregon winter in the open.

He had accomplished much, but he had been driven in. There was no place to go but back to his father's house, and there, living in close rooms with lungs that panted for all the air of the open sky, he was brought down by a third attack of pneumonia. He grew weaker even than before. In that tottering tabernacle of flesh, his brain collapsed. He lay like a corpse, too weak to stand the fatigue of speaking, too irritated and tired in his miserable brain to care to listen to the speech of others. The only act of will of which he was capable was to stick his fingers in his ears and resolutely to refuse to hear a single word that was spoken to him. They sent for the insanity experts. He was adjudged insane, and also the verdict was given that he would not live a month.

By one such mental expert he was carted off to a sanatorium on Mt. Tabor. Here, when they learned that he was harmless, they gave him his own way. They no longer dictated as to the food he ate, so he resumed his fruits and nuts—olive oil, peanut butter, and bananas the chief articles of his diet. As he regained his strength he made up his mind to live thenceforth his own life. If he lived like others, according to social conventions, he would surely die. And he did not want to die. The fear of death was one of the strongest factors in the genesis of the Nature Man. To live, he must have a natural diet, the open air, and the blessed sunshine.

Now an Oregon winter has no inducements for those who wish to return to Nature, so Darling started out in search of a climate. He mounted a bicycle and headed south for the sunlands. Stanford University claimed him for a year. Here he studied and worked his way, attending lectures in as scant garb as the authorities would allow and applying as much as possible the principles of living that he had learned in squirrel-town. His favourite method of study was to go off in the hills back of the University, and there to strip off his clothes and lie on the grass, soaking in sunshine and health at the same time that he soaked in knowledge.

But Central California has her winters, and the quest for a Nature Man's climate drew him on. He tried Los Angeles and Southern California, being arrested a few times and brought before the insanity commissions because, forsooth, his mode of life was not modelled after the mode of life of his fellow-men. He tried Hawaii, where, unable to prove him insane, the authorities deported him. It was not exactly a deportation. He could have remained by serving a year in prison. They gave him his choice. Now prison is death to the Nature Man, who thrives only in

the open air and in God's sunshine. The authorities of Hawaii are not to be blamed. Darling was
an undesirable citizen. Any man is undesirable
who disagrees with one. And that any man
should disagree to the extent Darling did in his
philosophy of the simple life is ample vindication
of the Hawaiian authorities' verdict of his un-
desirableness.

So Darling went thence in search of a climate
which would not only be desirable, but wherein
he would not be undesirable. And he found it,
in Tahiti, the garden-spot of garden-spots. And
so it was, according to the narrative as given, that
he wrote the pages of his book. He wears only
a loin-cloth and a sleeveless fish-net shirt. His
stripped weight is one hundred and sixty-five
pounds. His health is perfect. His eyesight,
that at one time was considered ruined, is excellent. The lungs that were practically destroyed
by three attacks of pneumonia have not only
recovered, but are stronger than ever before.

I shall never forget the first time, while talking
to me, that he squashed a mosquito. The stinging
pest had settled in the middle of his back between
his shoulders. Without interrupting the flow of
conversation, without dropping even a syllable, his
clenched fist shot up in the air, curved backward,
and smote his back between the shoulders, killing
the mosquito and making his frame resound like
a bass drum. It reminded me of nothing so
much as of horses kicking the woodwork in their
stalls.

"The gorilla in the African jungle pounds his
chest until the noise of it can be heard half a mile

away," he will announce suddenly, and thereat beat a hair-raising, devil's tattoo on his own chest.

One day he noticed a set of boxing-gloves hanging on the wall, and promptly his eyes brightened.

" Do you box ? " I asked.

" I used to give lessons in boxing when I was at Stanford," was the reply.

And there and then we stripped and put on the gloves. Bang ! a long, gorilla arm flashed out, landing the gloved end on my nose. Biff ! he caught me, in a duck, on the side of the head, nearly knocking me over sidewise. I carried the lump raised by that blow for a week. I ducked under a straight left, and landed a straight right on his stomach. It was a fearful blow. The whole weight of my body was behind it, and his body had been met as it lunged forward. I looked for him to crumple up and go down. Instead of which his face beamed approval, and he said, " That was beautiful." The next instant I was covering up and striving to protect myself from a hurricane of hooks, jolts, and uppercuts. Then I watched my chance and drove in for the solar plexus. I hit the mark. The Nature Man dropped his arms, gasped, and sat down suddenly.

" I'll be all right," he said. " Just wait a moment."

And inside thirty seconds he was on his feet—ay, and returning the compliment, for he hooked me in the solar plexus, and I gasped, dropped my hands, and sat down just a trifle more suddenly than he had.

All of which I submit as evidence that the man I boxed with was a totally different man from the poor, ninety-pound weight of eight years before, who, given up by physicians and alienists, lay gasping his life away in a closed room in Portland, Oregon. The book that Ernest Darling has written is a good book, and the binding is good, too.

Hawaii has wailed for years her need for desirable immigrants. She has spent much time, and thought, and money, in importing desirable citizens, and she has, as yet, nothing much to show for it. Yet Hawaii deported the Nature Man. She refused to give him a chance. So it is, to chasten Hawaii's proud spirit, that I take this opportunity to show her what she has lost in the Nature Man. When he arrived in Tahiti, he proceeded to seek out a piece of land on which to grow the food he ate. But land was difficult to find—that is, inexpensive land. The Nature Man was not rolling in wealth. He spent weeks in wandering over the steep hills, until, high up the mountain, where clustered several tiny canyons, he found eighty acres of brush-jungle which were apparently unrecorded as the property of any one. The government officials told him that if he would clear the land and till it for thirty years he would be given a title for it.

Immediately he set to work. And never was there such work. Nobody farmed that high up. The land was covered with matted jungle and overrrun by wild pigs and countless rats. The view of Papeete and the sea was magnificent, but the outlook was not encouraging. He spent weeks in building a road in order to make the plantation accessible. The pigs and the rats ate up whatever he planted as fast as it sprouted. He shot the pigs and trapped the rats. Of the latter, in two weeks he caught fifteen hundred. Everything had to be carried up on his back. He usually did his packhorse work at night.

Gradually he began to win out. A grass-walled house was built. On the fertile, volcanic soil he had wrested from the jungle and jungle beasts were growing five hundred cocoanut trees, five hundred papaia trees, three hundred mango trees, many breadfruit trees and alligator-pear trees, to say nothing of vines, bushes, and vegetables. He developed the drip of the hills in the canyons and worked out an efficient irrigation scheme, ditching the water from canyon to canyon and paralleling the ditches at different altitudes. His narrow canyons became botanical gardens. The arid shoulders of the hills, where formerly the blazing sun had parched the jungle and beaten it close to earth, blossomed into trees and shrubs and flowers. Not only had the Nature Man become self-supporting, but he was now a prosperous agriculturist with produce to sell to the city-dwellers of Papeete.

Then it was discovered that his land, which the government officials had informed him was without an owner, really had an owner, and that deeds, descriptions, etc., were on record. All his work bade fare to be lost. The land had been valueless when he took it up, and the owner, a large landholder, was unaware of the extent to which the Nature Man had developed it. A just price was agreed upon, and Darling's deed was officially filed.

Next came a more crushing blow. Darling's access to market was destroyed. The road he had built was fenced across by triple barb-wire fences. It was one of those jumbles in human affairs that is so common in this absurdest of social systems. Behind it was the fine hand of the same conservative element that haled the Nature Man before the Insanity Commission in Los Angeles and that deported him from Hawaii. It is so hard for self-satisfied men to understand any man whose satisfactions are fundamentally different. It seems clear that the officials have connived with the conservative element, for to this day the road the Nature Man built is closed; nothing has been done about it, while an adamant unwillingness to do anything about it is evidenced on every hand. But the Nature Man dances and sings along his way. He does not sit up nights thinking about the wrong which has been done him; he leaves the worrying to the doers of the wrong. He has no time for bitterness. He believes he is in the world for the purpose of being happy, and he has not a moment to waste in any other pursuit.

The road to his plantation is blocked. He cannot build a new road, for there is no ground on which he can build it. The government has restricted him to a wild-pig trail which runs precipitously up the mountain. I climbed the trail with him, and we had to climb with hands and feet in order to get up. Nor can that wild-pig trail be made into a road by any amount of toil less than that of an engineer, a steam-engine, and a steel cable. But what does the Nature Man care? In his gentle ethics the evil men do him he requites with goodness. And who shall say he is not happier than they?

"Never mind their pesky road," he said to me as we dragged ourselves up a shelf of rock and sat down, panting, to rest. "I'll get an air machine soon and fool them. I'm clearing a level space for a landing stage for the airships, and next time you come to Tahiti you will alight right at my door."

Yes, the Nature Man has some strange ideas besides that of the gorilla pounding his chest in the African jungle. The Nature Man has ideas about levitation. "Yes, sir," he said to me, "levitation is not impossible. And think of the glory of it—lifting one's self from the ground by an act of will. Think of it! The astronomers tell us that our whole solar system is dying; that, barring accidents, it will all be so cold that no life can live upon it. Very well. In that day all men will be accomplished levitationists, and they will leave this perishing planet and seek more hospitable worlds. How can levitation be accomplished? By progressive fasts. Yes, I have tried them, and toward the end I could feel myself actually getting lighter."

The man is a maniac, thought I.

"Of course," he added, "these are only theories of mine. I like to speculate upon the glorious future of man. Levitation may not be possible, but I like to think of it as possible."

One evening, when he yawned, I asked him how much sleep he allowed himself.

"Seven hours," was the answer. "But in ten years I'll be sleeping only six hours, and in twenty years only five hours. You see, I shall cut off an hour's sleep every ten years."

"Then when you are a hundred you won't be sleeping at all," I interjected.

"Just that. Exactly that. When I am a hundred I shall not require sleep. Also, I shall be living on air. There are plants that live on air, you know."

"But has any man ever succeeded in doing it?"

He shook his head.

"I never heard of him if he did. But it is only a theory of mine, this living on air. It would be fine, wouldn't it? Of course it may be impossible —most likely it is. You see, I am not unpractical. I never forget the present. When I soar ahead into the future, I always leave a string by which to find my way back again."

I fear me the Nature Man is a joker. At any rate he lives the simple life. His laundry bill cannot be large. Up on his plantation he lives on fruit the labour cost of which, in cash, he estimates at five cents a day. At present, because of his obstructed road and because he is head over heels in the propaganda of socialism, he is living in town, where his expenses, including rent, are twenty-five cents a day. In order to pay those expenses he is running a night school for Chinese.

The Nature Man is not bigoted. When there is nothing better to eat than meat, he eats meat, as, for instance, when in jail or on shipboard and the nuts and fruits give out. Nor does he seem to crystallize into anything except sunburn.

"Drop anchor anywhere and the anchor will drag—that is, if your soul is a limitless, fathomless sea, and not a dog-pound," he quoted to me, then added : " You see, my anchor is always dragging. I live for human health and progress, and I strive to drag my anchor always in that direction. To me, the two are identical. Dragging anchor is what has saved me. My anchor did not hold me to my death-bed. I dragged anchor into the brush and fooled the doctors. When I recovered health and strength, I started, by preaching and by example, to teach the people to become nature men and nature women. But they had deaf ears. Then, on the steamer coming to Tahiti, a quarter-master expounded socialism to me. He showed me that an economic square deal was necessary before men and women could live naturally. So I dragged anchor once more, and now I am working for the co-operative commonwealth. When that arrives, it will be easy to bring about nature living.

" I had a dream last night," he went on thoughtfully, his face slowly breaking into a glow. " It seemed that twenty-five nature men and nature women had just arrived on the steamer from California, and that I was starting to go with them up the wild-pig trail to the plantation."

Ah, me, Ernest Darling, sun-worshipper and nature man, there are times when I am compelled to envy you and your care-free existence. I see you now, dancing up the steps and cutting antics on the veranda ; your hair dripping from a plunge in the salt sea, your eyes sparkling, your sun-gilded body flashing, your chest resounding to the devil's own tattoo as you chant: "The gorilla in the African jungle pounds his chest until the noise of it can be heard half a mile away." And I shall see you always as I saw you that last day, when the *Snark* poked her nose once more through the passage in the smoking reef, outward bound, and I waved good-bye to those on shore. Not least in goodwill and affection was the wave I gave to the golden sun-god in the scarlet loin-cloth, standing upright in his tiny outrigger canoe.

CHAPTER XII

THE HIGH SEAT OF ABUNDANCE

On the arrival of strangers, every man endeavoured to obtain one as a friend and carry him off to his own habitation, where he is treated with the greatest kindness by the inhabitants of the district; they place him on a high seat and feed him with abundance of the finest food.—*Polynesian Researches*.

THE *Snark* was lying at anchor at Raiatea, just off the village of Uturoa. She had arrived the night before, after dark, and we were preparing to pay our first visit ashore. Early in the morning I had noticed a tiny outrigger canoe, with an impossible spritsail, skimming the surface of the lagoon. The canoe itself was coffin-shaped, a mere dugout, fourteen feet long, a scant twelve inches wide, and maybe twenty-four inches deep. It had no lines, except in so far that it was sharp at both ends. Its sides were perpendicular. Shorn of the outrigger, it would have capsized of itself inside a tenth of a second. It was the outrigger that kept it right side up.

I have said that the sail was impossible. It was. It was one of those things, not that you have to see to believe, but that you cannot believe

after you have seen it. The hoist of it and the
length of its boom were sufficiently appalling;
but, not content with that, its artificer had given
it a tremendous head. So large was the head
that no common sprit could carry the strain of
it in an ordinary breeze. So a spar had been
lashed to the canoe, projecting aft over the water.
To this had been made fast a sprit guy: thus,
the foot of the sail was held by the main-sheet,
and the peak by the guy to the sprit.

It was not a mere boat, not a mere canoe, but a
sailing machine. And the man in it sailed it by
his weight and his nerve—principally by the
latter. I watched the canoe beat up from leeward and run in toward the village, its sole
occupant far out on the outrigger and luffing up
and spilling the wind in the puffs.

"Well, I know one thing," I announced; "I
don't leave Raiatea till I have a ride in that
canoe."

A few minutes later Warren called down the
companionway, "Here's that canoe you were
talking about."

Promptly I dashed on deck and gave greeting to
its owner, a tall, slender Polynesian, ingenuous of
face, and with clear, sparkling, intelligent eyes.
He was clad in a scarlet loin-cloth and a straw hat.
In his hands were presents—a fish, a bunch of
greens, and several enormous yams. All of which
acknowledged by smiles (which are coinage still
in isolated spots of Polynesia) and by frequent
repetitions of *mauruuru* (which is the Tahitian
"thank you"), I proceeded to make signs that
I desired to go for a sail in his canoe.

His face lighted with pleasure and he uttered the single word, "Tahaa," turning at the same time and pointing to the lofty, cloud-draped peaks of an island three miles away—the island of Tahaa. It was fair wind over, but a head-beat back. Now I did not want to go to Tahaa. I had letters to deliver in Raiatea, and officials to see, and there was Charmian down below getting ready to go ashore. By insistent signs I indicated that I desired no more than a short sail on the lagoon. Quick was the disappointment in his face, yet smiling was the acquiescence.

"Come on for a sail," I called below to Charmian. "But put on your swimming suit. It's going to be wet."

It wasn't real. It was a dream. That canoe slid over the water like a streak of silver. I climbed out on the outrigger and supplied the weight to hold her down, while Tehei (pronounced Tayhayee) supplied the nerve. He, too, in the puffs, climbed part way out on the outrigger, at the same time steering with both hands on a large paddle and holding the mainsheet with his foot.

"Ready about!" he called.

I carefully shifted my weight inboard in order to maintain the equilibrium as the sail emptied.

"Hard a-lee!" he called, shooting her into the wind.

I slid out on the opposite side over the water on a spar lashed across the canoe, and we were full and away on the other tack.

"All right," said Tehei.

Those three phrases, "Ready about," "Hard a-lee," and "All right," comprised Tehei's English vocabulary and led me to suspect that at some time he had been one of a Kanaka crew under an American captain. Between the puffs I made signs to him and repeatedly and interrogatively uttered the word *sailor*. Then I tried it in atrocious French. *Marin* conveyed no meaning to him ; nor did *matelot*. Either my French was bad, or else he was not up in it. I have since concluded that both conjectures were correct. Finally, I began naming over the adjacent islands. He nodded that he had been to them. By the time my quest reached Tahiti, he caught my drift. His thought-processes were almost visible, and it was a joy to watch him think. He nodded his head vigorously. Yes, he had been to Tahiti, and he added himself names of islands such as Tikihau, Rangiroa, and Fakarava, thus proving that he had sailed as far as the Paumotus—undoubtedly one of the crew of a trading schooner.

After our short sail, when he had returned on board, he by signs inquired the destination of the *Snark*, and when I had mentioned Samoa, Fiji, New Guinea, France, England, and California in their geographical sequence, he said " Samoa," and by gestures intimated that he wanted to go along. Whereupon I was hard put to explain that there was no room for him. " *Petit bateau* " finally solved it, and again the disappointment in his face was accompanied by smiling ac-quiescence, and promptly came the renewed invitation to accompany him to Tahaa.

Charmian and I looked at each other. The exhilaration of the ride we had taken was still upon us. Forgotten were the letters to Raiatea,

the officials we had to visit. Shoes, a shirt, a
pair of trousers, cigarettes, matches, and a book
to read were hastily crammed into a biscuit tin
and wrapped in a rubber blanket, and we were
over the side and into the canoe.

" When shall we look for you ? " Warren called,
as the wind filled the sail and sent Tehei and me
scurrying out on the outrigger.

" I don't know," I answered.   " When we get
back, as near as I can figure it."

And away we went.   The wind had increased,
and with slacked sheets we ran off before it.   The
freeboard of the canoe was no more than two and
a half inches, and the little waves continually
lapped over the side. This required bailing.
Now bailing is one of the principal functions of
the *vahine*.   *Vahine* is the Tahitian for woman,
and Charmian being the only *vahine* aboard, the
bailing fell appropriately to her.   Tehei and I
could not very well do it, the both of us being
perched part way out on the outrigger and busied
with keeping the canoe bottom-side down.   So
Charmian bailed, with a wooden scoop of primitive
design, and so well did she do it that there were
occasions when she could rest off almost half the
time.

Raiatea and Tahaa are unique in that they lie
inside the same encircling reef.   Both are volcanic
islands, ragged of sky-line, with heaven-aspiring
peaks and minarets.   Since Raiatea is thirty miles
in circumference, and Tahaa fifteen miles, some
idea may be gained of the magnitude of the reef
that encloses them.   Between them and the reef
stretches from one to two miles of water, forming

a beautiful lagoon. The huge Pacific seas, extending in unbroken lines sometimes a mile or half as much again in length, hurl themselves upon the reef, overtowering and falling upon it with tremendous crashes, and yet the fragile coral structure withstands the shock and protects the land. Outside lies destruction to the mightiest ship afloat. Inside reigns the calm of untroubled water, whereon a canoe like ours can sail with no more than a couple of inches of free-board.

We flew over the water. And such water !— clear as the clearest spring-water, and crystalline in its clearness, all intershot with a maddening pageant of colours and rainbow ribbons more magnificently gorgeous than any rainbow. Jade green alternated with turquoise, peacock blue with emerald, while now the canoe skimmed over reddish purple pools, and again over pools of dazzling, shimmering white where pounded coral sand lay beneath and upon which oozed monstrous sea-slugs. One moment we were above wonder-gardens of coral, wherein coloured fishes disported, fluttering like marine butterflies ; the next moment we were dashing across the dark surface of deep channels, out of which schools of flying fish lifted their silvery flight ; and a third moment we were above other gardens of living coral, each more wonderful than the last. And above all was the tropic, trade-wind sky with its fluffy clouds racing across the zenith and heaping the horizon with their soft masses.

Before we were aware, we were close in to Tahaa (pronounced Tah-hah-ah, with equal accents), and Tehei was grinning approval of the *vahine's* proficiency at bailing. The canoe grounded on a shallow shore, twenty feet from land, and we waded out on a soft bottom where big slugs curled and writhed under our feet and where small octopuses advertised their existence by their superlative softness when stepped upon. Close to the beach, amid cocoanut palms and banana trees, erected on stilts, built of bamboo, with a grass-thatched roof, was Tehei's house. And out of the house came Tehei's *vahine*, a slender mite of a woman, kindly eyed and Mongolian of feature—when she was not North American Indian. " Bihaura," Tehei called her, but he did not pronounce it according to English notions of spelling. Spelled " Bihaura," it sounded like Bee-ah-oo-rah, with every syllable sharply emphasized.

She took Charmian by the hand and led her into the house, leaving Tehei and me to follow. Here, by sign-language unmistakable, we were informed that all they possessed was ours. No hidalgo was ever more generous in the expression of giving, while I am sure that few hidalgos were ever as generous in the actual practice. We quickly discovered that we dare not admire their possessions, for whenever we did admire a particular object it was immediately presented to us. The two *vahines*, according to the way of *vahines*, got together in a discussion and examination of feminine fripperies, while Tehei and I, manlike, went over fishing-tackle and wild-pig-hunting, to say nothing of the device whereby bonitas are caught on forty-foot poles from double canoes. Charmian admired a sewing basket—the best example she had seen of Polynesian basketry; it was hers. I admired a bonita hook, carved in one piece from a pearl-shell; it was mine. Charmian was attracted by a fancy braid of straw sennit, thirty feet of it in a roll, sufficient to make a hat of any design one wished; the roll of sennit was hers. My gaze lingered upon a poi-pounder that dated back to the old stone days; it was mine. Charmian dwelt a moment too long on a wooden poi-bowl, canoe-shaped, with four legs, all carved in one piece of wood; it was hers. I glanced a second time at a gigantic cocoanut calabash; it was mine. Then Charmian and I held a conference in which we resolved to admire no more—not because it did not pay well enough, but because it paid too well. Also, we were already racking our brains over the contents of the *Snark* for suitable return presents. Christmas is an easy problem compared with a Polynesian giving-feast.

We sat on the cool porch, on Bihaura's best mats, while dinner was preparing, and at the same time met the villagers. In twos and threes and groups they strayed along, shaking hands and uttering the Tahitian word of greeting—*Ioarana*, pronounced yo-rah-nah. The men, big strapping fellows, were in loin-cloths, with here and there no shirt, while the women wore the universal *ahu*, a sort of adult pinafore that flows in graceful lines from the shoulders to the ground. Sad to see was the elephantiasis that afflicted some of them. Here would be a comely woman of magnificent proportions, with the port of a queen, yet marred by one arm four times—or a dozen times—

the size of the other. Beside her might stand a six-foot man, erect, mighty-muscled, bronzed, with the body of a god, yet with feet and calves so swollen that they ran together, forming legs, shapeless, monstrous, that were for all the world like elephant legs.

No one seems really to know the cause of the South Sea elephantiasis. One theory is that it is caused by the drinking of polluted water. Another theory attributes it to inoculation through mosquito bites. A third theory charges it to predisposition plus the process of acclimatization. On the other hand, no one that stands in finicky dread of it and similar diseases can afford to travel in the South Seas. There will be occasions when such a one must drink water. There may be also occasions when the mosquitoes let up biting. But every precaution of the finicky one will be useless. If he runs barefoot across the beach to have a swim, he will tread where an elephantiasis case trod a few minutes before. If he closets himself in his own house, yet every bit of fresh food on his table will have been subjected to the contamination, be it flesh, fish, fowl, or vegetable. In the public market at Papeete two known lepers run stalls, and heaven alone knows through what channels arrive at that market the daily supplies of fish, fruit, meat, and vegetables. The only happy way to go through the South Seas is with a careless poise, without apprehension, and with a Christian Science-like faith in the resplendent fortune of your own particular star. When you see a woman, afflicted with elephantiasis wringing out cream from cocoanut meat with her naked hands, drink and reflect how good is the cream, forgetting the hands that pressed it out. Also, remember that diseases such as elephantiasis and leprosy do not seem to be caught by contact.

We watched a Raratongan woman, with swollen, distorted limbs, prepare our cocoanut cream, and then went out to the cook-shed where Tehei and Bihaura were cooking dinner. And then it was served to us on a drygoods box in the house. Our hosts waited until we were done and then spread their table on the floor. But our table! We were certainly in the high seat of abundance. First, there was glorious raw fish, caught several hours before from the sea and steeped the intervening time in lime-juice diluted with water. Then came roast chicken. Two cocoanuts, sharply sweet, served for drink. There were bananas that tasted like strawberries and that melted in the mouth, and there was banana-poi that made one regret that his Yankee forebears ever attempted puddings. Then there was boiled yam, boiled taro, and roasted *feis*, which last are nothing more or less than large, mealy, juicy, red-coloured cooking bananas. We marvelled at the abundance, and, even as we marvelled, a pig was brought on, a whole pig, a sucking pig, swathed in green leaves and roasted upon the hot stones of a native oven, the most honourable and triumphant dish in the Polynesian cuisine. And after that came coffee, black coffee, delicious coffee, native coffee grown on the hill-sides of Tahaa.

Tehei's fishing-tackle fascinated me, and after

we arranged to go fishing, Charmian and I decided to remain all night. Again Tehei broached Samoa, and again my *petit bateau* brought the disappointment and the smile of acquiescence to his face. Bora Bora was my next port. It was not so far away but that cutters made the passage back and forth between it and Raiatea. So I invited Tehei to go that far with us on the *Snark*. Then I learned that his wife had been born on Bora Bora and still owned a house there. She likewise was invited, and immediately came the counter invitation to stay with them in their house in Bora Bora. It was Monday. Tuesday we would go fishing and return to Raiatea. Wednesday we would sail by Tahaa and off a certain point, a mile away, pick up Tehei and Bihaura and go on to Bora Bora. All this we arranged in detail, and talked over scores of other things as well, and yet Tehei knew three phrases in English, Charmian and I knew possibly a dozen Tahitian words, and among the four of us there were a dozen or so French words that all understood. Of course, such polyglot conversation was slow, but, eked out with a pad, a lead pencil, the face of a clock Charmian drew on the back of a pad, and with ten thousand and one gestures, we managed to get on very nicely.

At the first moment we evidenced an inclination for bed the visiting natives, with soft *Iaoranas*, faded away, and Tehei and Bihaura likewise faded away. The house consisted of one large room, and it was given over to us, our hosts going elsewhere to sleep. In truth, their castle was ours. And right here, I want to say that of all the entertainment I have received in this world at the hands of all sorts of races in all sorts of places, I have never received entertainment that equalled this at the hands of this brown-skinned couple of Tahaa. I do not refer to the presents, the free-handed generousness, the high abundance, but to the fineness of courtesy and consideration and tact, and to the sympathy that was real sympathy in that it was understanding. They did nothing they thought ought to be done for us, according to their standards, but they did what they divined we wanted to be done for us, while their divination was most successful. It would be impossible to enumerate the hundreds of little acts of consideration they performed during the few days of our intercourse. Let it suffice for me to say that of all hospitality and entertainment I have known, in no case was theirs not only not excelled, but in no case was it quite equalled. Perhaps the most delightful feature of it was that it was due to no training, to no complex social ideals, but that it was the untutored and spontaneous outpouring from their hearts.

The next morning we went fishing, that is, Tehei, Charmian, and I did, in the coffin-shaped canoe; but this time the enormous sail was left behind. There was no room for sailing and fishing at the same time in that tiny craft. Several miles away, inside the reef, in a channel twenty fathoms deep, Tehei dropped his baited hooks and rock-sinkers. The bait was chunks of octopus flesh, which he bit out of a live octopus that writhed in the bottom of the canoe. Nine of these lines he set, each line attached to one end of a short length of bamboo floating on the surface. When a fish was hooked, the end of the bamboo was drawn under the water. Naturally, the other end rose up in the air, bobbing and waving frantically for us to make haste. And make haste we did, with whoops and yells and driving paddles, from one signalling bamboo to another, hauling up from the depths great glistening beauties from two to three feet in length.

Steadily, to the eastward, an ominous squall had been rising and blotting out the bright trade-wind sky. And we were three miles to leeward of home. We started as the first wind-gusts whitened the water. Then came the rain, such rain as only the tropics afford, when every tap and main in the sky is open wide, and when, to top it all, the very reservoir itself spills over in blinding deluge. Well, Charmian was in a swimming suit, I was in pyjamas, and Tehei wore only a loin-cloth. Bihaura was on the beach waiting for us, and she led Charmian into the house in much the same fashion that the mother leads in the naughty little girl who has been playing in mud-puddles.

It was a change of clothes and a dry and quiet smoke while *kai-kai* was preparing. *Kai-kai*, by the way, is the Polynesian for " food " or " to eat," or, rather, it is one form of the original root, whatever it may have been, that has been distributed far and wide over the vast area of the Pacific. It is *kai* in the Marquesas, Raratonga, Manahiki, Niuē, Fakaafo, Tonga, New Zealand, and Vaté. In Tahiti " to eat " changes to *amu*, in Hawaii and Samoa to *ai*, in Bau to *kana*, in

Niua to *kaina*, in Nongone to *kaka*, and in New Caledonia to *ki*. But by whatsoever sound or symbol, it was welcome to our ears after that long paddle in the rain. Once more we sat in the high seat of abundance until we regretted that we had been made unlike the image of the giraffe and the camel.

Again, when we were preparing to return to the *Snark*, the sky to windward turned black and another squall swooped down. But this time it was little rain and all wind. It blew hour after hour, moaning and screeching through the palms, tearing and wrenching and shaking the frail bamboo dwelling, while the outer reef set up a mighty thundering as it broke the force of the swinging seas. Inside the reef, the lagoon, sheltered though it was, was white with fury, and not even Tehei's seamanship could have enabled his slender canoe to live in such a welter.

By sunset, the back of the squall had broken, though it was still too rough for the canoe. So I had Tehei find a native who was willing to venture his cutter across to Raiatea for the outrageous sum of two dollars, Chili, which is equivalent in our money to ninety cents. Half the village was told off to carry presents, with which Tehei and Bihaura speeded their parting guests— captive chickens, fishes dressed and swathed in wrappings of green leaves, great golden bunches of bananas, leafy baskets spilling over with oranges and limes, alligator pears (the butter-fruit, also called the *avoca*), huge baskets of yams, bunches of taro and cocoanuts, and last of all, large branches and trunks of trees—firewood for the *Snark*.

While on the way to the cutter we met the only white man on Tahaa, and of all men, George Lufkin, a native of New England ! Eighty-six years of age he was, sixty-odd of which, he said, he had spent in the Society Islands, with occasional absences, such as the gold rush to Eldorado in 'forty-nine and a short period of ranching in California near Tulare. Given no more than three months by the doctors to live, he had returned to his South Seas and lived to eighty-six and to chuckle over the doctors aforesaid, who were all in their graves. *Fee-fee* he had, which is the native for elephantiasis and which is pronounced fay-fay. A quarter of a century before, the disease had fastened upon him, and it would remain with him until he died. We asked him about kith and kin. Beside him sat a sprightly damsel of sixty, his daughter. "She is all I have," he murmured plaintively, "and she has no children living."

The cutter was a small, sloop-rigged affair, but large it seemed alongside Tehei's canoe. On the other hand, when we got out on the lagoon and were struck by another heavy wind-squall, the cutter became liliputian, while the *Snark*, in our imagination, seemed to promise all the stability and permanence of a continent. They were good boatmen. Tehei and Bihaura had come along to see us home, and the latter proved a good boatwoman herself. The cutter was well ballasted, and we met the squall under full sail. It was getting dark, the lagoon was full of coral patches, and we were carrying on. In the height of the squall we had to go about, in order to make a short leg to windward to pass around a patch of coral no more than a foot under the surface. As the cutter filled on the other tack, and while she was in that "dead" condition that precedes gathering way, she was knocked flat. Jib-sheet and main-sheet were let go, and she righted into the wind. Three times she was knocked down, and three times the sheets were flung loose, before she could get away on that tack.

By the time we went about again, darkness had fallen. We were now to windward of the *Snark*, and the squall was howling. In came the jib, and down came the mainsail, all but a patch of it the size of a pillow-slip. By an accident we missed the *Snark*, which was riding it out to two anchors, and drove aground upon the inshore coral. Running the longest line on the *Snark* by means of the launch, and after an hour's hard work, we heaved the cutter off and had her lying safely astern.

The day we sailed for Bora Bora the wind was light, and we crossed the lagoon under power to the point where Tehei and Bihaura were to meet us. As we made in to the land between the coral banks, we vainly scanned the shore for our friends. There was no sign of them.

"We can't wait," I said. "This breeze won't fetch us to Bora Bora by dark, and I don't want to use any more gasolene than I have to."

You see, gasolene in the South Seas is a problem. One never knows when he will be able to replenish his supply.

But just then Tehei appeared through the trees as he came down to the water. He had peeled off his shirt and was wildly waving it. Bihaura apparently was not ready. Once aboard, Tehei informed us by signs that we must proceed along the land till we got opposite to his house. He took the wheel and conned the *Snark* through the coral, around point after point till we cleared the last point of all. Cries of welcome went up from the beach, and Bihaura, assisted by several of the villagers, brought off two canoe-loads of abundance. There were yams, taro, *feis*, bread-fruit, cocoanuts, oranges, limes, pineapples, water-melons, alligator pears, pomegranates, fish, chickens galore crowing and cackling and laying eggs on our decks, and a live pig that squealed infernally and all the time in apprehension of imminent slaughter.

Under the rising moon we came in through the perilous passage of the reef of Bora Bora and dropped anchor off Vaitapé village. Bihaura, with housewifely anxiety, could not get ashore too quickly to her house to prepare more abundance for us. While the launch was taking her and Tehei to the little jetty, the sound of music and of singing drifted across the quiet lagoon. Throughout the Society Islands we had been continually informed that we would find the Bora Borans very jolly. Charmian and I went ashore to see, and on the village green, by forgotten graves on the beach, found the youths and maidens dancing, flower-garlanded and flower-bedecked, with strange phosphorescent flowers in their hair that pulsed and dimmed and glowed in the moon-light. Farther along the beach we came upon a huge grass house, oval-shaped, seventy feet in length, where the elders of the village were singing *himines*. They, too, were flower-garlanded and jolly, and they welcomed us into the fold as little lost sheep straying along from outer darkness.

Early next morning Tehei was on board, with a string of fresh-caught fish and an invitation to dinner for that evening. On the way to dinner, we dropped in at the *himine* house. The same elders were singing, with here or there a youth or maiden that we had not seen the previous night. From all the signs, a feast was in preparation. Towering up from the floor was a mountain of fruits and vegetables, flanked on either side by numerous chickens tethered by cocoanut strips. After several *himines* had been sung, one of the men arose and made oration. The oration was made to us, and though it was Greek to us, we knew that in some way it connected us with that mountain of provender.

"Can it be that they are presenting us with all that?" Charmian whispered.

"Impossible," I muttered back. "Why should they be giving it to us? Besides, there is no room on the *Snark* for it. We could not eat a tithe of it. The rest would spoil. Maybe they are inviting us to the feast. At any rate, that they should give all that to us is impossible."

Nevertheless we found ourselves once more in the high seat of abundance. The orator, by gestures unmistakable, in detail presented every item in the mountain to us, and next he presented it to us *in toto*. It was an embarrassing moment. What would you do if you lived in a hall bedroom and a friend gave you a white elephant? Our *Snark* was no more than a hall bedroom, and already she was loaded down with the abundance of Tahaa. This new supply was too much. We blushed, and stammered, and *mauruuru'd*. We *mauruuru'd* with repeated *nui's* which conveyed the largeness and overwhelmingness of our thanks. At the same time, by signs, we committed the awful breach of etiquette of not accepting the present. The *himine* singers' disappointment was plainly betrayed, and that evening, aided by Tehei, we compromised by accepting one chicken, one bunch of bananas, one bunch of taro, and so on down the list.

But there was no escaping the abundance. I bought a dozen chickens from a native out in the country, and the following day he delivered thirteen chickens along with a canoe-load of fruit. The French storekeeper presented us with pomegranates and lent us his finest horse. The gendarme did likewise, lending us a horse that was the very apple of his eye. And everybody sent us flowers. The *Snark* was a fruit-stand and a greengrocer's shop masquerading under the guise of a conservatory. We went around flower-garlanded all the time. When the *himine* singers came on board to sing, the maidens kissed us welcome, and the crew, from captain to cabin-boy, lost its heart to the maidens of Bora Bora. Tehei got up a big fishing expedition in our honour, to which we went in a double canoe, paddled by a dozen strapping Amazons. We were relieved that no fish were caught, else the *Snark* would have sunk at her moorings.

The days passed, but the abundance did not diminish. On the day of departure, canoe after canoe put off to us. Tehei brought cucumbers and a young *papaia* tree burdened with splendid fruit. Also, for me he brought a tiny, double canoe with fishing apparatus complete. Further, he brought fruits and vegetables with the same lavishness as at Tahaa. Bihaura brought various special presents for Charmian, such as silk-cotton pillows, fans, and fancy mats. The whole population brought fruits, flowers, and chickens. And Bihaura added a live sucking pig. Natives whom I did not remember ever having seen before strayed over the rail and presented me with such things as fish-poles, fish-lines, and fish-hooks carved from pearl-shell.

As the *Snark* sailed out through the reef, she had a cutter in tow. This was the craft that was to take Bihaura back to Tahaa—but not Tehei. I had yielded at last, and he was one of the crew of the *Snark*. When the cutter cast off and headed east, and the *Snark's* bow turned toward the west, Tehei knelt down by the cockpit and breathed a silent prayer, the tears flowing down his cheeks. A week later, when Martin got around to developing and printing, he showed Tehei some of the photographs. And that brown-skinned son of Polynesia, gazing on the pictured lineaments of his beloved Bihaura, broke down in tears.

But the abundance ! There was so much of it. We could not work the *Snark* for the fruit that was in the way. She was festooned with fruit. The life-boat and launch were packed with it. The awning-guys groaned under their burdens. But once we struck the full trade-wind sea, the disburdening began. At every roll the *Snark* shook overboard a bunch or so of bananas and cocoanuts, or a basket of limes. A golden flood of limes washed about in the lee-scuppers. The big baskets of yams burst, and pineapples and pomegranates rolled back and forth. The chickens had got loose and were everywhere, roosting on the awnings, fluttering and squawking out on the jib-boom, and essaying the perilous feat of balancing on the spinnaker-boom. They were wild chickens, accustomed to flight. When attempts were made to catch them, they flew out over the ocean, circled about, and came back. Sometimes they did not come back. And in the confusion, unobserved, the little sucking pig got loose and slipped overboard.

" On the arrival of strangers, every man endeavoured to obtain one as a friend and carry him off to his own habitation, where he is treated with the greatest kindness by the inhabitants of the district : they place him on a high seat and feed him with abundance of the finest foods."

CHAPTER XIII

THE STONE-FISHING OF BORA BORA

AT five in the morning the conches began to blow. From all along the beach the eerie sounds arose, like the ancient voice of War, calling to the fishermen to arise and prepare to go forth. We on the *Snark* likewise arose, for there could be no sleep in that mad din of conches. Also, we were going stone-fishing, though our preparations were few.

Tautai-taora is the name for stone-fishing, *tautai* meaning a "fishing instrument." And *taora* meaning "thrown." But *tautai-taora*, in combination, means "stone-fishing," for a stone is the instrument that is thrown. Stone-fishing is in reality a fish-drive, similar in principle to a rabbit-drive or a cattle-drive, though in the latter affairs drivers and driven operate in the same medium, while in the fish-drive the men must be in the air to breathe and the fish are driven through the water. It does not matter if the water is a hundred feet deep, the men, working on the surface, drive the fish just the same.

This is the way it is done. The canoes form in line, one hundred to two hundred feet apart. In the bow of each canoe a man wields a stone, several pounds in weight, which is attached to a short rope. He merely smites the water with the stone, pulls up the stone, and smites again. He goes on smiting. In the stern of each canoe, another man paddles, driving the canoe ahead and at the same time keeping it in the formation. The line of canoes advances to meet a second line a mile or two away, the ends of the lines hurrying together to form a circle, the far edge of which is the shore. The circle begins to contract upon the shore, where the women, standing in a long row out into the sea, form a fence of legs, which serves to break any rushes of the frantic fish. At the right moment when the circle is sufficiently small, a canoe dashes out from shore, dropping overboard a long screen of cocoanut leaves and encircling the circle, thus reinforcing the palisade of legs. Of course, the fishing is always done inside the reef in the lagoon.

" *Très jolie*," the gendarme said, after explaining by signs and gestures that thousands of fish would be caught of all sizes from minnows to sharks, and that the captured fish would boil up and upon the very sand of the beach.

It is a most successful method of fishing, while its nature is more that of an outing festival, rather than of a prosaic, food-getting task. Such fishing parties take place about once a month at Bora Bora, and it is a custom that has descended from old time. The man who originated it is not remembered. They always did this thing. But one cannot help wondering about that forgotten savage of the long ago, into whose mind first flashed this scheme of easy fishing, of catching huge quantities of fish without hook, or net, or spear. One thing about him we can know : he was a radical. And we can be sure that he was considered feather-brained and anarchistic by his conservative tribesmen. His difficulty was much greater than that of the modern inventor, who has to convince in advance only one or two capitalists. That early inventor had to convince his whole tribe in advance, for without the co-operation of the whole tribe the device could not be tested. One can well imagine the nightly pow-wow-ings in that primitive island world, when he called his comrades antiquated moss-backs, and they called him a fool, a freak, and a crank, and charged him with having come from Kansas. Heaven alone knows at what cost of grey hairs and expletives he must finally have succeeded in winning over a sufficient number to give his idea a trial. At any rate, the experiment succeeded. It stood the test of truth—it worked ! And thereafter, we can be confident, there was no man to be found who did not know all along that it was going to work.

Our good friends, Tehei and Bihaura, who were giving the fishing in our honour, had promised to come for us. We were down below when the call came from on deck that they were coming. We dashed up the companionway, to be overwhelmed by the sight of the Polynesian barge in which we were to ride. It was a long double canoe, the canoes lashed together by timbers with an interval of water between, and the whole decorated with flowers and golden grasses. A dozen flower-crowned Amazons were at the paddles, while at the stern of each canoe was a strapping steersman. All were garlanded with gold and crimson and orange flowers, while each wore about the hips a scarlet *pareu*. There were flowers everywhere, flowers, flowers, flowers, without end. The whole thing was an orgy of colour. On the platform forward resting on the bows of the canoes, Tehei and Bihaura were dancing. All voices were raised in a wild song of greeting.

Three times they circled the *Snark* before coming alongside to take Charmian and me on board. Then it was away for the fishing-grounds, a five-mile paddle dead to windward. "Everybody is jolly in Bora Bora," is the saying throughout the Society Islands, and we certainly found everybody jolly. Canoe songs, shark songs, and fishing songs were sung to the dipping of the paddles, all joining in on the swinging choruses. Once in a while the cry *Mao !* was raised, whereupon all strained like mad at the paddles. *Mao* is shark, and when the deep-sea tigers appear, the natives paddle for dear life for the shore, knowing full well the danger they run of having their frail canoes overturned and of being devoured. Of course, in our case there were no sharks, but the cry of *mao* was used to incite them to paddle with as much energy as if a shark were really after them. "*Hoé ! Hoé !*" was another cry that made us foam through the water.

On the platform Tehei and Bihaura danced, accompanied by songs and choruses or by rhythmic hand-clappings. At other times a musical knocking of the paddles against the sides of the canoes marked the accent. A young girl dropped her paddle, leaped to the platform, and danced a hula, in the midst of which, still dancing, she swayed and bent, and imprinted on our cheeks the kiss of welcome. Some of the songs, or *himines*, were religious, and they were especially beautiful, the deep basses of the men mingling with the altos and thin sopranos of the women and forming a combination of sound that irresistibly reminded one of an organ. In fact, " kanaka organ " is the scoffer's description of the *himine*. On the other hand, some of the chants or ballads were very barbaric, having come down from pre-Christian times.

And so, singing, dancing, paddling, these joyous Polynesians took us to the fishing. The gendarme, who is the French ruler of Bora Bora, accompanied us with his family in a double canoe of his own, paddled by his prisoners ; for not only is he gendarme and ruler, but he is jailer as well, and in this jolly land when anybody goes fishing, all go fishing. A score of single canoes, with outriggers, paddled along with us. Around a point a big sailing-canoe appeared, running beautifully before the wind as it bore down to greet us. Balancing precariously on the outrigger, three young men saluted us with a wild rolling of drums.

The next point, half a mile farther on, brought us to the place of meeting. Here the launch, which had been brought along by Warren and Martin, attracted much attention. The Bora Borans could not see what made it go. The canoes were drawn upon the sand, and all hands went ashore to drink cocoanuts and sing and dance. Here our numbers were added to by many who arrived on foot from near-by dwellings, and a pretty sight it was to see the flower-crowned maidens, hand in hand and two by two, arriving along the sands.

"They usually make a big catch," Allicot, a half-caste trader, told us. "At the finish the water is fairly alive with fish. It is lots of fun. Of course you know all the fish will be yours."

"All?" I groaned, for already the *Snark* was loaded down with lavish presents, by the canoe-load, of fruits, vegetables, pigs, and chickens.

"Yes, every last fish," Allicot answered. "You see, when the surround is completed, you, being the guest of honour, must take a harpoon and impale the first one. It is the custom. Then everybody goes in with their hands and throws the catch out on the sand. There will be a mountain of them. Then one of the chiefs will make a speech in which he presents you with the whole kit and boodle. But you don't have to take them all. You get up and make a speech, selecting what fish you want for yourself and presenting all the rest back again. Then everybody says you are very generous."

"But what would be the result if I kept the whole present?" I asked.

"It has never happened," was the answer. "It is the custom to give and give back again."

The native minister started with a prayer for success in the fishing, and all heads were bared. Next, the chief fishermen told off the canoes and allotted them their places. Then it was into the canoes and away. No women, however, came

along, with the exception of Bihaura and Charmian. In the old days even they would have
been tabooed. The women remained behind to
wade out into the water and form the palisade
of legs.

The big double canoe was left on the beach,
and we went in the launch. Half the canoes
paddled off to leeward, while we, with the other
half, headed to windward a mile and a half, until
the end of our line was in touch with the reef.
The leader of the drive occupied a canoe midway
in our line. He stood erect, a fine figure of an
old man, holding a flag in his hand. He directed
the taking of positions and the forming of the
two lines by blowing on a conch. When all was
ready, he waved his flag to the right. With a
single splash the throwers in every canoe on that
side struck the water with their stones. While
they were hauling them back—a matter of a
moment, for the stones scarcely sank beneath the
surface—the flag waved to the left, and with
admirable precision every stone on that side
struck the water. So it went, back and forth,
right and left ; with every wave of the flag a long
line of concussion smote the lagoon. At the same
time the paddles drove the canoes forward ; and
what was being done in our line was being done in
the opposing line of canoes a mile and more away.

On the bow of the launch, Tehei, with eyes fixed
on the leader, worked his stone in unison with the
others. Once, the stone slipped from the rope,
and the same instant Tehei went overboard after
it. I do not know whether or not that stone
reached the bottom, but I do know that the next

instant Tehei broke surface alongside with the stone in his hand. I noticed this same accident occur several times among the near-by canoes, but in each instance the thrower followed the stone and brought it back.

The reef ends of our lines accelerated, the shore ends lagged, all under the watchful supervision of the leader, until at the reef the two lines joined, forming the circle. Then the contraction of the circle began, the poor frightened fish harried shoreward by the streaks of concussion that smote the water. In the same fashion elephants are driven through the jungle by motes of men who crouch in the long grasses or behind trees and make strange noises. Already the palisade of legs had been built. We could see the heads of the women, in a long line, dotting the placid surface of the lagoon. The tallest women went farthest out, thus, with the exception of those close inshore, nearly all were up to their necks in the water.

Still the circle narrowed, till canoes were almost touching. There was a pause. A long canoe shot out from shore, following the line of the circle. It went as fast as paddles could drive. In the stern a man threw overboard the long, continuous screen of cocoanut leaves. The canoes were no longer needed, and overboard went the men to reinforce the palisade with their legs. For the screen was only a screen, and not a net, and the fish could dash through it if they tried. Hence the need for legs that ever agitated the screen, and for hands that splashed and throats that yelled. Pandemonium reigned as the trap tightened.

But no fish broke surface or collided against the hidden legs. At last the chief fisherman entered the trap. He waded around everywhere, carefully. But there were no fish boiling up and out upon the sand. There was not a sardine, not a minnow, not a polly-wog. Something must have been wrong with that prayer ; or else, and more likely, as one grizzled fellow put it, the wind was not in its usual quarter and the fish were elsewhere in the lagoon. In fact, there had been no fish to drive.

"About once in five these drives are failures," Allicot consoled us.

Well, it was the stone-fishing that had brought us to Bora Bora, and it was our luck to draw the one chance in five. Had it been a raffle, it would have been the other way about. This is not pessimism. Nor is it an indictment of the plan of the universe. It is merely that feeling which is familiar to most fishermen at the empty end of a hard day.

CHAPTER XIV

THE AMATEUR NAVIGATOR

THERE are captains and captains, and some mighty fine captains, I know ; but the run of the captains on the *Snark* has been remarkably otherwise. My experience with them has been that it is harder to take care of one captain on a small boat than of two small babies. Of course, this is no more than is to be expected. The good men have positions, and are not likely to forsake their one-thousand-to-fifteen-thousand-ton billets for the *Snark* with her ten tons net. The *Snark* has had to cull her navigators from the beach, and the navigator on the beach is usually a congenital inefficient—the sort of man who beats about for a fortnight trying vainly to find an ocean isle and who returns with his schooner to report the island sunk with all on board, the sort of man whose temper or thirst for strong waters works him out of billets faster than he can work into them.

The *Snark* has had three captains, and by the grace of God she shall have no more. The first captain was so senile as to be unable to give a measurement for a boom-jaw to a carpenter. So utterly agedly helpless was he, that he was unable to order a sailor to throw a few buckets of salt water on the *Snark's* deck. For twelve days, at anchor, under an overhead tropic sun, the deck lay dry. It was a new deck. It cost me one hundred and thirty-five dollars to recaulk it. The second captain was angry. He was born angry. "Papa is always angry," was the description given him by his half-breed son. The third captain was so crooked that he couldn't hide behind a corkscrew. The truth was not in him, common honesty was not in him, and he was as far away from fair play and square-dealing as he was from his proper course when he nearly wrecked the *Snark* on the Ring-gold Isles.

It was at Suva, in the Fijis, that I discharged my third and last captain and took up again the rôle of amateur navigator. I had essayed it once before, under my first captain, who, out of San Francisco, jumped the *Snark* so amazingly over the chart that I really had to find out what was doing. It was fairly easy to find out, for we had a run of twenty-one hundred miles before us. I knew nothing of navigation; but, after several hours of reading up and half an hour's practice with the sextant, I was able to find the *Snark's* latitude by meridian observation and her longitude by the simple method known as "equal altitudes." This is not a correct method. It is not even a safe method, but my captain was attempting to navigate by it, and he was the only one on board who should have been able to tell me that it was a method to be eschewed. I brought the *Snark* to Hawaii, but the conditions favoured me. The sun was in northern declination and nearly overhead. The legitimate "chronometer-sight" method of ascertaining the longitude I had not heard of—yes, I had heard of it. My first captain mentioned it vaguely, but after one or two attempts at practice of it he mentioned it no more.

I had time in the Fijis to compare my chronometer with two other chronometers. Two weeks previous, at Pago Pago, in Samoa, I had asked my captain to compare our chronometer with the chronometers on the American cruiser, the *Annapolis*. This he told me he had done—of course he had done nothing of the sort ; and he told me that the difference he had ascertained was only a small fraction of a second. He told it to me with finely simulated joy and with words of praise for my splendid time-keeper. I repeat it now, with words of praise for his splendid and unblushing unveracity. For behold, fourteen days later, in Suva, I compared the chronometer with the one on the *Atua*, an Australian steamer, and found that mine was thirty-one seconds fast. Now thirty-one seconds of time, converted into arc, equals seven and one-quarter miles. That is to say, if I were sailing west, in the night-time, and my position, according to my dead reckoning from my afternoon chronometer sight, was shown to be seven miles off the land, why, at that very moment I would be crashing on the reef. Next I compared my chronometer with Captain Wooley's. Captain Wooley, the harbourmaster, gives the time to Suva, firing a gun signal at twelve, noon, three times a week. According to his chronometer mine was fifty-nine seconds fast, which is to say, that, sailing west, I should be crashing on the reef when I thought I was fifteen miles off from it.

I compromised by subtracting thirty-one seconds from the total of my chronometer's losing error, and sailed away for Tanna, in the New Hebrides, resolved, when nosing around the land on dark nights, to bear in mind the other seven miles I might be out according to Captain Wooley's instrument. Tanna lay some six hundred miles west-southwest from the Fijis, and it was my belief that while covering that distance I could quite easily knock into my head sufficient navigation to get me there. Well, I got there, but listen first to my troubles. Navigation *is* easy, I shall always contend that ; but when a man is taking three gasolene engines and a wife around the world and is writing hard every day to keep the engines supplied with gasolene and the wife with pearls and volcanoes, he hasn't much time left in which to study navigation. Also, it is bound to be easier to study said science ashore, where latitude and longitude are unchanging, in a house whose position never alters, than it is to study navigation on a boat that is rushing along day and night toward land that one is trying to find and which he is liable to find disastrously at a moment when he least expects it.

To begin with, there are the compasses and the setting of the courses. We sailed from Suva on Saturday afternoon, June 6, 1908, and it took us till after dark to run the narrow, reef-ridden passage between the islands of Viti Levu and Mbengha. The open ocean lay before me. There

was nothing in the way with the exception of
Vatu Leile, a miserable little island that persisted
in poking up through the sea some twenty miles
to the west-southwest—just where I wanted to go.
Of course, it seemed quite simple to avoid it by
steering a course that would pass it eight or ten
miles to the north.   It was a black night, and we
were running before the wind.   The man at the
wheel must be told what direction to steer in order
to miss Vatu Leile.   But what direction ?   I
turned me to the navigation books.   " True
Course " I lighted upon.   The very thing !   What
I wanted was the true course.   I read eagerly on :

" The True Course is the angle made with the
meridian by a straight line on the chart drawn
to connect the ship's position with the place
bound to."

Just what I wanted.   The *Snark's* position was
at the western entrance of the passage between
Viti Levu and Mbengha.   The immediate place
she was bound to was a place on the chart ten
miles north of Vatu Leile.   I pricked that place
off on the chart with my dividers, and with my
parallel rulers found that west-by-south was the
true course.   I had but to give it to the man at
the wheel and the *Snark* would win her way to
the safety of the open sea.

But alas and alack and lucky for me, I read on.
I discovered that the compass, that trusty, everlasting friend of the mariner, was not given to
pointing north.   It varied.   Sometimes it pointed
east of north, sometimes west of north, and on
occasion it even turned tail on north and pointed
south.   The variation at the particular spot on

the globe occupied by 'he *Snark* was 9° 40′ easterly. Well, that had to be taken into account before I gave the steering course to the man at the wheel. I read :

"The Correct Magne'ic Course is derived from the True Course by applying to it the variation."

Therefore, I reasoned, if the compass points 9° 40′ eastward of north, and I wanted to sail due north, I should have to steer 9° 40′ westward of the north indicated by the compass and which was not north at all. So I added 9° 40′ to the left of my west-by-south course, thus getting my correct Magnetic Course, and was ready once more to run to open sea.

Again alas and alack ! The Correct Magnetic Course was not the Compass Course. There was another sly little devil lying in wait to trip me up and land me smashing on the reefs of Vatu Leile. This little devil went by the name of Deviation. I read :

"The Compass Course is the course to steer, and is derived from the Correct Magnetic Course by applying to it the Deviation."

Now Deviation is the variation in the needle caused by the distribution of iron on board ship. This purely local variation I derived from the deviation card of my standard compass and then applied to the Correct Magnetic Course. The result was the Compass Course. And yet, not yet. My standard compass was amidships on the companionway. My steering compass was aft, in the cockpit, near the wheel. When the steering compass pointed west-by-south-three-quarters-south (the steering course), the standard compass pointed west-one-half-north, which was certainly not the steering course. I kept the *Snark* up till she was heading west-by-south-three-quarters-south on the standard compass, which gave, on the steering compass, south-west-by-west.

The foregoing operations constitute the simple little matter of setting a course. And the worst of it is that one must perform every step correctly or else he will hear "Breakers ahead!" some pleasant night, receive a nice sea-bath, and be given the delightful diversion of fighting his way to the shore through a horde of man-eating sharks.

Just as the compass is tricky and strives to fool the mariner by pointing in all directions except north, so does that guide-post of the sky, the sun, persist in not being where it ought to be at a given time. This carelessness of the sun is the cause of more trouble—at least it caused trouble for me. To find out where one is on the earth's surface, he must know, at precisely the same time, where the sun is in the heavens. That is to say, the sun, which is the timekeeper for men, doesn't run on time. When I discovered this, I fell into deep gloom and all the Cosmos was filled with doubt. Immutable laws, such as gravitation and the conservation of energy, became wobbly, and I was prepared to witness their violation at any moment and to remain unastonished. For see, if the compass lied and the sun did not keep its engagements, why should not objects lose their mutual attraction and why should not a few bushel baskets of force be annihilated? Even perpetual motion became possible, and I was in a frame of mind prone to purchase Keeley-Motor stock from the first enterprising agent that landed on the *Snark's* deck. And when I discovered that the earth really rotated on its axis 366 times a year, while there were only 365 sunrises and sunsets, I was ready to doubt my own identity.

This is the way of the sun. It is so irregular that it is impossible for man to devise a clock that will keep the sun's time. The sun accelerates and retards as no clock could be made to accelerate and retard. The sun is sometimes ahead of its schedule; at other times it is lagging behind; and at still other times it is breaking the speed limit in order to overtake itself, or, rather, to catch up with where it ought to be in the sky. In this last case it does not slow down quick enough, and, as a result, goes dashing ahead of where it ought to be. In fact, only four days in a year do the sun and the place where the sun ought to be happen to coincide. The remaining 361 days the sun is pothering around all over the shop. Man, being more perfect than the sun, makes a clock that keeps regular time. Also, he calculates how far the sun is ahead of its schedule or behind. The difference between the sun's position and the position where the sun ought to be if it were a decent, self-respecting sun, man calls the Equation of Time. Thus, the navigator endeavouring to find his ship's position on the sea, looks in his chronometer to see where precisely the sun ought to be according to the Greenwich custodian of the sun. Then to that location he applies the Equation of Time and finds out where the sun ought to be and isn't. This latter location, along with several other locations, enables him to find out what the man from Kansas demanded to know some years ago.

The *Snark* sailed from Fiji on Saturday, June 6, and the next day, Sunday, on the wide ocean, out of sight of land, I proceeded to endeavour to find out my position by a chronometer sight for longitude and by a meridian observation for latitude. The chronometer sight was taken in the morning, when the sun was some 21° above the horizon. I looked in the Nautical Almanac and found that on that very day, June 7, the sun was behind time 1 minute and 26 seconds, and that it was catching up at a rate of 14·67 seconds per hour. The chronometer said that at the precise moment of taking the sun's altitude it was twenty-five minutes after eight o'clock at Greenwich. From this date it would seem a schoolboy's task to correct the Equation of Time. Unfortunately, I was not a schoolboy. Obviously, at the middle of the day, at Greenwich, the sun was 1 minute and 26 seconds behind time. Equally obviously, if it were eleven o'clock in the morning, the sun would be 1 minute and 26 seconds behind time plus 14·67 seconds. If it were ten o'clock in the morning, twice 14·67 seconds would have to be added. And if it were 8 : 25 in the morning, then $3\frac{1}{2}$ times 14·67 seconds would have to be added. Quite clearly, then, if, instead of being 8 : 25 A.M., it were 8 : 25 P.M., then $8\frac{1}{2}$ times 14·67 seconds would have to be, not added, but *subtracted* ; for, if, at noon, the sun were 1 minute and 26 seconds behind time, and if it were catching up with where it ought to be at the rate of 14·67 seconds per hour, then at 8.25 P.M. it would be much nearer where it ought to be than it had been at noon.

So far, so good. But was that 8 : 25 of the chronometer A.M. or P.M. ? I looked at the *Snark's* clock. It marked 8 : 9, and it was certainly A.M., for I had just finished breakfast. Therefore, if it was eight in the morning on board the *Snark*, the eight o'clock of the chronometer (which was the time of the day at Greenwich) must be a different eight o'clock from the *Snark's* eight o'clock. But what eight o'clock was it ? It can't be the eight o'clock of this morning, I reasoned ; therefore, it must be either eight o'clock this evening or eight o'clock last night.

It was at this juncture that I fell into the bottomless pit of intellectual chaos. We are in east longitude, I reasoned, therefore we are ahead of Greenwich. If we are behind Greenwich, then to-day is yesterday ; if we are ahead of Greenwich, then yesterday is to-day, but if yesterday is to-day, what under the sun is to-day !—to-morrow ? Absurd ! Yet it must be correct. When I took the sun this morning at 8 : 25, the sun's custodians at Greenwich were just arising from dinner last night.

"Then correct the Equation of Time for yesterday," says my logical mind.

"But to-day is to-day," my literal mind insists. "I must correct the sun for to-day and not for yesterday."

"Yet to-day is yesterday," urges my logical mind.

"That's all very well," my literal mind continues. "If I were in Greenwich I might be in yesterday. Strange things happen in Greenwich. But I know as sure as I am living that I am here, now, in to-day, June 7, and that I took the sun here, now, to-day, June 7. Therefore, I must correct the sun here, now, to-day, June 7."

"Bosh!" snaps my logical mind. "Lecky says——"

"Never mind what Lecky says," interrupts my literal mind. "Let me tell you what the Nautical Almanac says. The Nautical Almanac says that to-day, June 7, the sun was 1 minute and 26 seconds behind time and catching up at the rate of 14˙67 seconds per hour. It says that yesterday, June 6, the sun was 1 minute and 36 seconds behind time and catching up at the rate of 15˙66 seconds per hour. You see, it is preposterous to think of correcting to-day's sun by yesterday's time-table."

"Fool!"

"Idiot!"

Back and forth they wrangle until my head is whirling around and I am ready to believe that I am in the day after the last week before next.

I remembered a parting caution of the Suva harbour-master : "*In east longitude take from the Nautical Almanac the elements for the preceding day.*"

Then a new thought came to me. I corrected the Equation of Time for Sunday and for Saturday, making two separate operations of it, and lo, when the results were compared, there was a difference only of four-tenths of a second. I was a changed man. I had found my way out of the crypt. The *Snark* was scarcely big enough to hold me and my experience. Four-tenths of a second would make a difference of only one-tenth of a mile—a cable-length !

All went merrily for ten minutes, when I chanced upon the following rhyme for navigators :

> " Greenwich time least
> Longitude east ;
> Greenwich best,
> Longitude west."

Heavens ! The *Snark's* time was not as good as Greenwich time. When it was 8 : 25 at Greenwich, on board the *Snark* it was only 8 : 9. " Greenwich time best, longitude west." There I was. In west longitude beyond a doubt.

" Silly ! " cries my literal mind. " You are 8 : 9 A.M. and Greenwich is 8 : 25 P.M."

" Very well," answers my logical mind. " To be correct, 8.25 P.M. is really twenty hours and twenty-five minutes, and that is certainly better than eight hours and nine minutes. No, there is no discussion ; you are in west longitude."

Then my literal mind triumphs.

" We sailed from Suva, in the Fijis, didn't we ? " it demands, and logical mind agrees. " And Suva is in east longitude ? " Again logical mind agrees. " And we sailed west (which would take us deeper into east longitude), didn't we ? Therefore, and you can't escape it, we are in east longitude."

" Greenwich time best, longitude west," chants my logical mind ; " and you must grant that twenty hours and twenty-five minutes is better than eight hours and nine minutes."

"All right," I break in upon the squabble; "we'll work up the sight and then we'll see."

And work it up I did, only to find that my longitude was 184° west.

"I told you so," snorts my logical mind.

I am dumbfounded. So is my literal mind, for several minutes. Then it enounces:

"But there is no 184° west longitude, nor east longitude, nor any other longitude. The largest meridian is 180° as you ought to know very well."

Having got this far, literal mind collapses from the brain strain, logical mind is dumb flabbergasted; and as for me, I get a bleak and wintry look in my eyes and go around wondering whether I am sailing toward the China coast or the Gulf of Darien.

Then a thin small voice, which I do not recognize, coming from nowhere in particular in my consciousness, says:

"The total number of degrees is 360. Subtract the 184° west longitude from 360°, and you will get 176° east longitude."

"That is sheer speculation," objects literal mind; and logical mind remonstrates. "There is no rule for it."

"Darn the rules!" I exclaim. "Ain't I here?

"The thing is self-evident," I continue. "184° west longitude means a lapping over in east longitude of four degrees. Besides I have been in east longitude all the time. I sailed from Fiji, and Fiji is in east longitude. Now I shall chart my position and prove it by dead reckoning."

But other troubles and doubts awaited me. Here is a sample of one. In south latitude, when the sun is in northern declination, chronometer sights may be taken early in the morning. I took mine at eight o'clock. Now, one of the necessary elements in working up such a sight is latitude. But one gets latitude at twelve o'clock, noon, by a meridian observation. It is clear that in order to work up my eight o'clock chronometer sight I must have my eight o'clock latitude. Of course, if the *Snark* were sailing due west at six knots per hour, for the intervening four hours her latitude would not change. But if she were sailing due south, her latitude would change to the tune of twenty-four miles. In which case a simple addition or subtraction would convert the twelve o'clock latitude into eight o'clock latitude. But suppose the *Snark* were sailing southwest. Then the traverse tables must be consulted.

This is the illustration. At eight A.M. I took my chronometer sight. At the same moment the distance recorded on the log was noted. At twelve M., when the sight for latitude was taken, I again noted the log, which showed me that since eight o'clock the *Snark* had run 24 miles. Her true course had been west ¾ south. I entered Table I, in the distance column, on the page for ¾ point courses, and stopped at 24, the number of miles run. Opposite, in the next two columns, I found that the *Snark* had made 3·5 miles of southing or latitude, and that she had made 23·7 miles of westing. To find my eight o'clock latitude was easy. I had but to subtract 3·5 miles from my noon latitude. All the elements being present, I worked up my longitude.

But this was my eight o'clock longitude. Since

then, and up till noon, I had made 23·7 miles of westing. What was my noon longitude? I followed the rule, turning to Traverse Table No. II. Entering the table, according to rule, and going through every detail, according to rule, I found the difference of longitude for the four hours to be 25 miles. I was aghast. I entered the table again, according to rule; I entered the table half a dozen times, according to rule, and every time found that my difference of longitude was 25 miles. I leave it to you, gentle reader. Suppose you had sailed 24 miles and that you had covered 3·5 miles of latitude, then how could you have covered 25 miles of longitude? Even if you had sailed due west 24 miles, and not changed your latitude, how could you have changed your longitude 25 miles? In the name of human reason, how could you cover one mile more of longitude than the total number of miles you had sailed?

It was a reputable traverse table, being none other than Bowditch's. The rule was simple (as navigators' rules go); I had made no error. I spent an hour over it, and at the end still faced the glaring impossibility of having sailed 24 miles, in the course of which I changed my latitude 3·5 miles and my longitude 25 miles. The worst of it was that there was nobody to help me out. Neither Charmian nor Martin knew as much as I knew about navigation. And all the time the *Snark* was rushing madly along toward Tanna, in the New Hebrides. Something had to be done.

How it came to me I know not—call it an inspiration if you will; but the thought arose in

me : if southing is latitude, why isn't westing
longitude ?   Why should I have to change westing
into longitude ?   And then the whole beautiful
situation dawned upon me.   The meridians of
longitude are 60 miles (nautical) apart at the
equator.   At the poles they run together.   Thus,
if I should travel up the 180° meridian of longitude until I reached the North Pole, and if the
astronomer at Greenwich travelled up the 0°
meridian of longitude to the North Pole, then,
at the North Pole, we could shake hands with
each other, though before we started for the North
Pole we had been some thousands of miles apart.
Again : if a degree of longitude was 60 miles
wide at the equator, and if the same degree, at
the point of the Pole, had no width, then somewhere between the Pole and the equator that
degree would be half a mile wide, and at other
places a mile wide, two miles wide, ten miles wide,
thirty miles wide, ay, and sixty miles wide.

All was plain again.   The *Snark* was in 19° south
latitude.   The world wasn't as big around there
as at the equator.   Therefore, every mile of
westing at 19° south was more than a minute of
longitude ; for sixty miles were sixty miles, but
sixty minutes are sixty miles only at the equator.
George Francis Train broke Jules Verne's record
of around the world.   But any man that wants
can break George Francis Train's record.   Such
a man would need only to go, in a fast steamer,
to the latitude of Cape Horn, and sail due east
all the way around.   The world is very small in
that latitude, and there is no land in the way to
turn him out of his course.   If his steamer main-

tained sixteen knots, he would circumnavigate the globe in just about forty days.

But there are compensations. On Wednesday evening, June 10, I brought up my noon position by dead reckoning to eight P.M. Then I projected the *Snark's* course and saw that she would strike Futuna, one of the easternmost of the New Hebrides, a volcanic cone two thousand feet high that rose out of the deep ocean. I altered the course so that the *Snark* would pass ten miles to the northward. Then I spoke to Wada, the cook, who had the wheel every morning from four to six.

"Wada San, to-morrow morning, your watch, you look sharp on weather-bow you see land."

And then I went to bed. The die was cast. I had staked my reputation as a navigator. Suppose, just suppose, that at daybreak there was no land. Then, where would my navigation be ? And where would we be ? And how would we ever find ourselves ? or find any land ? I caught ghastly visions of the *Snark* sailing for months through ocean solitudes and seeking vainly for land while we consumed our provisions and sat down with haggard faces to stare cannibalism in the face.

I confess my sleep was not

"... like a summer sky
That held the music of a lark."

Rather did "I waken to the voiceless dark," and listen to the creaking of the bulkheads and the rippling of the sea alongside as the *Snark* logged steadily her six knots an hour. I went over my calculations again and again, striving to find some mistake, until my brain was in such fever that it discovered dozens of mistakes. Suppose, instead of being sixty miles off Futuna, that my navigation was all wrong and that I was only six miles off ? In which case my course would be wrong, too, and for all I knew the *Snark* might be running straight at Futuna. For all I knew the *Snark* might strike Futuna the next moment. I almost sprang from the bunk at that thought ; and, though I restrained myself, I know that I lay for a moment, nervous and tense, waiting for the shock.

My sleep was broken by miserable nightmares. Earthquake seemed the favourite affliction, though there was one man, with a bill, who persisted in dunning me throughout the night. Also, he wanted to fight ; and Charmian continually persuaded me to let him alone. Finally, however, the man with the everlasting dun ventured into a dream from which Charmian was absent. It was my opportunity, and we went at it, gloriously, all over the sidewalk and street, until he cried enough. Then I said, "Now how about that bill ? " Having conquered, I was willing to pay. But the man looked at me and groaned. "It was all a mistake," he said ; "the bill is for the house next door."

That settled him, for he worried my dreams no more ; and it settled me, too, for I woke up chuckling at the episode. It was three in the morning. I went up on deck. Henry, the Rapa islander, was steering. I looked at the log. It recorded forty-two miles. The *Snark* had not

abated her six-knot gait, and she had not struck
Futuna yet. At half-past five I was again on
deck. Wada, at the wheel, had seen no land. I
sat on the cockpit rail, a prey to morbid doubt
for a quarter of an hour. Then I saw land, a
small, high piece of land, just where it ought to be,
rising from the water on the weather-bow. At six
o'clock I could clearly make it out to be the
beautiful volcanic cone of Futuna. At eight
o'clock, when it was abreast, I took its distance
by the sextant and found it to be 9·3 miles away.
And I had elected to pass it 10 miles away!

Then, to the south, Aneiteum rose out of the
sea, to the north, Aniwa, and, dead ahead, Tanna.
There was no mistaking Tanna, for the smoke of
its volcano was towering high in the sky. It was
forty miles away, and by afternoon, as we drew
close, never ceasing to log our six knots, we saw
that it was a mountainous, hazy land, with no
apparent openings in its coast-line. I was looking
for Port Resolution, though I was quite prepared
to find that as an anchorage, it had been destroyed. Volcanic earthquakes had lifted its
bottom during the last forty years, so that where
once the largest ships rode at anchor there was
now, by last reports, scarcely space and depth
sufficient for the *Snark*. And why should not
another convulsion, since the last report, have
closed the harbour completely?

I ran in close to the unbroken coast, fringed
with rocks awash upon which the crashing trade-
wind sea burst white and high. I searched with
my glasses for miles, but could see no entrance.
I took a compass bearing of Futuna, another of

Aniwa, and laid them off on the chart. Where the two bearings crossed was bound to be the position of the *Snark*. Then, with my parallel rulers, I laid down a course from the *Snark's* position to Port Resolution. Having corrected this course for variation and deviation, I went on deck, and lo, the course directed me towards that unbroken coast-line of bursting seas. To my Rapa islander's great concern, I held on till the rocks awash were an eighth of a mile away.

"No harbour this place," he announced, shaking his head ominously.

But I altered the course and ran along parallel with the coast. Charmian was at the wheel. Martin was at the engine, ready to throw on the propeller. A narrow slit of an opening showed up suddenly. Through the glasses I could see the seas breaking clear across. Henry, the Rapa man, looked with troubled eyes; so did Tehei, the Tahaa man.

"No passage there," said Henry. "We go there, we finish quick, sure."

I confess I thought so, too; but I ran on abreast, watching to see if the line of breakers from one side the entrance did not overlap the line from the other side. Sure enough, it did. A narrow place where the sea ran smooth appeared. Charmian put down the wheel and steadied for the entrance. Martin threw on the engine, while all hands and the cook sprang to take in sail.

A trader's house showed up in the bight of the bay. A geyser, on the shore, a hundred yards away, spouted a column of steam. To port, as we rounded a tiny point, the mission station appeared.

" Three fathoms," cried Wada at the lead-line.

" Three fathoms," " two fathoms," came in quick succession.

Charmian put the wheel down, Martin stopped the engine, and the *Snark* rounded to and the anchor rumbled down in three fathoms. Before we could catch our breaths a swarm of black Tannese was alongside and aboard—grinning, apelike creatures, with kinky hair and troubled eyes, wearing safety-pins and clay-pipes in their slitted ears : and as for the rest, wearing nothing behind and less than that before. And I don't mind telling that that night, when everybody was asleep, I sneaked up on deck, looked out over the quiet scene, and gloated—yes, gloated—over my navigation.

CHAPTER XV

CRUISING IN THE SOLOMONS

"WHY not come along now?" said Captain Jansen to us, at Penduffryn, on the island of Guadalcanar.

Charmian and I looked at each other and debated silently for half a minute. Then we nodded our heads simultaneously. It is a way we have of making up our minds to do things; and a very good way it is when one has no temperamental tears to shed over the last tin of condensed milk when it has capsized. (We are living on tinned goods these days, and since mind is rumoured to be an emanation of matter, our similes are naturally of the packing-house variety.)

"You'd better bring your revolvers along, and a couple of rifles," said Captain Jansen. "I've got five rifles aboard, though the one Mauser is without ammunition. Have you a few rounds to spare?"

We brought our rifles on board, several handfuls of Mauser cartridges, and Wada and Nakata, the *Snark's* cook and cabin-boy respectively. Wada and Nakata were in a bit of a funk. To say the least, they were not enthusiastic, though never did Nakata show the white feather in the face of danger. The Solomon Islands had not dealt kindly with them. In the first place, both had suffered from Solomon sores. So had the rest of us (at the time, I was nursing two fresh ones on a diet of corrosive sublimate); but the two Japanese had had more than their share. And the sores are not nice. They may be described as excessively active ulcers. A mosquito bite, a cut, or the slightest abrasion, serves for lodgment of the poison with which the air seems to be filled. Immediately the ulcer commences to eat. It eats in every direction, consuming skin and muscle with astounding rapidity. The pin-point ulcer of the first day is the size of a dime by the second day, and by the end of the week a silver dollar will not cover it.

Worse than the sores, the two Japanese had been afflicted with Solomon Island fever. Each had been down repeatedly with it, and in their weak, convalescent moments they were wont to huddle together on the portion of the *Snark* that happened to be nearest to faraway Japan, and to gaze yearningly in that direction.

But worst of all, they were now brought on board the *Minota* for a recruiting cruise along the savage coast of Malaita. Wada, who had the worse funk, was sure that he would never see Japan again, and with bleak, lack-lustre eyes he watched our rifles and ammunition going on board the *Minota*. He knew about the *Minota* and her Malaita cruises. He knew that she had been captured six months before on the Malaita coast, that her captain had been chopped to pieces with tomahawks, and that, according to the barbarian sense of equity on that sweet isle, she owed two more heads. Also, a labourer on Penduffryn Plantation, a Malaita boy, had just died of dysentery, and Wada knew that Penduffryn had been put in the debt of Malaita by one more head. Furthermore, in stowing our luggage away in the skipper's tiny cabin, he saw the axe gashes on the door where the triumphant bushmen had cut their way in. And, finally, the galley stove was without a pipe—said pipe having been part of the loot.

The *Minota* was a teak-built, Australian yacht, ketch-rigged, long and lean, with a deep fin-keel, and designed for harbour racing rather than for recruiting blacks. When Charmian and I came on board, we found her crowded. Her double boat's crew, including substitutes, was fifteen, and she had a score and more of "return" boys, whose time on the plantations was served and who were bound back to their bush villages. To look at, they were certainly true head-hunting cannibals. Their perforated nostrils were thrust through with bone and wooden bodkins the size of lead-pencils. Numbers of them had punctured the extreme meaty point of the nose, from which protruded, straight out, spikes of turtle-shell or of beads strung on stiff wire. A few had further punctured their noses with rows of holes following the curves of the nostrils from lip to point. Each ear of every man had from two to a dozen holes in it—holes large enough to carry wooden plugs three inches in diameter down to tiny holes in which were carried clay-pipes and similar trifles. In fact, so many holes did they possess that they lacked ornaments to fill them ; and when, the following day, as we neared Malaita, we tried out our rifles to see that they were in working order, there was a general scramble for the empty cartridges, which were thrust forthwith into the many aching voids in our passengers' ears.

At the time we tried out our rifles we put up our barbed wire railings. The *Minota*, crown-decked, without any house, and with a rail six inches high, was too accessible to boarders. So brass stanchions were screwed into the rail and a double row of barbed wire stretched around her from stem to stern and back again. Which was all very well as a protection from savages, but it was mighty uncomfortable to those on board when the *Minota* took to jumping and plunging in a sea-way. When one dislikes sliding down upon the lee-rail barbed wire, and when he dares not catch hold of the weather-rail barbed wire to save himself from sliding, and when, with these various disinclinations, he finds himself on a smooth flush-deck that is heeled over at an angle of forty-five degrees, some of the delights of Solomon Islands cruising may be comprehended. Also, it must be remembered, the penalty of a fall into the barbed wire is more than the mere scratches, for each scratch is practically certain to become a venomous ulcer. That caution will not save one from the wire was evidenced one fine morning when we were running along the Malaita coast with the breeze on our quarter. The wind was fresh, and a tidy sea was making. A black boy was at the wheel. Captain Jansen, Mr. Jacobsen (the mate), Charmian, and I had just sat down on deck to breakfast. Three unusually large seas caught us. The boy at the wheel lost his head. Three times the *Minota* was swept. The breakfast was rushed over the lee-rail. The knives and forks went through the scuppers; a boy aft went clean overboard and was dragged back; and our doughty skipper lay half inboard and half out, jammed in the barbed wire. After that, for the rest of the cruise, our joint use of the several remaining eating utensils was a splendid example of primitive communism. On the *Eugenie*, however, it was even worse, for we had but one teaspoon among four of us—but the *Eugenie* is another story.

Our first port was Su'u on the west coast of Malaita. The Solomon Islands are on the fringe of things. It is difficult enough sailing on dark nights through reef-spiked channels and across erratic currents where there are no lights to guide (from northwest to southeast the Solomons extend across a thousand miles of sea, and on all the thousands of miles of coasts there is not one lighthouse); but the difficulty is seriously enhanced by the fact that the land itself is not correctly charted. Su'u is an example. On the Admiralty chart of Malaita the coast at this point runs a straight, unbroken line. Yet across this straight, unbroken line the *Minota* sailed in twenty fathoms of water. Where the land was alleged to be, was a deep indentation. Into this we sailed, the mangroves closing about us, till we dropped anchor in a mirrored pond. Captain Jansen did not like the anchorage. It was the first time he had been there, and Su'u had a bad reputation. There was no wind with which to get away in case of attack, while the crew could be bushwhacked to a man if they attempted to tow out in the whale-boat. It was a pretty trap, if trouble blew up.

"Suppose the *Minota* went ashore—what would you do?" I asked.

"She's not going ashore," was Captain Jansen's answer.

"But just in case she did?" I insisted.

He considered for a moment and shifted his glance from the mate buckling on a revolver to the boat's crew climbing into the whale-boat each man with a rifle.

"We'd get into the whale-boat, and get out of here as fast as God'd let us," came the skipper's delayed reply.

He explained at length that no white man was sure of his Malaita crew in a tight place; that the bushmen looked upon all wrecks as their personal property; that the bushmen possessed plenty of Snider rifles; and that he had on board a dozen "return" boys for Su'u who were certain to join in with their friends and relatives ashore when it came to looting the *Minota*.

The first work of the whale-boat was to take the "return" boys and their trade-boxes ashore. Thus one danger was removed. While this was being done, a canoe came alongside manned by three naked savages. And when I say naked, I mean naked. Not one vestige of clothing did they have on, unless nose-rings, ear-plugs, and shell armlets be accounted clothing. The head man in the canoe was an old chief, one-eyed, reputed to be friendly, and so dirty that a boat-scraper would have lost its edge on him. His mission was to warn the skipper against allowing any of his people to go ashore. The old fellow repeated the warning again that night.

In vain did the whale-boat ply about the shores of the bay in quest of recruits. The bush was full of armed natives, all willing enough to talk with the recruiter, but not one would engage to sign on for three years' plantation labour at six pounds per year. Yet they were anxious enough to get our people ashore. On the second day they raised a smoke on the beach at the head of the bay. This being the customary signal of men desiring to recruit, the boat was sent. But nothing resulted. No one recruited, nor were any of our men lured ashore. A little later we caught glimpses of a number of armed natives moving about on the beach.

Outside of these rare glimpses, there was no telling how many might be lurking in the bush. There was no penetrating that primeval jungle with the eye. In the afternoon, Captain Jansen, Charmian, and I went dynamiting fish. Each one of the boat's crew carried a Lee-Enfield. "Johnny," the native recruiter, had a Winchester beside him at the steering sweep. We rowed in close to a portion of the shore that looked deserted. Here the boat was turned around and backed in ; in case of attack, the boat would be ready to dash away. In all the time I was on Malaita I never saw a boat land bow on. In fact, the recruiting vessels use two boats—one to go in on the beach, armed, of course, and the other to lie off several hundred feet and " cover " the first boat. The *Minota*, however, being a small vessel, did not carry a covering boat.

We were close in to the shore and working in closer, stern-first, when a school of fish was sighted. The fuse was ignited and the stick of dynamite thrown. With the explosion, the surface of the water was broken by the flash of leaping fish. At the same instant the woods broke into life. A score of naked savages, armed with bows and arrows, spears, and Sniders, burst out upon the shore. At the same moment our boat's crew lifted their rifles. And thus the opposing parties faced each other, while our extra boys dived over after the stunned fish.

Three fruitless days were spent at Su'u. The *Minota* got no recruits from the bush, and the bushmen got no heads from the *Minota*. In fact, the only one who got anything was Wada, and his was a nice dose of fever. We towed out with the whale-boat, and ran along the coast to Langa Langa, a large village of salt-water people, built with prodigious labour on a lagoon sand-bank— literally *built up*, an artificial island reared as a refuge from the blood-thirsty bushmen. Here, also, on the shore side of the lagoon, was Binu, the place where the *Minota* was captured half a year previously and her captain killed by the bushmen. As we sailed in through the narrow entrance, a canoe came alongside with the news that the man-of-war had just left that morning after having burned three villages, killed some thirty pigs, and drowned a baby. This was the *Cambrian*, Captain Lewes commanding. He and

I had first met in Korea during the Japanese-Russian War, and we had been crossing each other's trail ever since without ever a meeting. The day the *Snark* sailed into Suva, in the Fijis, we made out the *Cambrian* going out. At Vila, in the New Hebrides, we missed each other by one day. We passed each other in the night-time off the island of Santo. And the day the *Cambrian* arrived at Tulagi, we sailed from Penduffryn, a dozen miles away. And here at Langa Langa we had missed by several hours.

The *Cambrian* had come to punish the murderers of the *Minota's* captain, but what she had succeeded in doing we did not learn until later in the day, when a Mr. Abbot, a missionary, came alongside in his whale-boat. The villages had been burned and the pigs killed. But the natives had escaped personal harm. The murderers had not been captured, though the *Minota's* flag and other of her gear had been recovered. The drowning of the baby had come about through a misunderstanding. Chief Johnny, of Binu, had declined to guide the landing party into the bush, nor could any of his men be induced to perform that office. Whereupon Captain Lewes, righteously indignant, had told Chief Johnny that he deserved to have his village burned. Johnny's *bêche de mer* English did not include the word "deserve." So his understanding of it was that his village was to be burned anyway. The immediate stampede of the inhabitants was so hurried that the baby was dropped into the water. In the meantime Chief Johnny hastened to Mr. Abbot. Into his hand he put fourteen sovereigns and requested him to go on board the *Cambrian* and buy Captain Lewes off. Johnny's village was not burned. Nor did Captain Lewes get the fourteen sovereigns, for I saw them later in Johnny's possession when he boarded the *Minota*. The excuse Johnny gave me for not guiding the landing party was a big boil which he proudly revealed. His real reason, however, and a perfectly valid one, though he did not state it, was fear of revenge on the part of the bushmen. Had he, or any of his men, guided the marines, he could have looked for bloody reprisals as soon as the *Cambrian* weighed anchor.

As an illustration of conditions in the Solomons, Johnny's business on board was to turn over, for a tobacco consideration, the sprit, mainsail, and jib of a whale-boat. Later in the day, a Chief Billy came on board and turned over, for a tobacco consideration, the mast and boom. This gear belonged to a whale-boat which Captain Jansen had recovered the previous trip of the *Minota*. The whale-boat belonged to Meringe Plantation on the island of Ysabel. Eleven contract labourers, Malaita men and bushmen at that, had decided to run away. Being bushmen, they knew nothing of salt water nor of the way of a boat in the sea. So they persuaded two natives of San Cristoval, salt-water men, to run away with them. It served the San Cristoval men right. They should have known better. When they had safely navigated the stolen boat to Malaita, they had their heads hacked off for their pains. It was this boat and gear that Captain Jansen had recovered.

Not for nothing have I journeyed all the way to the Solomons. At last I have seen Charmian's proud spirit humbled and her imperious queendom of femininity dragged in the dust. It happened at Langa Langa, ashore, on the manufactured island which one cannot see for the houses. Here, surrounded by hundreds of unblushing naked men, women, and children, we wandered about and saw the sights. We had our revolvers strapped on, and the boat's crew, fully armed, lay at the oars, stern in ; but the lesson of the man-of-war was too recent for us to apprehend trouble. We walked about everywhere and saw everything until at last we approached a large tree trunk that served as a bridge across a shallow estuary. The blacks formed a wall in front of us and refused to let us pass. We wanted to know why we were stopped. The blacks said we could go on. We misunderstood, and started. Explanations became more definite. Captain Jansen and I, being men, could go on. But no Mary was allowed to wade around that bridge, much less cross it. "Mary" is *bêche de mer* for woman. Charmian was a Mary. To her the bridge was *tambo*, which is the native for taboo. Ah, how my chest expanded ! At last my manhood was vindicated. In truth I belonged to the lordly sex. Charmian could trapse along at our heels, but we were MEN, and we could go right over that bridge while she would have to go around by whale-boat.

Now I should not care to be misunderstood by what follows ; but it is a matter of common knowledge in the Solomons that attacks of fever are often brought on by shock.   Inside half an hour after Charmian had been refused the right of way, she was being rushed aboard the *Minota*, packed in blankets, and dosed with quinine.   I don't know what kind of shock had happened to Wada and Nakata, but at any rate they were down with fever as well.   The Solomons might be healthfuller.

Also, during the attack of fever, Charmian developed a Solomon sore.   It was the last straw. Every one on the *Snark* had been afflicted except her.   I had thought that I was going to lose my foot at the ankle by one exceptionally malignant boring ulcer.   Henry and Tehei, the Tahitian sailors, had had numbers of them.   Wada had been able to count his by the score.   Nakata had had single ones three inches in length.   Martin had been quite certain that necrosis of his shin-bone had set in from the roots of the amazing colony he elected to cultivate in that locality. But Charmian had escaped.   Out of her long immunity had been bred a contempt for the rest of us.   Her ego was flattered to such an extent that one day she shyly informed me that it was all a matter of pureness of blood.   Since all the rest of us cultivated the sores, and since she did not— well, anyway, hers was the size of a silver dollar, and the pureness of her blood enabled her to cure it after several weeks of strenuous nursing.   She pins her faith to corrosive sublimate.   Martin swears by iodoform.   Henry uses lime-juice un-diluted.   And I believe that when corrosive sublimate is slow in taking hold, alternate dressings of peroxide of hydrogen are just the thing.   There are white men in the Solomons who stake all upon boracic acid, and others who are prejudiced in favour of lysol. I also have the weakness of a panacea. It is California. I defy any man to get a Solomon Island sore in California.

We ran down the lagoon from Langa Langa, between mangrove swamps, through passages scarcely wider than the *Minota*, and past the reef villages of Kaloka and Auki. Like the founders of Venice, these salt-water men were originally refugees from the mainland. Too weak to hold their own in the bush, survivors of village massacres, they fled to the sand-banks of the lagoon. These sand-banks they built up into islands. They were compelled to seek their provender from the sea, and in time they became salt-water men. They learned the ways of the fish and the shell-fish, and they invented hooks and lines, nets and fish-traps. They developed canoe-bodies. Unable to walk about, spending all their time in the canoes, they became thick-armed and broad-shouldered, with narrow waists and frail spindly legs. Controlling the sea-coast, they became wealthy, trade with the interior passing largely through their hands. But perpetual enmity exists between them and the bushmen. Practically their only truces are on market-days, which occur at stated intervals, usually twice a week. The bushwomen and the salt-water women do the bartering. Back in the bush, a hundred yards away, fully armed, lurk the bushmen, while to seaward, in the canoes, are the salt-water men. There are very rare instances of the market-day truces being broken. The bushmen like their fish too well, while the salt-water men have an organic craving for the vegetables they cannot grow on their crowded islets.

Thirty miles from Langa Langa brought us to the passage between Bassakanna Island and the mainland. Here, at nightfall, the wind left us, and all night, with the whale-boat towing ahead and the crew on board sweating at the sweeps, we strove to win through. But the tide was against us. At midnight, midway in the passage, we came up with the *Eugenie*, a big recruiting schooner, towing with two whale-boats. Her skipper, Captain Keller, a sturdy young German of twenty-two, came on board for a "gam," and the latest news of Malaita was swapped back and forth. He had been in luck, having gathered in twenty recruits at the village of Fiu. While lying there, one of the customary courageous killings had taken place. The murdered boy was what is called a salt-water bushman—that is, a salt-water man who is half bushman and who lives by the sea but does not live on an islet. Three bushmen came down to this man where he was working in his garden. They behaved in friendly fashion, and after a time suggested *kai-kai*. *Kai-kai* means food. He built a fire and started to boil some taro. While bending over the pot, one of the bushmen shot him through the head. He fell into the flames, whereupon they thrust a spear through his stomach, turned it around, and broke it off.

"My word," said Captain Keller, "I don't want ever to be shot with a Snider. Spread! You could drive a horse and carriage through that hole in his head."

Another recent courageous killing I heard of on Malaita was that of an old man.   A bush chief had died a natural death.   Now the bushmen don't believe in natural deaths.   No one was ever known to die a natural death.   The only way to die is by bullet, tomahawk, or spear thrust.   When a man dies in any other way, it is a clear case of having been charmed to death.   When the bush chief died naturally, his tribe placed the guilt on a certain family.   Since it did not matter which one of the family was killed, they selected this old man who lived by himself.   This would make it easy.   Furthermore, he possessed no Snider.   Also, he was blind.   The old fellow got an inkling of what was coming and laid in a large supply of arrows.   Three brave warriors, each with a Snider, came down upon him in the night-time.   All night they fought valiantly with him. Whenever they moved in the bush and made a noise or a rustle, he discharged an arrow in that direction.   In the morning, when his last arrow was gone, the three heroes crept up to him and blew his brains out.

Morning found us still vainly toiling through the passage.   At last, in despair, we turned tail, ran out to sea, and sailed clear round Bassakanna to our objective, Malu.   The anchorage at Malu was very good, but it lay between the shore and an ugly reef, and while easy to enter, it was difficult to leave.   The direction of the southeast trade necessitated a beat to windward ; the point of the reef was widespread and shallow ; while a current bore down at all times upon the point.

Mr. Caulfeild, the missionary at Malu, arrived

in his whale-boat from a trip down the coast.   A slender, delicate man he was, enthusiastic in his work, level-headed and practical, a true twentieth-century soldier of the Lord.   When he came down to this station on Malaita, as he said, he agreed to come for six months.   He further agreed that if he were alive at the end of that time, he would continue on.   Six years had passed and he was still continuing on.   Nevertheless he was justified in his doubt as to living longer than six months.   Three missionaries had preceded him on Malaita, and in less than that time two had died of fever and the third had gone home a wreck.

" What murder are you talking about ? " he asked suddenly, in the midst of a confused conversation with Captain Jansen.

Captain Jansen explained.

" Oh, that's not the one I have reference to," quoth Mr. Caulfeild.   " That's old already.   It happened two weeks ago."

It was here at Malu that I atoned for all the exulting and gloating I had been guilty of over the Solomon sore Charmian had collected at Langa Langa.   Mr. Caulfeild was indirectly responsible for my atonement.   He presented us with a chicken, which I pursued into the bush with a rifle.   My intention was to clip off its head.   I succeeded, but in doing so fell over a log and barked my shin.   Result : three Solomon sores.   This made five all together that were adorning my person.   Also, Captain Jansen and Nakata had caught *gari-gari*.   Literally translated, *gari-gari* is scratch-scratch.   But translation was not necessary for the rest of us.   The skipper's and Nakata's gymnastics served as a translation without words.

(No, the Solomon Islands are not as healthy as they might be. I am writing this article on the island of Ysabel, where we have taken the *Snark* to careen and clean her copper. I got over my last attack of fever this morning, and I have had only one free day between attacks. Charmian's are two weeks apart. Wada is a wreck from fever. Last night he showed all the symptoms of coming down with pneumonia. Henry, a strapping giant of a Tahitian, just up from his last dose of fever, is dragging around the deck like a last year's crab-apple. Both he and Tehei have accumulated a praiseworthy display of Solomon sores. Also, they have caught a new form of *gari-gari*, a sort of vegetable poisoning like poison oak or poison ivy. But they are not unique in this. A number of days ago Charmian, Martin, and I went pigeon-shooting on a small island, and we have had a foretaste of eternal torment ever since. Also, on that small island, Martin cut the soles of his feet to ribbons on the coral while chasing a shark—at least, so he says, but from the glimpse I caught of him I thought it was the other way about. The coral-cuts have all become Solomon sores. Before my last fever I knocked the skin off my knuckles while heaving on a line, and I now have three fresh sores. And poor Nakata! For three weeks he has been unable to sit down. He sat down yesterday for the first time, and managed to stay down for fifteen minutes. He says cheerfully that he expects to be cured of his *gari-gari* in another month.

Furthermore, his *gari-gari*, from too enthusiastic scratch-scratching, has furnished footholds for countless Solomon sores. Still furthermore, he has just come down with his seventh attack of fever. If I were a king, the worst punishment I could inflict on my enemies would be to banish them to the Solomons. On second thought, king or no king, I don't think I'd have the heart to do it.)

Recruiting plantation labourers on a small, narrow yacht, built for harbour sailing, is not any too nice. The decks swarm with recruits and their families. The main cabin is packed with them. At night they sleep there. The only entrance to our tiny cabin is through the main cabin, and we jam our way through them or walk over them. Nor is this nice. One and all, they are afflicted with every form of malignant skin disease. Some have ringworm, others have *bukua*. This latter is caused by a vegetable parasite that invades the skin and eats it away. The itching is intolerable. The afflicted ones scratch until the air is filled with fine dry flakes. Then there are yaws and many other skin ulcerations. Men come aboard with Solomon sores in their feet so large that they can walk only on their toes, or with holes in their legs so terrible that a fist could be thrust in to the bone. Blood-poisoning is very frequent, and Captain Jansen, with sheath-knife and sail needle, operates lavishly on one and all. No matter how desperate the situation, after opening and cleansing, he claps on a poultice of sea-biscuit soaked in water. Whenever we see a particularly horrible case, we retire to a corner and deluge our own sores with corrosive sublimate. And so we live and eat and sleep on the *Minota*, taking our chance and " pretending it is good."

At Suava, another artificial island, I had a second crow over Charmian. A big fella marster belong Suava (which means the high chief of Suava) came on board. But first he sent an emissary to Captain Jansen for a fathom of calico with which to cover his royal nakedness. Meanwhile he lingered in the canoe alongside. The regal dirt on his chest I swear was half an inch thick, while it was a good wager that the underneath layers were anywhere from ten to twenty years of age. He sent his emissary on board again, who explained that the big fella marster belong Suava was condescendingly willing enough to shake hands with Captain Jansen and me and cadge a stick or so of trade tobacco, but that nevertheless his high-born soul was still at so lofty an altitude that it could not sink itself to such a depth of degradation as to shake hands with a mere female woman. Poor Charmian! Since her Malaita experiences she has become a changed woman. Her meekness and humbleness are appallingly becoming, and I should not be surprised, when we return to civilization and stroll along a sidewalk, to see her take her station, with bowed head, a yard in the rear.

Nothing much happened at Suava. Bichu, the native cook, deserted. The *Minota* dragged anchor. It blew heavy squalls of wind and rain. The mate, Mr. Jacobsen, and Wada were prostrated with fever. Our Solomon sores increased and multiplied. And the cockroaches on board held a combined Fourth of July and Coronation Parade. They selected midnight for the time, and our tiny cabin for the place. They were from two to three inches long; there were hundreds of them, and they walked all over us. When we attempted to pursue them, they left solid footing, rose up in the air, and fluttered about like humming-birds. They were much larger than ours on the *Snark*. But ours are young yet, and haven't had a chance to grow. Also, the *Snark* has centipedes, big ones, six inches long. We kill them occasionally, usually in Charmian's bunk. I've been bitten twice by them, both times foully, while I was asleep. But poor Martin had worse luck. After being sick in bed for three weeks, the first day he sat up he sat down on one. Sometimes I think they are the wisest who never go to Carcassonne.

Later on we returned to Malu, picked up seven recruits, hove up anchor, and started to beat out the treacherous entrance. The wind was chopping about, the current upon the ugly point of reef setting strong. Just as we were on the verge of clearing it and gaining open sea, the wind broke off four points. The *Minota* attempted to go about, but missed stays. Two of her anchors had been lost at Tulagi. Her one remaining anchor was let go. Chain was let out to give it a hold on the coral. Her fin keel struck bottom, and her main topmast lurched and shivered as if about to come down upon our heads. She fetched up on the slack of the anchors at the moment a big comber smashed her shoreward.

The chain parted. It was our only anchor. The *Minota* swung around on her heel and drove headlong into the breakers.

Bedlam reigned. All the recruits below, bushmen and afraid of the sea, dashed panic-stricken on deck and got in everybody's way. At the same time the boat's crew made a rush for the rifles. They knew what going ashore on Malaita meant—one hand for the ship and the other hand to fight off the natives. What they held on with I don't know, and they needed to hold on as the *Minota* lifted, rolled, and pounded on the coral. The bushmen clung in the rigging, too witless to watch out for the topmast. The whale-boat was run out with a tow-line endeavouring in a puny way to prevent the *Minota* from being flung farther in toward the reef, while Captain Jansen and the mate, the latter pallid and weak with fever, were resurrecting a scrap-anchor from out the ballast and rigging up a stock for it. Mr. Caulfeild, with his mission boys, arrived in his whale-boat to help.

When the *Minota* first struck, there was not a canoe in sight ; but like vultures circling down out of the blue, canoes began to arrive from every quarter. The boat's crew, with rifles at the ready, kept them lined up a hundred feet away with a promise of death if they ventured nearer. And there they clung, a hundred feet away, black and ominous, crowded with men, holding their canoes with their paddles on the perilous edge of the breaking surf. In the meantime the bushmen were flocking down from the hills, armed with spears, Sniders, arrows, and clubs, until the beach was massed with them. To complicate matters, at least ten of our recruits had been enlisted from the very bushmen ashore who were waiting hungrily for the loot of the tobacco and trade goods and all that we had on board.

The *Minota* was honestly built, which is the first essential for any boat that is pounding on a reef. Some idea of what she endured may be gained from the fact that in the first twenty-four hours she parted two anchor-chains and eight hawsers. Our boat's crew was kept busy diving for the anchors and bending new lines. There were times when she parted the chains reinforced with hawsers. And yet she held together. Tree trunks were brought from ashore and worked under her to save her keel and bilges, but the trunks were gnawed and splintered and the ropes that held them frayed to fragments, and still she pounded and held together. But we were luckier than the *Ivanhoe*, a big recruiting schooner, which had gone ashore on Malaita several months previously and been promptly rushed by the natives. The captain and crew succeeded in getting away in the whale-boats, and the bushmen and salt-water men looted her clean of everything portable.

Squall after squall, driving wind and blinding rain, smote the *Minota*, while a heavier sea was making. The *Eugenie* lay at anchor five miles to windward, but she was behind a point of land and could not know of our mishap. At Captain Jansen's suggestion, I wrote a note to Captain Keller, asking him to bring extra anchors and

gear to our aid. But not a canoe could be persuaded to carry the letter. I offered half a case
of tobacco, but the blacks grinned and held their
canoes bow-on to the breaking seas. A half a
case of tobacco was worth three pounds. In two
hours, even against the strong wind and sea, a
man could have carried the letter and received in
payment what he would have laboured half a
year for on a plantation. I managed to get into
a canoe and paddle out to where Mr. Caulfeild
was running an anchor with his whale-boat. My
idea was that he would have more influence over
the natives. He called the canoes up to him,
and a score of them clustered around and heard
the offer of half a case of tobacco. No one
spoke.

" I know what you think," the missionary called
out to them. " You think plenty tobacco on the
schooner and you're going to get it. I tell you
plenty rifles on schooner. You no get tobacco,
you get bullets."

At last, one man, alone in a small canoe, took
the letter and started. Waiting for relief, work
went on steadily on the *Minota*. Her water-tanks
were emptied, and spars, sails, and ballast started
shoreward. There were lively times on board
when the *Minota* rolled one bilge down and then
the other, a score of men leaping for life and legs
as the trade-boxes, booms, and eighty-pound
pigs of iron ballast rushed across from rail to rail
and back again. The poor pretty harbour yacht !
Her decks and running rigging were a raffle.
Down below everything was disrupted. The
cabin floor had been torn up to get at the ballast,

and rusty bilge-water swashed and splashed. A bushel of limes, in a mess of flour and water, charged about like so many sticky dumplings escaped from a half-cooked stew. In the inner cabin, Nakata kept guard over our rifles and ammunition.

Three hours from the time our messenger started, a whale-boat, pressing along under a huge spread of canvas, broke through the thick of a shrieking squall to windward. It was Captain Keller, wet with rain and spray, a revolver in his belt, his boat's crew fully armed, anchors and hawsers heaped high amidships, coming as fast as wind could drive—the white man, the inevitable white man, coming to a white man's rescue.

The vulture line of canoes that had waited so long broke and disappeared as quickly as it had formed. The corpse was not dead after all. We now had three whale-boats, two plying steadily between the vessel and shore, the other kept busy running out anchors, rebending parted hawsers, and recovering the lost anchors. Later in the afternoon, after a consultation, in which we took into consideration that a number of our boat's crew, as well as ten of the recruits, belonged to this place, we disarmed the boat's crew. This, incidently, gave them both hands free to work for the vessel. The rifles were put in the charge of five of Mr. Caulfeild's mission boys. And down below in the wreck of the cabin the missionary and his converts prayed to God to save the *Minota*. It was an impressive scene : the unarmed man of God praying with cloudless faith, his savage followers leaning on their rifles and mumbling amens. The cabin walls reeled about them. The vessel lifted and smashed upon the coral with every sea. From on deck came the shouts of men heaving and toiling, praying, in another fashion, with purposeful will and strength of arm.

That night Mr. Caulfeild brought off a warning. One of our recruits had a price on his head of fifty fathoms of shell-money and forty pigs. Baffled in their desire to capture the vessel, the bushmen decided to get the head of the man. When killing begins, there is no telling where it will end, so Captain Jansen armed a whale-boat and rowed in to the edge of the beach. Ugi, one of his boat's crew, stood up and orated for him. Ugi was excited. Captain Jansen's warning that any canoe sighted that night would be pumped full of lead, Ugi turned into a bellicose declaration of war, which wound up with a peroration somewhat to the following effect : "You kill my captain, I drink his blood and die with him ! "

The bushmen contented themselves with burning an unoccupied mission house, and sneaked back to the bush. The next day the *Eugenie* sailed in and dropped anchor. Three days and two nights the *Minota* pounded on the reef ; but she held together, and the shell of her was pulled off at last and anchored in smooth water. There we said good-bye to her and all on board, and sailed away on the *Eugenie*, bound for Florida Island.[1]

[1] To point out that we of the *Snark* are not a crowd of weaklings, which might be concluded from our divers afflic.

tions, I quote the following, which I gleaned verbatim from the *Eugenie's* log and which may be considered as a sample of Solomon Islands cruising :

Ulava, Thursday, March 12, 1908.
Boat went ashore in the morning. Got two loads ivory nut, 4000 copra. Skipper down with fever.

Ulava, Friday, March 13, 1908.
Buying nuts from bushmen, 1½ ton. Mate and skipper down with fever.

Ulava, Saturday, March 14, 1908.
At noon hove up and proceeded with a very light E.N.E. wind for Ngora-Ngora. Anchored in 8 fathoms—shell and coral. Mate down with fever.

Ngora-Ngora, Sunday, March 15, 1908.
At daybreak found that the boy Bagua had died during the night, on dysentery. He was about 14 days sick. At sunset, big N.W. squall. (Second anchor ready) Lasting one hour and 30 minutes.

At sea, Monday, March 16, 1908.
Set course for Sikiana at 4 P.M. Wind broke off. Heavy squalls during the night. Skipper down on dysentery, also one man.

At sea, Tuesday, March 17, 1908.
Skipper and 2 crew down on dysentery. Mate fever.

At sea, Wednesday, March 18, 1908.
Big sea. Lee-rail under water all the time. Ship under reefed mainsail, staysail, and inner jib. Skipper and 3 men dysentery. Mate fever.

At sea, Thursday, March 19, 1908.
Too thick to see anything. Blowing a gale all the time. Pump plugged up and bailing with buckets. Skipper and five boys down on dysentery.

At sea, Friday, March 20, 1908.
During night squalls with hurricane force. Skipper and six men down on dysentery.

At sea, Saturday, March 21, 1908.
Turned back from Sikiana. Squalls all day with heavy rain and sea. Skipper and best part of crew on dysentery. Mate fever.

And so, day by day, with the majority of all on board prostrated, the *Eugenie's* log goes on. The only variety occurred on March 31, when the mate came down with dysentery and the skipper was floored by fever.

CHAPTER XVI

BÊCHE DE MER ENGLISH

GIVEN a number of white traders, a wide area of land, and scores of savage languages and dialects, the result will be that the traders will manufacture a totally new, unscientific, but perfectly adequate, language. This the traders did when they invented the Chinook lingo for use over British Columbia, Alaska, and the Northwest Territory. So with the lingo of the Kroo-boys of Africa, the pigeon English of the Far East, and the bêche de mer of the westerly portion of the South Seas. This latter is often called pigeon English, but pigeon English it certainly is not. To show how totally different it is, mention need be made only of the fact that the classic *piecee* of China has no place in it.

There was once a sea captain who needed a dusky potentate down in his cabin. The potentate was on deck. The captain's command to the Chinese steward was : " Hey, boy, you go top-side catchee one piecee king." Had the steward been a New Hebridean or a Solomon islander, the command would have been : " Hey, you fella boy, go look 'm eye belong you along deck, bring 'm me fella one big fella marster belong bla k man."

It was the first white men who ventured through Melanesia after the early explorers, who developed bêche de mer English—men such as the bêche de mer fishermen, the sandalwood traders, the pearl hunters, and the labour recruiters. In the Solomons, for instance, scores of languages and dialects are spoken. Unhappy the trader who tried to learn them all; for in the next group to which he might wander he would find scores of additional tongues. A common language was necessary—a language so simple that a child could learn it, with a vocabulary as limited as the intelligence of the savages upon whom it was to be used. The traders did not reason this out. Bêche de mer English was the product of conditions and circumstances. Function precedes organ; and the need for a universal Melanesian lingo preceded bêche de mer English. Bêche de mer was purely fortuitous, but it was fortuitous in the deterministic way. Also, from the fact that out of the need the lingo arose, bêche de mer English is a splendid argument for the Esperanto enthusiasts.

A limited vocabulary means that each word shall be overworked. Thus, *fella*, in bêche de mer, means all that *piecee* does and quite a bit more, and is used continually in every possible connection. Another overworked word is *belong*. Nothing stands alone. Everything is related. The thing desired is indicated by its relationship with other things. A primitive vocabulary means primitive expression, thus, the continuance of rain is expressed as *rain he stop*. *Sun he come up* cannot possibly be misunderstood, while the phrase-structure itself can be used without mental exertion in ten thousand different ways, as, for instance, a native who desires to tell you that there are fish in the water and who says *fish he stop*. It was while trading on Ysabel island that I learned the excellence of this usage. I wanted two or three pairs of the large clam-shells (measuring three feet across), but I did not want the meat inside. Also, I wanted the meat of some of the smaller clams to make a chowder. My instruction to the natives finally ripened into the following : "You fella bring me fella big fella clam—*kai-kai* he no stop, he walk about. You fella bring me fella small fella clam—*kai-kai* he stop."

Kai-kai is the Polynesian for *food, meat, eating,* and *to eat ;* but it would be hard to say whether it was introduced into Melanesia by the sandal-wood traders or by the Polynesian westward drift. *Walk about* is a quaint phrase. Thus, if one orders a Solomon sailor to put a tackle on a boom, he will suggest, "That fella boom he walk about too much." And if the said sailor asks for shore liberty, he will state that it is his desire to walk about. Or if said sailor be seasick, he will explain his condition by stating, "Belly belong me walk about too much."

Too much, by the way, does not indicate anything excessive. It is merely the simple superlative. Thus, if a native is asked the distance to a certain village, his answer will be one of these four : "Close up"; "long way little bit"; "long way big bit"; or "long way too much." *Long way too much* does not mean that one cannot walk to the village ; it means that he will have to walk farther than if the village were a long way big bit.

Gammon is to lie, to exaggerate, to joke. *Mary* is a woman. Any woman is a Mary. All women are Marys. Doubtlessly the first dim white adventurer whimsically called a native woman Mary, and of similar birth must have been many other words in bêche de mer. The white men were all seamen, and so *capsize* and *sing out* were introduced into the lingo. One would not tell a Melanesian cook to empty the dish-water, but he would tell him to capsize it. To *sing out* is to cry loudly, to call out, or merely to speak. *Sing-sing* is a song. The native Christian does not think of God calling for Adam in the Garden of Eden ; in the native's mind, God sings out for Adam.

Savvee or *catchee* are practically the only words which have been introduced straight from pigeon English. Of course, *pickaninny* has happened along, but some of its uses are delicious. Having bought a fowl from a native in a canoe, the native asked me if I wanted " Pickaninny stop along him fella." It was not until he showed me a handful of hen's eggs that I understood his meaning. *My word*, as an exclamation with a thousand significances, could have arrived from nowhere else than Old England. A paddle, a sweep, or an oar, is called *washee*, and *washee* is also the verb.

Here is a letter, dictated by one Peter, a native trader at Santa Anna, and addressed to his employer. Harry, the schooner captain, started to write the letter, but was stopped by Peter at the end of the second sentence. Thereafter the letter runs in Peter's own words, for Peter was afraid that Harry gammoned too much, and he wanted the straight story of his needs to go to head-quarters.

"SANTA ANNA

"Trader Peter has worked 12 months for your firm and has not received any pay yet. He hereby wants £12." (At this point Peter began dicta-tion). "Harry he gammon along him all the time too much. I like him 6 tin biscuit, 4 bag rice, 24 tin bullamacow. Me like him 2 rifle, me savvee look out along boat, some place me go man he no good, he *kai-kai* along me.

"PETER."

Bullamacow means tinned beef. This word was corrupted from the English language by the Samoans, and from them learned by the traders, who carried it along with them into Melanesia. Captain Cook and the other early navigators made a practice of introducing seeds, plants, and do-mestic animals amongst the natives. It was at Samoa that one such navigator landed a bull and a cow. "This is a bull and cow," said he to the Samoans. They thought he was giving the name of the breed, and from that day to this, beef on the hoof and beef in the tin is called *bullamacow*.

A Solomon islander cannot say *fence*, so, in bêche de mer, it becomes *fennis*; store is *sittore*, and box is *bokkis*. Just now the fashion in chests, which are known as boxes, is to have a bell arrangement on the lock so that the box cannot be opened without sounding an alarm. A box so equipped is not spoken of as a mere box, but as the *bokkis belong bell*.

Fright is the bêche de mer for fear. If a native appears timid and one asks him the cause, he is liable to hear in reply : " Me fright along you too much." Or the native may be *fright* along storm, or wild bush, or haunted places. *Cross* covers every form of anger. A man may be cross at one when he is feeling only petulant ; or he may be cross when he is seeking to chop off your head and make a stew out of you. A recruit, after having toiled three years on a plantation, was returned to his own village on Malaita. He was clad in all kinds of gay and sportive garments. On his head was a top-hat. He possessed a trade-box full of calico, beads, porpoise-teeth, and tobacco. Hardly was the anchor down, when the villagers were on board. The recruit looked anxiously for his own relatives, but none was to be seen. One of the natives took the pipe out of his mouth. Another confiscated the strings of beads from around his neck. A third relieved him of his gaudy loin-cloth, and a fourth tried on the top-hat and omitted to return it. Finally, one of them took his trade-box, which represented three years' toil, and dropped it into a canoe alongside. " That fella belong you ? " the captain asked the recruit, referring to the thief. " No belong me," was the answer. " Then why in Jericho do you let him take the box ? " the captain demanded indignantly. Quoth the recruit, " Me speak along him, say bokkis he stop, that fella he cross along me "—which was the recruit's way of saying that the other man would murder him. God's wrath, when He sent the Flood, was merely a case of being cross along mankind.

What name? is the great interrogation of bêche de mer. It all depends on how it is uttered. It may mean : What is your business ? What do you mean by this outrageous conduct ? What do you want ? What is the thing you are after ? You had best watch out ; I demand an explanation ; and a few hundred other things. Call a native out of his house in the middle of the night, and he is likely to demand, " What name you sing out along me ? "

Imagine the predicament of the Germans on the plantations of Bougainville Island, who are compelled to learn bêche de mer English in order to handle the native labourers. It is to them an unscientific polyglot, and there are no text-books by which to study it. It is a source of unholy delight to the other white planters and traders to hear the German wrestling stolidly with the circumlocutions and short-cuts of a language that has no grammar and no dictionary.

Some years ago large numbers of Solomon islanders were recruited to labour on the sugar plantations of Queensland. A missionary urged one of the labourers, who was a convert, to get up and preach a sermon to a shipload of Solomon islanders who had just arrived. He chose for his subject the Fall of Man, and the address he gave became a classic in all Australasia. It proceeded somewhat in the following manner :

" Altogether you boy belong Solomons you no savvee white man. Me fella me savvee him. Me fella me savvee talk along white man.

" Before long time altogether no place he stop. God big fella marster belong white man, him fella He make 'm altogether. God big fella marster belong white man, He make 'm big fella garden. He good fella too much. Along garden plenty yam he stop, plenty cocoanut, plenty taro, plenty *kumara* (sweet potatoes), altogether good fella *kai-kai* too much.

" Bimeby God big fella marster belong white man He make 'm one fella man and put 'm along garden belong Him. He call 'm this fella man Adam. He name belong him. He put him this fella man Adam along garden, and He speak, ' This fella garden he belong you.' And He look 'm this fella Adam he walk about too much. Him fella Adam all the same sick ; he no savvee *kai-kai* ; he walk about all the time. And God He no savvee. God big fella marster belong white man, He scratch 'm head belong Him. God say : ' What name ? Me no savvee what name this fella Adam he want.'

" Bimeby God He scratch 'm head belong Him too much, and speak : ' Me fella me savvee, him fella Adam him want 'm Mary.' So He make Adam he go asleep, He take one fella bone belong him, and He make 'm one fella Mary along bone. He call him this fella Mary, Eve. He give 'm this fella Eve along Adam, and He speak along him fella Adam : ' Close up altogether along this fella garden belong you two fella. One fella tree he tambo (taboo) along you altogether. This fella tree belong apple.'

" So Adam Eve two fella stop along garden, and they two fella have 'm good time too much.

Bimeby, one day, Eve she come along Adam, and she speak, 'More good you me two fella we eat 'm this fella apple.' Adam he speak, 'No,' and Eve she speak, 'What name you no like 'm me?' And Adam he speak, 'Me like 'm you too much, but me fright along God.' And Eve she speak, 'Gammon! What name? God He no savvee look along us two fella all 'm time. God big fella marster, He gammon along you.' But Adam he speak, 'No.' But Eve she talk, talk, talk, allee time—allee same Mary she talk along boy along Queensland and make 'm trouble along boy. And bimeby Adam he tired too much, and he speak, 'All right.' So these two fella they go eat 'm. When they finish eat 'm, my word, they fright like hell, and they go hide along scrub.

"And God He come walk about along garden, and He sing out, 'Adam!' Adam he no speak. He too much fright. My word! And God He sing out, 'Adam!' And Adam he speak, 'You call 'm me?' God He speak, 'Me call 'm you too much.' Adam he speak, 'Me sleep strong fella too much.' And God He speak, 'You been eat 'm this fella apple.' Adam he speak, 'No, me no been eat 'm.' God He speak. 'What name you gammon along me? You been eat 'm.' And Adam he speak, 'Yes, me been eat 'm.'

"And God big fella marster He cross along Adam Eve two fella too much, and He speak, 'You two fella finish along me altogether. You go catch 'm bokkis (box) belong you, and get to hell along scrub.'

"So Adam Eve these two fella go along scrub. And God He make 'm one big fennis (fence) all around garden and He put 'm one fella marster belong God along fennis. And He give this fella marster belong God one big fella musket, and He speak, ' S'pose you look 'm these two fella Adam Eve, you shoot 'm plenty too much.' "

CHAPTER XVII

THE AMATEUR M.D.

WHEN we sailed from San Francisco on the *Snark* I knew as much about sickness as the Admiral of the Swiss Navy knows about salt water. And here, at the start, let me advise any one who meditates going to out-of-the-way tropic places. Go to a first-class druggist— the sort that have specialists on their salary list who know everything. Talk the matter over with such an one. Note carefully all that he says. Have a list made of all that he recommends. Write out a cheque for the total cost, and tear it up.

I wish I had done the same. I should have been far wiser, I know now, if I had bought one of those ready-made, self-acting, fool-proof medicine chests such as are favoured by fourth-rate ship-masters. In such a chest each bottle has a number. On the inside of the lid is placed a simple table of directions: No. 1, toothache; No. 2, smallpox; No. 3, stomachache; No. 4, cholera; No. 5, rheumatism; and so on, through the list of human ills. And I might have used it as did a certain venerable skipper, who, when No. 3 was empty, mixed a dose from No. 1 and

No. 2, or, when No. 7 was all gone, dosed his crew with 4 and 3 till 3 gave out, when he used 5 and 2.

So far, with the exception of corrosive sublimate (which was recommended as an antiseptic in surgical operations, and which I have not yet used for that purpose), my medicine-chest has been useless. It has been worse than useless, for it has occupied much space which I could have used to advantage.

With my surgical instruments it is different. While I have not yet had serious use for them, I do not regret the space they occupy. The thought of them makes me feel good. They are so much life insurance, only, fairer than that last grim game, one is not supposed to die in order to win. Of course, I don't know how to use them, and what I don't know about surgery would set up a dozen quacks in prosperous practice. But needs must when the devil drives, and we of the *Snark* have no warning when the devil may take it into his head to drive, ay, even a thousand miles from land and twenty days from the nearest port.

I did not know anything about dentistry, but a friend fitted me out with forceps and similar weapons, and in Honolulu I picked up a book upon teeth. Also, in that sub-tropical city I managed to get hold of a skull, from which I extracted the teeth swiftly and painlessly. Thus equipped, I was ready, though not exactly eager, to tackle any tooth that got in my way. It was in Nuku-hiva, in the Marquesas, that my first case presented itself in the shape of a little, old Chinese. The first thing I did was to get the buck fever, and I leave it to any fair-minded person if buck fever, with its attendant heart-palpitations and arm-tremblings, is the right condition for a man to be in who is endeavouring to pose as an old hand at the business. I did not fool the aged Chinaman. He was as frightened as I and a bit more shaky. I almost forgot to be frightened in the fear that he would bolt. I swear, if he had tried to, that I would have tripped him up and sat on him until calmness and reason returned.

I wanted that tooth. Also, Martin wanted a snap-shot of me getting it. Likewise Charmian got her camera. Then the procession started. We were stopping at what had been the club-house when Stevenson was in the Marquesas on the *Casco*. On the veranda, where he had passed so many pleasant hours, the light was not good—for snapshots, I mean. I led on into the garden, a chair in one hand, the other hand filled with forceps of various sorts, my knees knocking together disgracefully. The poor old Chinaman came second, and he was shaking, too. Charmian and Martin brought up the rear, armed with kodaks. We dived under the avocado trees, threaded our way through the cocoanut palms, and came on a spot that satisfied Martin's photographic eye.

I looked at the tooth, and then discovered that I could not remember anything about the teeth I had pulled from the skull five months previously. Did it have one prong? two prongs? or three prongs? What was left of the part that showed appeared very crumbly, and I knew that I should have to take hold of the tooth deep down in the gum. It was very necessary that I should know how many prongs that tooth had. Back to the house I went for the book on teeth. The poor old victim looked like photographs I had seen of fellow-countrymen of his, criminals, on their knees, waiting the stroke of the beheading sword.

"Don't let him get away," I cautioned to Martin. "I want that tooth."

"I sure won't," he replied with enthusiasm, from behind his camera. "I want that photo-graph."

For the first time I felt sorry for the Chinaman. Though the book did not tell me anything about pulling teeth, it was all right, for on one page I found drawings of all the teeth, including their prongs and how they were set in the jaw. Then came the pursuit of the forceps. I had seven pairs, but was in doubt as to which pair I should use. I did not want any mistake. As I turned the hardware over with rattle and clang, the poor victim began to lose his grip and to turn a greenish yellow around the gills. He complained about the sun, but that was necessary for the photo-graph, and he had to stand it. I fitted the forceps around the tooth, and the patient shivered and began to wilt.

"Ready ? " I called to Martin.

"All ready," he answered.

I gave a pull. Ye gods ! The tooth was loose ! Out it came on the instant. I was jubilant as I held it aloft in the forceps.

"Put it back, please, oh, put it back," Martin pleaded. "You were too quick for me."

And the poor old Chinaman sat there while I

put the tooth back and pulled over. Martin
snapped the camera. The deed was done.
Elation ? Pride ? No hunter was ever prouder
of his first pronged buck than I was of that three-
pronged tooth. I did it ! I did it ! With my
own hands and a pair of forceps I did it, to say
nothing of the forgotten memories of the dead
man's skull.

My next case was a Tahitian sailor. He was a
small man, in a state of collapse from long days
and nights of jumping toothache. I lanced the
gums first. I didn't know how to lance them, but
I lanced them just the same. It was a long pull
and a strong pull. The man was a hero. He
groaned and moaned, and I thought he was going
to faint. But he kept his mouth open and let
me pull. And then it came.

After that I was ready to meet all comers—just
the proper state of mind for a Waterloo. And
it came. Its name was Tomi. He was a strapping giant of a heathen with a bad reputation.
He was addicted to deeds of violence. Among
other things he had beaten two of his wives to
death with his fists. His father and mother had
been naked cannibals. When he sat down and
I put the forceps into his mouth, he was nearly
as tall as I was standing up. Big men, prone
to violence, very often have a streak of fat in their
make-up, so I was doubtful of him. Charmian
grabbed one arm and Warren grabbed the other.
Then the tug of war began. The instant the
forceps closed down on the tooth, his jaws closed
down on the forceps. Also, both his hands flew
up and gripped my pulling hand. I held on,

and he held on. Charmian and Warren held on. We wrestled all about the shop.

It was three against one, and my hold on an aching tooth was certainly a foul one ; but in spite of the handicap he got away with us. The forceps slipped off, banging and grinding along against his upper teeth with a nerve-scraping sound. Out of his mouth flew the forceps, and he rose up in the air with a blood-curdling yell. The three of us fell back. We expected to be massacred. But that howling savage of sanguinary reputation sank back in the chair. He held his head in both his hands, and groaned and groaned and groaned. Nor would he listen to reason. I was a quack. My painless tooth-extraction was a delusion and a snare and a low advertising dodge. I was so anxious to get that tooth that I was almost ready to bribe him. But that went against my professional pride and I let him depart with the tooth still intact, the only case on record up to date of failure on my part when once I had got a grip. Since then I have never·let a tooth go by me. Only the other day I volunteered to beat up three days to windward to pull a woman missionary's tooth. I expect, before the voyage of the *Snark* is finished, to be doing bridge work and putting on gold crowns.

I don't know whether they are yaws or not—a physician in Fiji told me they were, and a missionary in the Solomons told me they were not ; but at any rate I can vouch for the fact that they are most uncomfortable. It was my luck to ship in Tahiti a French sailor, who, when we got to sea, proved to be afflicted with a vile skin disease,

The *Snark* was too small and too much of a family party to permit retaining him on board ; but perforce, until we could reach land and discharge him, it was up to me to doctor him. I read up the books and proceeded to treat him, taking care afterwards always to use a thorough antiseptic wash. When we reached Tutuila, far from getting rid of him, the port doctor declared a quarantine against him and refused to allow him ashore. But at Apia, Samoa, I managed to ship him off on a steamer to New Zealand. Here at Apia my ankles were badly bitten by mosquitoes, and I confess to having scratched the bites—as I had a thousand times before. By the time I reached the island of Savaii, a small sore had developed on the hollow of my instep. I thought it was due to chafe and to acid fumes from the hot lava over which I tramped. An application of salve would cure it—so I thought. The salve did heal it over, whereupon an astonishing inflammation set in, the new skin came off, and a larger sore was exposed. This was repeated many times. Each time new skin formed, an inflammation followed, and the circumference of the sore increased. I was puzzled and frightened. All my life my skin had been famous for its healing powers, yet here was something that would not heal. Instead, it was daily eating up more skin, while it had eaten down clear through the skin and was eating up the muscle itself.

By this time the *Snark* was at sea on her way to Fiji. I remembered the French sailor, and for the first time became seriously alarmed. Four other similar sores had appeared—or ulcers, rather, and the pain of them kept me awake at night. All my plans were made to lay up the *Snark* in Fiji and get away on the first steamer to Australia and professional M.D.'s. In the meantime, in my amateur M.D. way, I did my best. I read through all the medical works on board. Not a line nor a word could I find descriptive of my affliction. I brought common horse-sense to bear on the problem. Here were malignant and excessively active ulcers that were eating me up. There was an organic and corroding poison at work. Two things I concluded must be done. First, some agent must be found to destroy the poison. Secondly, the ulcers could not possibly heal from the outside in ; they must heal from the inside out. I decided to fight the poison with corrosive sublimate. The very name of it struck me as vicious. Talk of fighting fire with fire ! I was being consumed by a corrosive poison, and it appealed to my fancy to fight it with another corrosive poison. After several days I alternated dressings of corrosive sublimate with dressings of peroxide of hydrogen. And behold, by the time we reached Fiji four of the five ulcers were healed, while the remaining one was no bigger than a pea.

I now felt fully qualified to treat yaws. Likewise I had a wholesome respect for them. Not so the rest of the crew of the *Snark*. In their case, seeing was not believing. One and all, they had seen my dreadful predicament ; and all of them, I am convinced, had a subconscious certitude that their own superb constitutions and glorious personalities would never allow lodgment of so vile a poison in their carcasses as my anæmic constitution and mediocre personality had allowed to lodge in mine.   At Port Resolution, in the New Hebrides, Martin elected to walk barefooted in the bush and returned on board with many cuts and abrasions, especially on his shins.

"You'd better be careful," I warned him. "I'll mix up some corrosive sublimate for you to wash those cuts with.   An ounce of prevention, you know."

But Martin smiled a superior smile.   Though he did not say so, I nevertheless was given to understand that he was not as other men (I was the only man he could possibly have had reference to), and that in a couple of days his cuts would be healed.   He also read me a dissertation upon the peculiar purity of his blood and his remarkable healing powers.   I felt quite humble when he was done with me.   Evidently I was different from other men in so far as purity of blood was concerned.

Nakata, the cabin-boy, while ironing one day, mistook the calf of his leg for the ironing-block and accumulated a burn three inches in length and half an inch wide.   He, too, smiled the superior smile when I offered him corrosive sublimate and reminded him of my own cruel experience.   I was given to understand, with all due suavity and courtesy, that no matter what was the matter with my blood, his number-one, Japanese, Port-Arthur blood was all right and scornful of the festive microbe.

Wada, the cook, took part in a disastrous landing of the launch, when he had to leap overboard and fend the launch off the beach in a smashing surf. By means of shells and coral he cut his legs and feet up beautifully. I offered him the corrosive sublimate bottle. Once again I suffered the superior smile and was given to understand that his blood was the same blood that had licked Russia and was going to lick the United States some day, and that if his blood wasn't able to cure a few trifling cuts, he'd commit hari-kari in sheer disgrace.

From all of which I concluded that an amateur M.D. is without honour on his own vessel, even if he has cured himself. The rest of the crew had begun to look upon me as a sort of mild monomaniac on the question of sores and sublimate. Just because my blood was impure was no reason that I should think everybody else's was. I made no more overtures. Time and microbes were with me, and all I had to do was wait.

"I think there's some dirt in those cuts," Martin said tentatively, after several days. "I'll wash them out and then they'll be all right," he added, after I had refused to rise to the bait.

Two more days passed, but the cuts did not pass, and I caught Martin soaking his feet and legs in a pail of hot water.

"Nothing like hot water," he proclaimed enthusiastically. "It beats all the dope the doctors ever put up. These sores will be all right in the morning."

But in the morning he wore a troubled look, and I knew that the hour of my triumph approached.

"I think I *will* try some of that medicine," he announced later on in the day. "Not that I think it'll do much good," he qualified, "but I'll just give it a try anyway."

Next came the proud blood of Japan to beg medicine for its illustrious sores, while I heaped coals of fire on all their houses by explaining in minute and sympathetic detail the treatment that should be given. Nakata followed instructions implicitly, and day by day his sores grew smaller. Wada was apathetic, and cured less readily. But Martin still doubted, and because he did not cure immediately, he developed the theory that while doctor's dope was all right, it did not follow that the same kind of dope was efficacious with everybody. As for himself, corrosive sublimate had no effect. Besides, how did I know that it was the right stuff? I had had no experience. Just because I happened to get well while using it was not proof that it had played any part in the cure. There were such things as coincidences. Without doubt there was a dope that would cure the sores, and when he ran across a real doctor he would find what that dope was and get some of it.

About this time we arrived in the Solomon Islands. No physician would ever recommend the group for invalids or sanitoriums. I spent but little time there ere I really and for the first time in my life comprehended how frail and unstable is human tissue. Our first anchorage was Port Mary, on the island of Santa Anna. The one lone white man, a trader, came alongside. Tom Butler was his name, and he was a beautiful example of what the Solomons can do to a strong man. He lay in his whale-boat with the helplessness of a dying man. No smile and little intelligence illumined his face. He was a sombre death's-head, too far gone to grin. He, too, had yaws, big ones. We were compelled to drag him over the rail of the *Snark*. He said that his health was good, that he had not had the fever for some time, and that with the exception of his arm he was all right and trim. His arm appeared to be paralysed. Paralysis he rejected with scorn. He had had it before, and recovered. It was a common native disease on Santa Anna, he said, as he was helped down the companion ladder, his dead arm dropping, bump-bump, from step to step. He was certainly the ghastliest guest we ever entertained, and we've had not a few lepers and elephantiasis victims on board.

Martin inquired about yaws, for here was a man who ought to know. He certainly did know, if we could judge by his scarred arms and legs and by the live ulcers that corroded in the midst of the scars. Oh, one got used to yaws, quoth Tom Butler. They were never really serious until they had eaten deep into the flesh. Then they attacked the walls of the arteries, the arteries burst, and there was a funeral. Several of the natives had recently died that way ashore. But what did it matter? If it wasn't yaws, it was something else—in the Solomons.

I noticed that from this moment Martin displayed a swiftly increasing interest in his own yaws. Dosings with corrosive sublimate were more frequent, while, in conversation, he began to revert with growing enthusiasm to the clean climate of Kansas and all other things Kansan.

Charmian and I thought that California was a little bit of all right. Henry swore by Rapa, and Tehei staked all on Bora Bora for his own blood's sake ; while Wada and Nakata sang the sanitary pæan of Japan.

One evening, as the *Snark* worked around the southern end of the island of Ugi, looking for a reputed anchorage, a Church of England missionary, a Mr. Drew, bound in his whale-boat for the coast of San Cristoval, came alongside and stopped for dinner. Martin, his legs swathed in Red Cross bandages till they looked like a mummy's, turned the conversation upon yaws. Yes, said Mr. Drew, they were quite common in the Solomons. All white men caught them.

" And have you had them ? " Martin demanded, in the soul of him quite shocked that a Church of England missionary could possess so vulgar an affliction.

Mr. Drew nodded his head and added that not only had he had them, but at that moment he was doctoring several.

" What do you use on them ? " Martin asked like a flash.

My heart almost stood still waiting the answer. By that answer my professional medical prestige stood or fell. Martin, I could see, was quite sure it was going to fall. And then the answer—O blessed answer !

" Corrosive sublimate," said Mr. Drew.

Martin gave in handsomely, I'll admit, and I am confident that at that moment, if I had asked permission to pull one of his teeth, he would not have denied me.

All white men in the Solomons catch yaws, and every cut or abrasion practically means another yaw. Every man I met had had them, and nine out of ten had active ones. There was but one exception, a young fellow who had been in the islands five months, who had come down with fever ten days after he arrived, and who had since then been down so often with fever that he had had neither time nor opportunity for yaws.

Every one on the *Snark* except Charmian came down with yaws. Hers was the same egotism that Japan and Kansas had displayed. She ascribed her immunity to the pureness of her blood, and as the days went by she ascribed it more often and more loudly to the pureness of her blood. Privately I ascribed her immunity to the fact that, being a woman, she escaped most of the cuts and abrasions to which we hard-working men were subject in the course of working the *Snark* around the world. I did not tell her so. You see, I did not wish to bruise her ego with brutal facts. Being an M.D., if only an amateur one, I knew more about the disease than she, and I knew that time was my ally. But alas, I abused my ally when it dealt a charming little yaw on the shin. So quickly did I apply antiseptic treatment, that the yaw was cured before she was convinced that she had one. Again, as an M.D., I was without honour on my own vessel; and, worse than that, I was charged with having tried to mislead her into the belief that she had had a yaw. The pureness of her blood was more rampant than ever, and I poked my nose into my navigation books and kept quiet. And then came the day. We were cruising along the coast of Malaita at the time.

"What's that abaft your ankle-bone ? " said I.

"Nothing," said she.

"All right," said I ; "but put some corrosive sublimate on it just the same. And some two or three weeks from now, when it is well and you have a scar that you will carry to your grave, just forget about the purity of your blood and your ancestral history and tell me what you think about yaws anyway."

It was as large as a silver dollar, that yaw, and it took all of three weeks to heal. There were times when Charmian could not walk because of the hurt of it ; and there were times upon times when she explained that abaft the ankle-bone was the most painful place to have a yaw. I explained, in turn, that, never having experienced a yaw in that locality, I was driven to conclude the hollow of the instep was the most painful place for yaw-culture. We left it to Martin, who disagreed with both of us and proclaimed passionately that the only truly painful place was the shin. No wonder horse-racing is so popular.

But yaws lose their novelty after a time. At the present moment of writing I have five yaws on my hands and three more on my shin. Charmian has one on each side of her right instep. Tehei is frantic with his. Martin's latest shin-cultures have eclipsed his earlier ones. And Nakata has several score casually eating away at his tissue. But the history of the *Snark* in the Solomons has been the history of every ship since the early discoverers. From the "Sailing Directions" I quote the following:

"The crews of vessels remaining any considerable time in the Solomons find wounds and sores liable to change into malignant ulcers."

Nor on the question of fever were the "Sailing Directions" any more encouraging, for in them I read:

"New arrivals are almost certain sooner or later to suffer from fever. The natives are also subject to it. The number of deaths among the whites in the year 1897 amounted to 9 among a population of 50."

Some of these deaths, however, were accidental. Nakata was the first to come down with fever. This occurred at Penduffryn. Wada and Henry followed him. Charmian surrendered next. I managed to escape for a couple of months; but when I was bowled over, Martin sympathetically joined me several days later. Out of the seven of us all told Tehei is the only one who has escaped; but his sufferings from nostalgia are worse than fever. Nakata, as usual, followed instructions faithfully, so that by the end of his third attack he could take a two hours' sweat, consume thirty or forty grains of quinine, and be weak but all right at the end of twenty-four hours.

Wada and Henry, however, were tougher patients with which to deal. In the first place, Wada got in a bad funk. He was of the firm conviction that his star had set and that the Solomons would receive his bones. He saw that life about him was cheap. At Penduffryn he saw the ravages of dysentery, and, unfortunately for him, he saw one victim carried out on a strip of galvanized sheet-iron and dumped without coffin or funeral into a hole in the ground. Everybody had fever, everybody had dysentery, everybody had everything. Death was common. Here to-day and gone to-morrow—and Wada forgot all about to-day and made up his mind that to-morrow had come.

He was careless of his ulcers, neglected to sublimate them, and by uncontrolled scratching spread them all over his body. Nor would he follow instructions with fever, and, as a result, would be down five days at a time, when a day would have been sufficient. Henry, who is a strapping giant of a man, was just as bad. He refused point blank to take quinine, on the ground that years before he had had fever and that the pills the doctor gave him were of different size and colour from the quinine tablets I offered him. So Henry joined Wada.

But I fooled the pair of them, and dosed them with their own medicine, which was faith-cure. They had faith in their funk that they were going to die. I slammed a lot of quinine down their throats and took their temperature. It was the first time I had used my medicine-chest thermometer, and I quickly discovered that it was worthless, that it had been produced for profit and not for service. If I had let on to my two patients that the thermometer did not work, there would have been two funerals in short order. Their temperature I swear was 105°. I solemnly made one and then the other smoke the thermometer, allowed an expression of satisfaction to irradiate my countenance, and joyfully told them that their temperature was 94°. Then I slammed more quinine down their throats, told them that any sickness or weakness they might experience would be due to the quinine, and left them to get well. And they did get well, Wada in spite of himself. If a man can die through a misapprehension, is there any immorality in making him live through a misapprehension?

Commend me the white race when it comes to grit and surviving. One of our two Japanese and both our Tahitians funked and had to be slapped on the back and cheered up and dragged along by main strength toward life. Charmian and Martin took their afflictions cheerfully, made the least of them, and moved with calm certitude along the way of life. When Wada and Henry were convinced that they were going to die, the funeral atmosphere was too much for Tehei, who prayed dolorously and cried for hours at a time. Martin, on the other hand, cursed and got well, and Charmian groaned and made plans for what she was going to do when she got well again.

Charmian had been raised a vegetarian and a sanitarian. Her Aunt Netta, who brought her up and who lived in a healthful climate, did not believe in drugs. Neither did Charmian. Besides, drugs disagreed with her. Their effects were worse than the ills they were supposed to alleviate. But she listened to the argument in favour of quinine, accepted it as the lesser evil, and in consequence had shorter, less painful, and less frequent attacks of fever. We encountered a Mr. Caulfeild, a missionary, whose two predecessors had died after less than six months' residence in the Solomons. Like them he had been a firm believer in homeopathy, until after his first fever, whereupon, unlike them, he made a grand slide back to allopathy and quinine, catching fever and carrying on his Gospel work.

But poor Wada! The straw that broke the cook's back was when Charmian and I took him along on a cruise to the cannibal island of Malaita, in a small yacht, on the deck of which the captain had been murdered half a year before. *Kai-kai* means to eat, and Wada was sure he was going to be *kai-kai'd*. We went about heavily armed, our vigilance was unremitting, and when we went for a bath in the mouth of a fresh-water stream, black boys, armed with rifles, did sentry duty about us. We encountered English war vessels burning and shelling villages in punishment for murders. Natives with prices on their heads sought shelter on board of us. Murder stalked abroad in the land. In out-of-the-way places we received warnings from friendly savages of impending attacks. Our vessel owed two heads to Malaita, which were liable to be collected any time. Then to cap it all, we were wrecked on a reef, and with rifles in one hand warned the canoes of wreckers off while with the other hand we toiled to save the ship. All of which was too much for Wada, who went daffy, and who finally quitted the *Snark* on the island of Ysabel, going ashore for good in a driving rain-storm, between two attacks of fever, while threatened with pneumonia. If he escapes being *kai-kai'd*, and if he can survive sores and fever which are riotous ashore, he can expect, if he is reasonably lucky, to get away from that place to the adjacent island in anywhere from six to eight weeks. He never did think much of my medicine, despite the fact that I successfully and at the first trial pulled two aching teeth for him.

The *Snark* has been a hospital for months, and I confess that we are getting used to it. At Meringe Lagoon, where we careened and cleaned the *Snark's* copper, there were times when only one man of us was able to go into the water, while the three white men on the plantation ashore were all down with fever. At the moment of writing this we are lost at sea somewhere northeast of Ysabel and trying vainly to find Lord Howe Island, which is an atoll that cannot be sighted unless one is on top of it. The chronometer has gone wrong. The sun does not shine anyway, nor can I get a star observation at night, and we have had nothing but squalls and rain for days and days. The cook is gone. Nakata, who has been trying to be both cook and cabin boy, is down on his back with fever. Martin is just up from fever, and going down again. Charmian, whose fever has become periodical, is looking up in her date book to find when the next attack will be. Henry has begun to eat quinine in an expectant mood. And, since my attacks hit me with the suddenness of bludgeon-blows, I do not know from moment to moment when I shall be brought down. By a mistake we gave our last flour away to some white men who did not have any flour. We don't know when we'll make land. Our Solomon sores are worse than ever, and more numerous. The corrosive sublimate was accidentally left ashore at Penduffryn; the peroxide of hydrogen is exhausted; and I am experimenting with boracic acid, lysol, and antiphlogystine. At any rate, if I fail in becoming a reputable M.D., it won't be from lack of practice.

P.S. It is now two weeks since the foregoing was written, and Tehei, the only immune on board, has been down ten days with far severer fever than any of us and is still down. His temperature has been repeatedly as high as 104, and his pulse 115.

P.S. At sea, between Tasman atoll and Manning Straits.

Tehei's attack developed into black water fever —the severest form of malarial fever, which, the doctor-book assures me, is due to some outside infection as well. Having pulled him through his fever, I am now at my wit's end, for he has lost his wits altogether. I am rather recent in practice to take up the cure of insanity. This makes the second lunacy case on this short voyage.

P.S. Some day I shall write a book (for the profession), and entitle it, "Around the World on the Hospital Ship *Snark*." Even our pets have not escaped. We sailed from Meringe Lagoon with two, an Irish terrier and a white cockatoo. The terrier fell down the cabin companionway and lamed its nigh hind leg, then repeated the manœuvre and lamed its off fore leg. At the present moment it has but two legs to walk on. Fortunately, they are on opposite sides and ends, so that she can still dot and carry two. The cockatoo was crushed under the cabin skylight and had to be killed. This was our first funeral—though for that matter, the several chickens we had, and which would have made welcome broth for the convalescents, flew overboard and were drowned. Only the cockroaches flourish. Neither illness nor accident ever befalls them, and they grow larger and more carnivorous day by day, gnawing our finger-nails and toe-nails while we sleep.

P.S. Charmian is having another bout with fever. Martin, in despair, has taken to horse-doctoring his yaws with bluestone and to blessing the Solomons. As for me, in addition to navigating, doctoring, and writing short stories, I am far from well. With the exception of the insanity cases, I'm the worst off on board. I shall catch the next steamer to Australia and go on the operating table. Among my minor afflictions, I may mention a new and mysterious one. For the past week my hands have been swelling as with dropsy. It is only by a painful effort that I can close them. A pull on a rope is excruciating. The sensations are like those that accompany severe chilblains. Also, the skin is peeling off both hands at an alarming rate, besides which the new skin underneath is growing hard and thick. The doctor-book fails to mention this disease. Nobody knows what it is.

P.S. Well, anyway, I've cured the chronometer. After knocking about the sea for eight squally, rainy days, most of the time hove to, I succeeded in catching a partial observation of the sun at midday. From this I worked up my latitude, then headed by log to the latitude of Lord Howe, and ran both that latitude and the island down together. Here I tested the chronometer by longitude sights and found it something like three minutes out. Since each minute is equivalent to fifteen miles, the total error can be appreciated. By repeated observations at Lord Howe I rated the chronometer, finding it to have a daily losing error of seven-tenths of a second. Now it happens that a year ago, when we sailed from Hawaii, that selfsame chronometer had that selfsame losing error of seven-tenths of a second. Since that error was faithfully added every day, and since that error, as proved by my observations at Lord Howe, has not changed, then what under the sun made that chronometer all of a sudden accelerate and catch up with itself three minutes? Can such things be? Expert watchmakers say no; but I say that they have never done any expert watchmaking and watch-rating in the Solomons. That it is the climate is my only diagnosis. At any rate, I have successfully doctored the chronometer, even if I have failed with the lunacy cases and with Martin's yaws.

P.S. Martin has just tried burnt alum, and is blessing the Solomons more fervently than ever.

P.S. Between Manning Straits and Pavuvu Islands.

Henry has developed rheumatism in his back, ten skins have peeled off my hands and the eleventh is now peeling, while Tehei is more lunatic than ever and day and night prays God not to kill him. Also, Nakata and I are slashing away at fever again. And finally up to date, Nakata last evening had an attack of ptomaine poisoning, and we spent half the night pulling him through.

BACKWORD

THE *Snark* was forty-three feet on the water-line and fifty-five over all, with fifteen feet beam (tumble-home sides) and seven feet eight inches draught. She was ketch-rigged, carrying flying-jib, jib, fore-staysail, main-sail, mizzen, and spinnaker. There were six feet of head-room below, and she was crown-decked and flush-decked. There were four alleged *water-tight* compartments. A seventy-horse power auxiliary gas-engine sporadically furnished locomotion at an approximate cost of twenty dollars per mile. A five-horse power engine ran the pumps when it was in order, and on two occasions proved capable of furnishing juice for the search-light. The storage batteries worked four or five times in the course of two years. The fourteen-foot launch was rumoured to work at times, but it invariably broke down whenever I stepped on board.

But the *Snark* sailed. It was the only way she could get anywhere. She sailed for two years, and never touched rock, reef, nor shoal. She had no inside ballast, her iron keel weighed five tons, but her deep draught and high freeboard made her very stiff. Caught under full sail in tropic squalls, she buried her rail and deck many times, but stubbornly refused to turn turtle. She steered easily, and she could run day and night, without steering, close-by, full-and-by, and with the wind abeam. With the wind on her quarter and the sails properly trimmed, she steered herself within two points, and with the wind almost astern she required scarcely three points for self-steering.

The *Snark* was partly built in San Francisco. The morning her iron keel was to be cast was the morning of the great earthquake. Then came anarchy. Six months overdue in the building, I sailed the shell of her to Hawaii to be finished, the engine lashed to the bottom, building materials lashed on deck. Had I remained in San Francisco for completion, I'd still be there. As it was, partly built, she cost four times what she ought to have cost.

The *Snark* was born unfortunately. She was libelled in San Francisco, had her cheques protested as fraudulent in Hawaii, and was fined for breach of quarantine in the Solomons. To save themselves, the newspapers could not tell the truth about her. When I discharged an incompetent captain, they said I had beaten him to a pulp. When one young man returned home to continue at college, it was reported that I was a regular Wolf Larsen, and that my whole crew had deserted because I had beaten it to a pulp. In fact the only blow struck on the *Snark* was when the cook was manhandled by a captain who had shipped with me under false pretences, and whom I discharged in Fiji. Also, Charmian and I boxed for exercise ; but neither of us was seriously maimed.

The voyage was our idea of a good time. I

built the *Snark* and paid for it, and for all expenses. I contracted to write thirty-five thousand words descriptive of the trip for a magazine which was to pay me the same rate I received for stories written at home. Promptly the magazine advertised that it was sending me especially around the world for itself. It was a wealthy magazine. And every man who had business dealings with the *Snark* charged three prices because forsooth the magazine could afford it. Down in the uttermost South Sea isle this myth obtained, and I paid accordingly. To this day everybody believes that the magazine paid for everything and that I made a fortune out of the voyage. It is hard, after such advertising, to hammer it into the human understanding that the whole voyage was done for the fun of it.

I went to Australia to go into hospital, where I spent five weeks. I spent five months miserably sick in hotels. The mysterious malady that afflicted my hands was too much for the Australian specialists. It was unknown in the literature of medicine. No case like it had ever been reported. It extended from my hands to my feet so that at times I was as helpless as a child. On occasion my hands were twice their natural size, with seven dead and dying skins peeling off at the same time. There were times when my toe-nails, in twenty-four hours, grew as thick as they were long. After filing them off, inside another twenty-four hours they were as thick as before.

The Australian specialists agreed that the malady was non-parasitic, and that, therefore, it must be nervous. It did not mend, and it was impossible for me to continue the voyage. The only way I could have continued it would have been by being lashed in my bunk, for in my helpless condition, unable to clutch with my hands, I could not have moved about on a small rolling boat. Also, I said to myself that while there were many boats and many voyages, I had but one pair of hands and one set of toe-nails. Still further, I reasoned that in my own climate of California I had always maintained a stable nervous equilibrium. So back I came.

Since my return I have completely recovered. And I have found out what was the matter with me. I encountered a book by Lieutenant-Colonel Charles E. Woodruff of the United States Army entitled "Effects of Tropical Light on White Men." Then I knew. Later, I met Colonel Woodruff, and learned that he had been similarly afflicted. Himself an Army surgeon, seventeen Army surgeons sat on his case in the Philippines, and, like the Australian specialists, confessed themselves beaten. In brief, I had a strong predisposition toward the tissue-destructiveness of tropical light. I was being torn to pieces by the ultra-violet rays just as many experimenters with the X-ray have been torn to pieces.

In passing, I may mention that among the other afflictions that jointly compelled the abandonment of the voyage, was one that is variously called *the healthy man's disease, European Leprosy*, and *Biblical Leprosy*. Unlike *True Leprosy*, nothing is known of this mysterious malady. No doctor has ever claimed a cure for a case of it, though spontaneous cures are recorded. It comes,

they know not how. It is, they know not what.
It goes, they know not why. Without the use of
drugs, merely by living in the wholesome California
climate, my silvery skin vanished. The only hope
the doctors had held out to me was a spontaneous
cure, and such a cure was mine.

A last word : the test of the voyage. It is easy
enough for me or any man to say that it was en-
joyable. But there is a better witness, the one
woman who made it from beginning to end. In
hospital when I broke the news to Charmian that
I must go back to California, the tears welled into
her eyes. For two days she was wrecked and
broken by the knowledge that the happy, happy
voyage was abandoned.

Glen Ellen, California,
     April 7, 1911.